Keeping House
in Lusaka

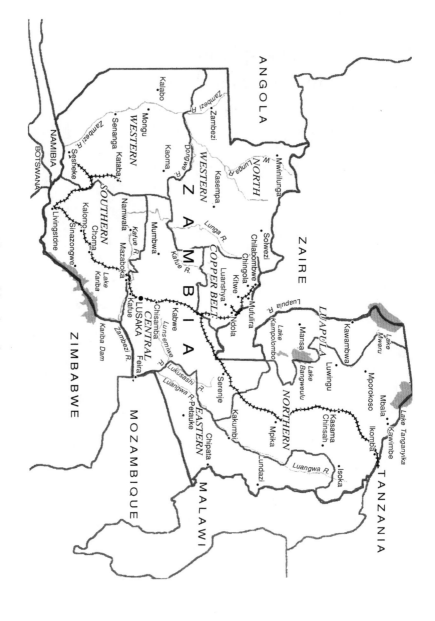

The Republic of Zambia

Keeping House in Lusaka

Karen Tranberg Hansen

Columbia University Press

NEW YORK

Columbia University Press
Publishers since 1893
New York   Chichester, West Sussex
Copyright © 1997 Columbia University Press
All rights reserved

Library of Congress Cataloging-in-Publication Data
Hansen, Karen Tranberg.
    Keeping house in Lusaka / Karen Tranberg Hansen.
        p.   cm.
    Includes bibliographical references and index.
    ISBN 0–231–08142–1 (cloth : alk. paper). — ISBN 0–231–08143–X
(pbk. : alk. paper)
    1. Urban anthropology—Zambia—Mtendere Township (Lusaka).
2. Urbanization—Zambia—Mtendere Township (Lusaka)—History—20th
century. 3. Public housing—Zambia—Mtendere Township (Lusaka)
4. Women—Housing—Zambia—Mtendere Township   5. Mtendere Township
(Lusaka, Zambia)—History—20th century.   6. Mtendere Township
(Lusaka, Zambia)—Economic conditions.   7. Mtendere Township
(Lusaka, Zambia)—Social life and customs.   I. Title.
GN657.R4H36   1996   96-21351
307.76'096894—dc20   CIP

Casebound editions of Columbia University Press books are printed on permanent and
durable acid-free paper.

Printed in the United States of America

c 10 9 8 7 6 5 4 3 2 1
p 10 9 8 7 6 5 4 3 2 1

Contents

Plates, Maps, and Tables   *vii*

Preface   *ix*

INTRODUCTION: AFRICAN URBANISM   1

1. Colonial Lusaka   21

2. A House of One's Own   47

3. Urban Arrangements for Living   70

4. On the Home Front   94

5. Private Troubles and Public Issues   118

6. City Limits   141

7. The Makings of a Research Project   165

CONCLUSION: A VIEW FROM LUSAKA   183

Notes   *195*

Bibliography   *201*

Index   *221*

Plates, Maps, and Tables

Plates

Mrs. Manda and her children playing *nsolo* in the front yard   x

Cairo Road in the 1980s   2

Women and children on the way to the independence day celebration
in 1971, with headquarters of Anglo-American corporation in
the background   3

Core house under construction in stage 1 of Kaunda Square
site-and-service scheme, 1972   54

View of core houses at Kaunda Square, stage 1   54

Various stages of house construction in Mtendere   66, 67

Different types of houses in Mtendere   74

Woman informal trader operating from her yard, selling beans   82

Woman informal trader operating from her yard, selling
munkoyo (a homemade, slightly fermented beverage)   83

Young men informal hawkers operating a roulette game   89

Young men informal hawkers selling cigarettes   90

Women neighbors with their children at bath time   108

Mrs. Sakala doing laundry   108

Children hawking vegetables in the street   149

Older sister watching younger siblings   149

Young men doing radio repair   153

Young man doing piecework in garden on the outskirts of Mtendere   153

Mrs. Lungu Jr. in the living room   159

Mrs. Mumba doing wool embroidery of her own design on mealie
   meal plastic sacking   160

Women and children relaxing. Different house types in the
   background. House constructed of wood boards and metal sheets   186

Women and children relaxing. Different house types in the
   background. Unfinished brick building constructed with rental of
   single rooms in view   186

Maps

The Republic of Zambia   ii

Lusaka Town Planning Scheme, 1954   26

Lusaka on the Eve of Independence, 1963   52

Lusaka, 1985   62

Layout of Mtendere Township, 1967   63

Tables

1.1 Population Growth in Lusaka, 1921–1956   32

2.1 Urban Population Growth in Zambia, 1963–1990   49

2.2 Growth of Squatter Settlements in Lusaka, 1954–1980   56

3.1 Ethnic Background of Mtendere Sample, 1971   75

3.2 Men's Occupations, Mtendere Sample, 1971   78

Preface

Some things never end. The concerns that are central to this book continue to preoccupy me in my ongoing research in Zambia. In the time it has taken for me actually to write it, I have accumulated many debts of inspiration and authorship that have shaped the nature and the outcome of this volume.

There is, first, my professional gratitude to Colin Murray for allowing me to rework the title of his unpublished dissertation, "Keeping House in Lesotho," into the title of this book. His published work (Murray 1981), a modern classic, is written with enviable clarity and grace. In my hope to engage my readers actively with the contemporary reality of one of Africa's rapidly growing metropolises, I have striven for a narrative that combines ethnography and theory with ease and without encumbrance. The book is intended for people who are interested in contemporary Africa and Third World cities, regional specialists or otherwise. Specifically, I have written it to bridge a gap I experience as a college teacher between ethnographies of thick description and politico-economic studies of macroeconomic changes in Africa. In short, this book opens a window on how one of the most rapid and most dramatic economic declines in Africa during the postcolonial era has been experienced by people who have lived through it. My special perspective is a result of repeated follow-up research I conducted over a period of twenty years about the lives and times of residents in one of Lusaka's many low-income areas.

Above all, I owe personal gratitude to the residents of Mtendere township in Lusaka, who tolerated my comings and goings over the years while taking me into their confidence about their lives as householders, residents of Lusaka, and citizens of Zambia. Spanning two generations, their experiences encapsulate Zambia's post–World War II history, and knowing them personalized my understanding of it. My assistant through all these years, Mrs. Norah Rice of Mtendere township, nurtured my interest in the cultural politics of urban life and has been my friend and confidante. I am deeply indebted to her. On and off, several members of her spatially extended household also facilitated my activities, and I thank them as well.

It was the pioneering urban research conducted during the late colonial period that attracted me to Zambia. I have learned much from the insights that A. L. Epstein and J. Clyde Mitchell shared with me. During all my stays in Zambia I have been a research affiliate of the Institute for African Studies at the University of Zambia in Lusaka. I am grateful to the institute's directors for supporting me whenever I returned, and most especially to Ilse Mwanza, the research affiliate officer, who has provided me with help, encouragement, and friend-

Mrs. Manda and her children playing *nsolo* in the front yard

ship throughout the years. She mediated many contacts, as did colleagues at the University of Zambia, particularly Hugh Macmillan and Mwelwa Musambachime, who whetted my interest in the history of the region. Their friendship is important to me. So is that of Susan and Henry Antkiewicz, Judy Butterman, Kusum and Ansu Datta, Kathy and Paul Freund, and Bonnie Keller, who at one time or another opened their Lusaka homes to me.

The initial phase of this research was made possible thanks to a graduate fellowship from Rotary International (1971–1972). Later stages were supported by faculty grants from the University of Minnesota (1981) and Northwestern University (1989 and 1992), and the Social Science Research Council (1988); some of my research in Mtendere was conducted while I held a National Science Foundation grant (1983–1984 and 1985) for a study of domestic service. I am grateful to all these bodies for their support. Parts of this book were written while I was a guest researcher at the Centre for Development Research in Copenhagen (1992), and I thank my colleagues for supporting this work and for sharpening my insights into development issues. I also wish to acknowledge the William and Marion Haas Fund for supporting the production of maps, which were prepared by the Geography Program at Northwestern University.

Because this project has spanned several years, some of my observations have found their way into print. Some of the discussion in chapter 2 draws from my article "Lusaka's Squatters: Past and Present" (1982a), and some of the legal case material that I discuss in chapter 5 is included in my essay "Washing Dirty Laundry in Public: Local Court, Custom, and Gender Relations in Post-Colonial Zambia" (forthcoming). Beyond these very identifiable influences, this book has been deeply inspired by my previously published works and extends those interests in new directions.

Last but not least, several persons influenced the shaping of this undertaking at various stages. They include George Bond, Jeremy Gould, Roger Sanjek, and Luise White. Friends and colleagues in the Chicago-area Africanist community, Paul Berliner, Jean and John Comaroff, Cheryl Odim-Johnson, Gianna and Hans Panofsky, Mette Shayne, and Peg Strobel have been both patient and supportive in seeing this project through. And Leslie Ashbaugh, Elizabeth Colson, Maria Grosz-Ngate, Jane Guyer, Robert Launay, Hugh Macmillan, and Carter Roeber read the entire manuscript. I wish to thank them all for their insightful advice and constructive comments. For the challenge of writing this book I thank my students at Northwestern University, whose enlightenment agenda is shared by the people to whom this book introduces them. If I have not listened well enough, they will all know whom to blame.

I dedicate this book to the memory of J. Clyde Mitchell.

Keeping House
in Lusaka

Introduction: African Urbanism

The towering cityscape of Lusaka's central business district leaves the impression of a modern city, surrounded by light industrial areas on the west and by government offices on the east. When viewed from a distance, the tall office buildings of Zambia's capital have much in common with those of other African capitals that—like Lusaka—arose as administrative headquarters in European settler colonies at the beginning of the twentieth century.

The legacy of Lusaka's planning as the capital of colonial Northern Rhodesia in the 1930s is clearly apparent in the grid pattern of the city's postcolonial geography. Wide avenues lined with trees and high-cost residential areas surrounded by open spaces or small parks bear out the claim of the capital's garden-city design. Then, as now, the low-cost residential areas where the majority of the capital's population lived were out of sight. But regardless of their visual prominence, neither the tree-lined streets with flowering blue jacarandas and red flamboyants with puttees of whitewash nor the garden hedges of multicolored bougainvillea and hibiscus can conceal that the colonial garden city built for European comforts is only one element in the developments that have turned Lusaka into a bustling African metropolis.

At independence in 1964, many street names in Lusaka were changed. New names such as Freedom Way and Chachacha Road celebrated the struggle for independence.[1] International alliances were marked, as in Haile Selassie Avenue, and altered, as in the renaming of Sadam Hussain Boulevard to Los Angeles Boulevard after the Gulf War in 1991. But the colonial name of Lusaka's main thoroughfare, Cairo Road, still remains. It rings with imperial echoes of Lusaka as a colonial outpost of Europe, a small part of a grand plan to link the British colonies in Africa, from the Cape of Good Hope in South Africa to Cairo in Egypt. Although that dream faded long ago, Zambia, with its capital, Lusaka, retains a central position on the regional map. That map today features a rapidly changing southern African subcontinent where processes set in motion in the broader global world are shaping people's livelihoods and engaging their desires.

While the preoccupations of Lusaka's residents resonate with the past in many ways, their projects and plans are building a new society. Nearly two decades of economic upheaval since independence have changed Lusaka from a relatively prosperous capital by African standards into a Third World city with many of the attendant problems, including housing shortages, unemployment, crime, and disease. There is no escaping the difficulties that these conditions created

Cairo Road in the 1980s

for the people who lived in the city throughout the economic decline that set in during the early 1970s. The process has its own agony, which is experienced differently according to one's gender, age, and class. But above all, such experiences are shaping urbanism as an African way of life as Zambia enters the next century. This book focuses on the complexity of ordinary urban lives, on women, men, and young adults and the hard choices they have made in order to live in postcolonial Lusaka since the early 1970s.

How does one capture the changing pulse of a rapidly growing African metropolis like Lusaka in all its varied aspects, among them political economy, urban planning, informal-sector developments, and legal dynamics? *Keeping House in Lusaka* approaches this question through a study of how residents in one of Lusaka's many low-income townships reacted to one of Africa's most dreadful economic downturns. The book gathers research that I undertook over approximately twenty years in Mtendere, a settlement on the outskirts of Lusaka, between 1971 and 1989, and it is informed as well by shorter visits I made during 1992 and 1993. Using detailed, long-term obser-

Women and children on the way to the independence day celebration in 1971, with headquarters of Anglo-American corporation in the background

vations of the lives and times of Mtendere residents, I discuss the sociocultural ramifications of economic decline in a part of Africa that has experienced one of the most extensive rates of urbanization in the postcolonial period.

My special issues of concern in this book are the gender and generational relations that are shaping access to urban housing and work. I focus on members of households in Mtendere, whose projects for making a living are transforming the opportunity structure through daily activities and utilization of material, social, and cultural resources. Mtendere is not an urban enclave that can be studied as if it were a self-contained community. Instead, its women, men, and youth engage in complex interactions with other population segments in the city and beyond it, as well as with agents of their state. Contributing to scholarship on Third World urbanization in general and to work on transformations of African livelihoods in particular, this study's politico-economically informed analysis of cultural practices within urban households offers striking insights into the cultural and gendered experiences of contemporary urban life in Africa, a focus that is missing from much recent work on development.

The book's title, *Keeping House in Lusaka*, highlights the centrality of both housing and relations within households to the outcome of urban projects for making a living. Housing is a staging area for many aspects of life that bring together household members in accommodation or conflict around a variety of activities, linking them with other actors within the same household and with still others outside households (Sanjek 1982:58). Contemporary legacies of a racially segregated colonial housing market tied to wage employment have turned a house of one's own in a rapidly growing African metropolis like Lusaka into an important hedge against socioeconomic adversity for urban residents with limited resources. But housing provides much more than shelter (Amis and Lloyd 1990; Tipple and Willis 1991). Its built environment is often inseparable from a host of activities and social relations. While a house can support social and economic activities, it can also complicate such efforts, especially when access depends on gender and women obtain it through men (Moser 1987; Larsson and Schlyter 1993). In short, houses, the kinds of households they host, and their members' relationships to changing resource structures provide the entry point for study of the urban experience of development in postcolonial Lusaka.

Economic Crisis, Third World Urbanization, and Experiences of Development

"Among all the nations of Sub-Saharan Africa, Zambia," according to well-informed observers of the country's political economy, "has suffered one of the greatest—and most rapid—economic declines" (Bates and Collier 1993:388). When Zambia became independent from British colonial rule in 1964, it initially experienced a period of economic growth, and until 1975 it was one of the most prosperous countries of Africa south of the Sahara. But twenty years after independence, relative prosperity had given way to a dramatic economic decline that changed its economic ranking in the World Bank's categorization from a high-income to a low-income country.

What is more, among all the nations of sub-Saharan Africa, Zambia has experienced one of the highest—and most rapid—urbanization rates (Wood 1986). The country's urbanization is a product of the colonial period, during which newly established towns first grew by a trickle, increased considerably during the World War II and postwar periods, and expanded rapidly after independence. In terms of formal estimates, the population that lived in urban areas increased from 21 percent to 40 percent of the total population from the eve of independence to 1980, a figure nearly twice that of the rest of sub-Saharan Africa (Republic of Zambia 1990:5–7). Informed estimates suggest that almost half of Zambia's total population of some eight million today is urban (World Bank 1992:663). Between 1963 and 1990, the population of the capital alone grew from 123,146 to close to one million.

A long history of rural to urban migration and, more recently, a high annual population growth rate of 3.2 percent over the 1980–1990 decade account for Zambia's high urbanization rate (Republic of Zambia 1990:6). Extensive rural out-migration was set into motion by British colonial policy, which for a long time attempted to restrict African migration to men. While colonial policy gave white farmers preferential access to land, extension services, and attractive producer prices, it discouraged the development of African commercial agriculture until the 1940s. The economic policies of the postcolonial government have largely replicated this pattern. More than 90 percent of the country's export revenue derives from mining. Agricultural policy favors a small group of commercial farmers at the expense of the peas-

ants who make up some 90 percent of the rural population. The low
priority given to agriculture—and to peasant production in particular—is exemplified by the extremely small budget allocations to agriculture during the 1980s (Geisler and Hansen 1994:97).

Rural-urban disparities in Zambia narrowed in the wake of the
overall economic decline during the first half of the 1970s. There is
some evidence of recent return migration from urban to rural areas,
mainly from the copperbelt, and of migration from the copperbelt to
Lusaka Province, no doubt influenced by recent employment
retrenchment in the mining industry (Republic of Zambia 1985:10,
12, 17–19, 33). Although it may have slowed somewhat, the migration process continues. Projections indicate that by the end of this
century, more people will live in Zambia's towns than in the countryside (UNDP 1993:155).

Zambia's dramatic economic decline and rapid urbanization provide the context for this book's discussion of the experience of development from the perspective of an urban, low-income population. As
such, the book seeks to complement the partial understandings of the
effects of socioeconomic decline provided by macroeconomic, sectoral,
or target group–oriented research. The existing work on Africa's
ongoing economic decline has provided stark macroeconomic evidence of declining gross national products, deteriorating terms of
trade, falling wage employment, and growing debt burdens (Bates and
Krueger 1993; Gibbon, Havnevik, and Hermele 1993; Onimode 1989;
Sandbrook 1993). Aside from the focus on deteriorating macroeconomic indicators, some work has paid attention to distinct sectors of
the economy, noting in recent years economic declines in both urban
and rural areas and increasing problems in feeding urban populations
(Guyer 1987; Jamal and Weeks 1988). But policy prescriptions have
overwhelmingly focused on the rural effects of Africa's economic crisis, whereas the changing nature of urban-rural relations has drawn
little attention (Amis 1990:4; Commins, Lofchie, and Payne 1986).
Finally, some research has targeted specific groups, for example,
women, single heads of households, and youth (Elson 1991; Palmer
1991; Tumbo-Masabo and Liljeström 1994). Although such work has
identified a frightening range of adverse effects of economic decline,
its findings have rarely been fully explained in relation to the increasing socioeconomic differentiation that has become characteristic of
many African societies at large (Peters 1983).

A growing body of academic research has begun to examine development priorities, strategies, and projects, identifying many shortcomings of the development enterprise at the level of national policy, multinational and international agencies, nongovernmental organizations (NGOs), or combinations thereof (Crehan and von Oppen 1988; Dahl and Hjort 1984; Ferguson 1990a; Rogers 1980). Much empirical work on the ongoing economic decline in Africa has concentrated on the rural crisis (Davison 1988; Gladwin 1991). This important work needs to reckon with special cases such as Zambia, where the rapid urbanization rate poses challenging questions not only about the viability of urban livelihoods but also about rural-urban interactions (Ashbaugh 1996; Geisler and Hansen 1994; Stren et al. 1992). But above all, and with few exceptions (Colson and Scudder 1988; Ferguson 1985; Roeber 1995), this scholarship has had little to say about the cultural side of the development process, specifically, about how the ongoing economic decline has been experienced by the people who are actually living through it.

Zambia's dramatic economic decline and rapid urbanization provide the two main strands to my preoccupation with the experiences of urban living among low-income Lusaka residents between the early 1970s and the late 1980s. The economic and urban strands overlap in my effort to describe urbanism in Zambia in local terms rather than through Western referential assumptions about what the city ought to be like (Wirth 1938). The colonial era's economic history and today's international context set Third World urbanization apart from the circumstances that prompted the growth of cities in the industrialized West (Flanagan 1993:110). Whereas Wirth's urbanism as a way of life was a cultural product of industrialization, the growth of the market economy, and the routinization of modern society, urbanism as a way of life in Lusaka is an expression of the distinctive aggregation of economic activity that postcolonial economic development in society at large has set into motion across Lusaka's colonial-built environment. This urbanism has its own spatial features, as evidenced in striking contrasts and sharp discontinuities, with very high and very low residential densities side by side and a large proportion of high-density areas located on the urban fringe (Wood 1986:179). Because Mtendere is located next to a low-density residential area, thereby creating a highly visible juxtaposition of poverty and wealth, the township is the very image of postcolonial urban Lusaka.

Lusaka's spatial and economic features require attention because they are important in shaping people's experience of urban life. At the center of this book is my attempt to characterize the livelihoods of Mtendere residents in their changing local context without losing sight of individual agency and to demonstrate how their social and cultural practices have helped to mediate the urban economic decline that they have experienced. In short, through my discussion of their changing interactions with work, gender, and time, I seek to describe Zambia's evolving urbanism from within Lusaka.

To be sure, in many ways Lusaka is just another Third World city, characterized by high formal unemployment, mushrooming squatter settlements, and proliferation of informal-sector activity (Drakakis-Smith 1990; Gilbert and Gugler 1992). In effect, a certain degree of homogenization of cities is taking place across Africa, regardless of their precolonial or colonial origin, and between them and Third World cities elsewhere (Flanagan 1993:110–16). Yet these cities are lodged in their specific historical, regional, and cultural contexts, appropriating some of the tools and practices of the world at large but on terms that are shaped by local cultural and interactional complexities (King 1990; Appadurai 1990). Urban residents in Africa are everywhere experiencing transformations of their livelihoods as a result of changes in their national economies and the world beyond them. Still, "one is struck," in the words of one observer, "by the creative hybridization of endogenous concepts and modern (western) patterns of behavior" that is taking place (Geschiere 1992:162).

Attention to cultural change helps to balance the emphasis on the economy as the driving force so characteristic of dependency and world-systems analyses of Third World urbanization (Armstrong and McGee 1985; Timberlake 1985). While existing social-organizational forms are influencing the way urban Africans respond to their altered circumstances, such forms themselves sometimes change in the process. In this way, they help to constitute new social relationships and institutions that do not necessarily coincide with or draw on existing ones (Berry 1985:152). As I suggest for the case of Lusaka, this transformative encounter must be analyzed on its own terms for what it is, rather than for what it is not—that is, merely derivative, not fully Western or modern.

But local-level observations do not replace grand questions about the economy; we must also reckon with the wider structural relations and social forces that have shaped and are changing the urban opportunity structure in a country like Zambia. To link these two levels, I ground the actions of Mtendere residents in the household, which I view as a crossover point between biography and history, the intersection of what C. Wright Mills perceptively termed private troubles and public issues (1970:9–25). Examining the connections that Mtendere householders make between their changing experiences and the economic and political system in which they live, this book casts revealing light on the nature of urban household dynamics and on how they and the cultural practices that shape them are influencing urbanism as a way of life in postcolonial Lusaka.

Local-level experiences of economic change in a township like Mtendere feed on and engage public issues that are being placed on household agendas by socioeconomic and political change in the wider setting. Interaction in Mtendere spills over beyond the township, while the politics of the city and the nation cross the thresholds of homes. Although individual lives and personal projects and plans are mediated by township residence, they have much in common with township livelihoods elsewhere in Zambia. Thus, the development experiences of residents in a low-income township such as Mtendere are of urban and national, rather than only local, proportions. As such, they speak about the problems of the "common man," the gender-biased generic term used by the one-party state and the media when referring to the great majority of Zambia's urban population. As I point out in the concluding chapter, the urban and national experiences that are filtered through the lives of Mtendere residents give the observations I make in this book comparative rather than merely local implications.

Modalities of Time

In this study of African urbanism in Lusaka, the special issues of concern—housing, work, households, and gender relations—are examined with reference to time. Time has a dual nature as both a local experiential category and an analytical construct. The question of how to account for time and its experience is a vexing issue in long-term anthropological research. Depending on the context, people's experience of linear time may become convoluted, making time appear to be discontinuous or to "zig-zag," as Monica Wilson once suggested (1976), or even to suspend the sense of its passing entirely. Colson's discussion of the "reordering of experience" in the mutual involvement with time by anthropologists and the people we study offers perceptive insights into the dilemma of studying experiences of change (1984). My own long-term involvement in this study makes the unraveling of the effects of time doubly challenging, because Mtendere residents and I shared significant periods of time, all the while aging and maturing ourselves; yet we were positioned so differently in global terms: they have been constantly engaged in an unrelenting struggle to make ends meet, whereas I have been upwardly mobile.

In order to understand the impact of time on households, we must tease apart several interacting processes. Not only must we know something about the historical processes that have set changes into motion, about the dynamics of household development cycles and the position of members at the point of change, but we must also investigate individual if not idiosyncratic reactions. In thinking about how to account for the effects of time and its experience, it is helpful to consider distinct temporalities. Depending on the level of analysis, time has at least three referents: large-scale historical time, which has to do with societal transformations; biographical time, which hinges on the stage in the life cycle; and situational time, which entails personal agency (Gugler and Flanagan 1978:97–117).[2]

It is difficult to speak of time without calling on spatial metaphors (Giddens 1983:204). Considering time in the sense of large-scale historical transformation involves reckoning with the worldwide expansion of Western industrial capitalism, asymmetrical center-periphery relations, rural-urban inequality, and neighborhood differentiation, especially as a result of struggles over housing access (1983:206). All these processes have affected the lives of urban residents in a township like Mtendere, but not in the same manner.

Individual experiences of historical change are shaped by biographical time, which captures the unfolding of social reproduction over the life span of individuals that we commonly call the life cycle (Giddens 1983:205). Important spatial metaphors of this dimension of time are households, educational institutions, and workplaces. Haraven (1982), who characterizes biographical time as family time, has noted that life trajectories cannot be understood without taking account of how family needs rather than individual preferences may influence—for example, who studies or goes to work, gets married or helps out at home, moves away or stays in the hometown. But although families and households have their own built-in time scale, their "cycle" must not be interpreted too literally to imply a return to the same point or that no change takes place between the experiences of generations and across biographies (Murray 1987). For instance, growing up into young adulthood in Mtendere meant different things to different adolescent girls in the 1970s and the 1980s.

The spatial metaphors of situational change arise from human agency, which prompts social practices that in turn may develop into routinized or institutionalized forms (Giddens 1983:215–25). An excellent example of this is women's small-scale trading activities, which have developed from individually instigated initiatives into routinized patterns (Hansen 1975).

None of the spatial metaphors suggested above are static; rather they are experienced differently depending on gender, age, and socioeconomic position. As this book demonstrates, unequal access readily turns the spatial metaphors just described into political issues that cause considerable friction both within households and on the wider urban scene.[3] I have incorporated the three senses of time and their spatial metaphors into the organization of this book. The first two chapters, on the colonial city and housing, are concerned with historical time, whereas the chapters on the informal sector, households, and gender are lodged in biographical and situational time. The last two chapters discuss the intersection of time in the diverging experiences of senior Mtendere residents and their young adult children as well as in the context of this project's unfolding.

Themes

What unites the themes of *Keeping House in Lusaka* is that they are observed from within households—hence the book's title. Throughout it, I have striven to synthesize my understanding of Mtendere residents' economic and sociocultural struggles for a living in a manner that reckons with the changing politico-economic and historical context they have lived through without losing sight of the individual actor. The chief period of my concern stretches between two significant events that had profound effects on their lives: the formation of the one-party state at the end of 1972 and the dismantling of it by multiparty elections in October 1991. The particular configurations of Zambia's political economy during those years were crucial in shaping the nature and course of the country's economic deterioration. While these processes have been documented extensively elsewhere, a few observations are in order here.[4]

Briefly, by the early 1970s import-substitution-led industrialization had failed to produce economic growth, and the trickle-down effects predicted by modernization theory never materialized. Government revenue continued to depend on mineral exports from a mining industry that had been nationalized in the late 1960s. Plummeting world market copper prices, combined with the oil crisis of the early 1970s, sent the economy into a downslide from which it has never recovered. Developments during the 1970s did not result in economic growth sufficient even to meet basic needs but instead increased them. Despite considerable development intervention in agriculture, Zambia was rarely able to feed its own growing population, let alone export. These problems were accentuated by recurring drought and political destabilization in neighboring countries within the southern African region. By the early 1980s, the economy had increasingly been tied over by foreign loans, which turned Zambia's per capita debt burden into one of the highest in the developing world.

This book is not a historical account but rather one that situates my observations in time while highlighting a number of important issues that have been central to recent scholarship on Third World urbanization concerned with housing, work, and gender relations. Taking a thematic approach, the book shifts perspective in each chapter, moving between different levels of analysis from the planning of colonial Lusaka to gender dynamics within and across households, the national economy, and on to questions about what kind of city Lusaka represents today in the context of development and Third World urbanization. Establishing connections between these themes that arose as my long-term study took shape over the years, I conclude by raising questions about their broader significance. Each chapter also discusses particular conceptual arguments, which I briefly preview below.

The Colonial City

Chapter 1, "Colonial Lusaka," concerns the development of the capital into an African city. Between 1931 and 1964, the year Northern

Rhodesia became independent from British colonial rule under the name of Zambia, Lusaka was a city in rapid transformation. The planning and building activity that began in the wake of the colonial government's 1931 decision to move the site of the capital from Livingstone to Lusaka transformed a small town that had grown from its slender beginnings in 1905 as a railway siding to service the needs of nearby European farmers into an African metropolis. Between the official opening of the capital in 1935 and independence in 1964, Lusaka was affected in many ways by the political and economic developments in the neighboring countries and by the world economy. This period of nearly three decades of transition drew Lusaka's African residents into processes of constructing and reconstructing new arrangements for living through which they made this colonial city their own.

The opening paragraph of this book noted how legacies of Lusaka's colonial-built environment are still visible on the capital's cityscape more than thirty years after Northern Rhodesia became independent. I argue in chapter 1 that these legacies, and the name of Cairo Road, are deceiving, for they conjure up misleading notions of straightforward continuity between past and present, especially in the fields of housing and work.

I begin by suggesting that scholarly notions of Lusaka as a textbook example of a colonial city (E. Wilson 1992:126–27) hide its history as an African town. What is more, this characterization glosses over historical differences in urban planning practices between Zambia and South Africa, which are important for our understanding of the direction of postcolonial urban developments in Zambia. Manifestations of these differences are Lusaka's earlier and far more extensive development of squatter settlements and informal-sector activity.

In fact, squatting and informal-sector developments also make a major difference between Lusaka and the copperbelt towns, where they were far less extensive, since the mining companies were the major employer and landlord. Chapter 1 uses these observations to invite some qualification of established statements about the nature of colonial urbanization in Zambia. I argue that African urbanism in colonial Lusaka differs in important respects from the influential version of African urban life portrayed in a number of very prominent studies of the mining towns conducted by a group of anthropologists associated with the Rhodes-Livingstone Institute during the late colonial period.

Combining the limited scholarship conducted in colonial Lusaka with African recollections, I trace out a sense of how African women and men used their colonial-planned city, making it their own. In this way, my study pushes observations about gender relations and households, only hinted at in the work on the mining towns, into new directions by making gender the central relationship in the analysis of the overall effects and experiences of urbanization and social and economic change in Lusaka. I also suggest that my observations about the early growth of squatter settlements have implications for our understanding of the processes that in the postcolonial era are contributing to erase former distinctions between Lusaka and the towns on the copperbelt.

Housing

While chapter 1 sets the scene historically and foreshadows current processes, it also introduces the themes of housing and work, which are discussed in the two subsequent chapters. In fact, neither housing nor work can be understood without reference to employment practices and state policy, which in both the past and the present created a close link between housing and work in this part of Africa. Chapter 2, "A House of One's Own," discusses the low-income housing question in Lusaka after independence and the mismatch between the availability to Lusaka's rapidly growing population of employer- and state-provided housing and newly built housing at affordable cost.

Squatting increased dramatically in scope, and in the early 1970s attempts were made to upgrade some of Lusaka's many squatter settlements. Site-and-service schemes, where the city council demarcated plots and established basic services, were introduced as well. The chapter's focus next turns to Mtendere, one of the earliest of these efforts undertaken in Lusaka. The settlement fell from official grace and was for a while considered a squatter settlement; during that time its development was completed by planned and organized squatting, supervised by the party.

At the center of my discussion is private house ownership for low-income urban residents, something rarely allowed Africans in colonial Lusaka, and the importance of housing to attempts at securing urban arrangements for living. A house of one's own was a singularly important stake in the city, not only in the physical sense of providing shelter but also as a facilitator of income-generating work, especially for women. What is more, a house of one's own hosted a variety of social relations that were part of the different resource networks on which women and men drew, as I discuss in subsequent chapters.

The Informal Sector

In chapter 3, "Urban Arrangements for Living," I discuss how Mtendere residents established themselves socioeconomically in the township and how over the course of the years women and men sought to make an income to secure the well-being of those within their closest circles. Their access to the city's opportunity structure differed significantly in that men more readily found wage employment, largely in low-skilled manual labor occupations, and women carried out informal income-generating work, mainly in small-scale trading.

Chapter 3 provides a Zambian and gendered perspective on the informal sector, that part of the unregulated economy hailed by many development planners as a natural arena for productive absorption of workers. My observations over more than twenty years do not substantiate this scenario, nor do those of other scholarship on Lusaka. In fact, women's crowding of informal-sector markets readily confuses activity with prosperity. Women's success depends critically on their access to resources, and in this regard age and gender are important differentiating criteria. So are social-organizational practices that shape the different claims women and men can make on resources.

It has been common in recent scholarship to analyze informal-sector developments as responses to the declining economic scope of the state (e.g., Rothchild and Chazan 1988; Clark 1988). While the state must not drop out of analysis, its declining economic capacity is not the only driving force behind informal-sector developments. My long-term observations of women's changing economic involvement in a low-income urban area like Mtendere demonstrate clearly that these dynamics are not only economic but also social and cultural. Informal-sector developments are significantly influenced by gender dynamics within Zambian households that are shaping the direction in which the informal sector changes in important ways. In particular, these dynamics have to do with cultural practices that both on the home front and in Zambian society at large tend to privilege men over women.

Households

Mtendere households are not bounded units whose members see eye to eye on what needs to be done. Chapter 4, "On the Home Front," discusses the household as a locus of competing interests, claims, and resources, demonstrating how members negotiate access to resources, in the process interacting with one another and members of other households, as well as with persons from beyond the township, including the city at large and the countryside. These observations have implications for interaction beyond households and work in settings that also channel resources. The chapter discusses a variety of largely gender-segregated interactional settings, including neighborhood, church, and voluntary associations. Explaining the limited role that ethnicity plays in township interaction, I point out how urban initiation rites and kitchen parties (bridal showers) reinvoke tradition while mediating thoroughly modern gender experiences.

My observations about household developments in Mtendere township give evidence of an ongoing battle in which women and men of different generations grapple with questions of what marriage and households should be like in a rapidly deteriorating economy. The private troubles of women and men about these issues and their efforts to strategize around them also involve the postcolonial state because of its inability to create jobs, provide affordable housing, improve agriculture, and offer education. The state becomes intimately implicated in private household affairs because of its reluctance to reform customary marriage and inheritance laws. The residents' personal battles thus are also public struggles, and the home front becomes a public stage on which the impact of larger social, economic, and political processes can be studied at close range.

Gender Relations

Ongoing economic deterioration accentuates gender and generational tensions within urban Zambian households. A woman's access to productive resources was in the past, as it still is today, mediated through men—her father, uncle, brother, or husband—and this applies across class and ethnic groups in both rural and urban areas. Cultural norms continue to make women dependent on men for basic household allowances and access to services, including housing, loans, insurance, and bank accounts. When tensions between women and men are not solved through informal mediation within the township, their battles are sometimes fought in local courts, the successors to the urban native courts of the colonial era.

In chapter 5, "Private Troubles and Public Issues," I follow some Mtendere residents to court, analyzing court cases for what they may tell us about the relationship between "custom" and gender relations in postcolonial urban Zambian society. Women and men making claims and counterclaims in the language of custom, and women fighting women over men reveal how normative gender relations are shot through with ambiguities because of ongoing socioeconomic change. I demonstrate how claims about custom provide legitimation for men's control of women's sexual behavior. The reverse does not apply; in divorce cases women have no customary right to support from estranged spouses.

Yet the local court is not a static instrument but an institution that interacts with a changing society. This is evident in the practice I observed in local court in which the presiding justice awarded divorced "properly married" wives some economic support from their former husbands. In short, while some of the battles between the sexes continue to be fought in the language of custom, they are at times settled to reckon with contemporary needs that arise because of socioeconomic change.

Generations, Localization, and Globalization

Political developments in Zambia during the economic decline of the 1970s and 1980s have provoked considerable conflict between the generations in a low-income urban setting such as Mtendere. The present generation of young adults, who were children when I first met their parents in the early 1970s, are encountering an opportunity structure that differs from that of their parents and shares little with that of their older siblings, who received education and readily found jobs during the economic growth period immediately after independence. The second generation has been exposed to a broader scope of global influences than their parents were, and their diminished access to resources in today's depressed economy is evident in several domains of life.

Mtendere was never a self-contained community. Political discord within and between residents and the local party organization developed as part of the political upheaval experienced in Zambia between the late 1980s and 1991, when multiparty elections dismantled the almost-twenty-year reign of the one-party state. The fragile political compromise of the present has as yet to assuage the painful and impatient awareness held by Lusaka's young adults, including youth in Mtendere, of a world of global opportunity that is within reach yet not readily accessible to them.

Chapter 6, "City Limits," takes us full circle, to the end of the development cycle of several of the households I followed through the years, examining both the actions of senior women and men at the dissolution point of households and the prospects for new household formation by their young adult children. Some senior householders are returning to the countryside, though rarely to agricultural pursuits, and women and men take strikingly different action at this point of their life cycle, prioritizing individual designs on life over those of the household.

Because of the depressed economy, many young women and men are in a bind, having insufficient resources to set up independent households. Parents' frustrations on account of their children's limited job prospects prompt some to take different actions in supporting young daughters and sons. And mothers' disillusionment over their young daughters' premarital pregnancies provokes conservative reinvents of tradition aimed at instilling notions of women's proper place. I suggest that such reinvented traditions as urban initiation ceremonies and kitchen parties mediate deeply felt tensions between local and global influences, which in turn are constituting gendered notions about what being Zambian means in our late-twentieth-century world.

Long-Term Urban Research

It was through long-term research that I recognized the issue that ultimately constitutes this book's major challenge: the entanglement of historical, biographical, and situational time within the experiences of individuals who had lived through dramatic change in their society.

Yet few scholars begin their research with the explicit intention of making it into a long-term undertaking. Chapter 7, "The Makings of a Research Project," discusses how the development of this study into a long-term research project has had a determining effect on the themes and overall orientation of this book. I have very deliberately placed this discussion toward the end of the book in order to highlight the mutual interaction between field research and intellectual consid-erations that occurs in any research project but becomes an important part of a long-term project's development. A methodology chapter placed at the beginning of the book would not fully reveal the logic of this process. In fact, the chapter does double duty, reflecting on—and thus summarizing—my research and in that way anticipating the more formal observations I make in the concluding chapter.

As this project developed beyond its original conception as an exploratory study of women's work, it combined survey work with qualitative interviews and participant observation. Chapter 7 dis-cusses the twists and turns of my research, the planned and fortuitous shifts it underwent, and the formal survey methods that I employed. Above all, it discusses this study's interactive element: the nature of my own involvement with residents in ways that both affect and are influenced by my evolving understanding of the processes in which I became implicated. The themes I have singled out are based on my understanding of their local importance and relevance. This selection process inevitably colors the discussions pursued here.

Much has been written about intersubjectivity in anthropological research experiences, about anthropologists and the people we study sharing the same time, and about writing conventions that readily erase this dimension from the published record (Dumont 1992; Fabian 1983:25–35; Stoller 1994). In the final analysis, and in rela-tionship to this particular project, I believe that the Mtendere resi-dents whose lives I have followed and I were mutually involved both in structuring and in constructing the flow of life that I describe here.

Because my understanding of township life in Lusaka has evolved in an ongoing dialogue with Mtendere residents, this book privileges qualitative description over charts, graphs, and tables in an effort to provide insights into both the joys and the agonies of lived experi-ences. It is in close and careful analysis of residents' experiences through time that this book speaks to and about the local meanings, in gender and generational terms, of a dramatic economic decline, which macroeconomic, sectoral, or target-group development studies barely have the conceptual apparatus to uncover.

A View from Lusaka

Since long-term field study engages the researcher with ongoing transformations of society at many levels, it readily provokes questions about powerful assumptions that curtail our understanding of both the directionality and the effects of change. Among the assumptions that became intellectual issues as this study unfolded over the years were widely held notions about urban bias that not only simplify the complexities of postcolonial economic developments in a country like Zambia but also pose problems for development intervention. The chapter identifies some of the insights that long-term research brings to this and several other assumptions about the nature and direction of change of African urban life and of rural-urban dynamics.

In concluding this book, I discuss the broader relevance of the themes that each chapter has laid out, drawing on my detailed observations of the lives and times of Mtendere residents over a twenty-year period. Although my findings are significantly colored by their specific historical, regional, and cultural context, they pertain to experiences that are transforming the livelihoods of urban residents elsewhere in Africa and in the Third World's rapidly growing cities. I briefly identify the salient issues, pointing to the challenge of incorporating scholarship on local development experiences into the development enterprise, and above all calling into question the low priority given to the urban agenda in interventions aimed at improving African livelihoods. Because the development literature on these issues is so highly programmatic, both it and my discussion of them tend to be tedious. Bringing these issues to bear on lived experiences that I have observed over the long term, I end by commenting on what I consider to be very recognizably Zambian urban experiences in our late-twentieth-century global world.

1 | Colonial Lusaka

L usaka is but one of the Third World's rapidly growing capitals, yet it is lodged in its own historical,
regional, and cultural context. How do we depict the
changing historical character of a city like Lusaka? The way in which
we describe a city depends a great deal on who we are. Outside
observers have different perspectives from urban residents, whose
views in turn differ, most certainly by race, class, and gender but also
to some extent by religious and ethnic background. Mr. Zulu and Mrs.
Mubanga,[1] whose recollections of life in Lusaka from the late 1930s
onward I turn to shortly, provide distinctly gendered versions of the
African experience of life in the colonial capital.

Beginning this chapter with a characterization of colonial Lusaka
by outside observers, I first discuss how the concerns of a previous
generation of scholars have contributed to hiding Lusaka's story as an
African city. Seeking to shed light on urbanism as an African way of
life, I explore in the second part of the chapter what kind of place colonial Lusaka was for its African inhabitants in the period after World
War II and leading up to independence in 1964.

Lusaka's story as an African city has been hidden from view in
many previous scholarly accounts of this region, for two main reasons. One is a tendency to view Lusaka as a "created colonial city par
excellence" (Western 1985:357), rooted in general British colonial
practice and, in particular, developed along the lines of the racially
segregated towns in South Africa and what was then Southern

Rhodesia (now Zimbabwe). Because such accounts are concerned largely with the political and economic effects of colonialism, they unwittingly privilege European interests. Finding familiar landmarks and contours of the colonial city both on the copperbelt and in Lusaka, such studies miss taking notice of the local character of urban developments, and therefore they barely explore how Africans made such European-planned towns into places of their own.

The other reason that the African side of Lusaka has been hidden from view is also academic. It has to do with the special shape and concerns of the most significant localized contribution to urban anthropology ever undertaken, namely the research conducted in this region under the auspices of the Rhodes-Livingstone Institute between the 1930s and the 1950s, associated particularly, but not only, with the work of Wilson, Mitchell, and Epstein, some of it inspired by Gluckman (1945). The urban world that these anthropologists sought to understand was one of rapidly growing mining towns, including Broken Hill (now Kabwe) but especially the copperbelt towns, and their concerns lay with the process of urbanization, the impact of the urban industrial environment on African lives, and African reactions to town. This period's limited scholarship on colonial Lusaka consists largely of social surveys (Bettison 1959). The capital was not the site of anthropological field research until 1964 (Boswell 1969). By far the majority of the subsequent work on Zambia's social and economic history has focused on mine workers and their activities.[2] The version of colonial urban life in Northern Rhodesia that results from these studies draws disproportionately on copperbelt experiences. This space- and time-bound version of urban life during the colonial period begs to be qualified by a fuller view from Lusaka.

Comparisons, Contrasts, Contexts: North and South

To an outside observer writing on the eve of Zambia's independence, Lusaka left the "general appearance of having been dumped in the middle of the African bush" (E. Wilson 1963:411). European accounts, whether by local residents or travelers, of Lusaka prior to its days as a colonial capital converge in a descriptive mode very similar to this early note from 1909: "Lusaka was nothing more than a wayside dorp [Afrikaans for *village*] with a railway station of corrugated iron . . .

one hotel, one store, a lime works and a few other ramshackle buildings" (Copeman 1956:141).

The overall European character of Lusaka changed only slowly.
Recalling his impressions when transferred to the new capital as a
young colonial officer, Vernon Brelsford commented on the "somewhat grandiose town plan [that] had been drawn up, but the
Depression held it back . . . and the only buildings on the Ridgeway
[the "first-class" European residential area] were a few new houses
for civil servants. For the rest it was just bush. . . . There was bush all
round [the new *boma*] . . . on Cairo Road." "Lusaka could have been
a Transvaal 'dorp,' " he continued, "only the golf course . . . gave it a
certain British imprint. There were probably no more than 200
Europeans, among them Jewish and Greek traders, Italian lime burn-
ers, South African railwaymen and an Afrikaans settlement at the
north end of town grouped round the Dutch Reformed Church"
(Hobson 1985:8–9).

Beyond acknowledging that the city took its name from a local
headman, Lusaakas, which in the Lenje language means "thorn
bush," contemporary descriptions contain little reference to the
African society that was an important part of the town's early life
(Sampson [1960] 1982). The 1921 census tells another story of Lusaka
when listing 1,280 African men in employment, compared to only
243 European residents (Bettison 1959:8–9). Yet the built environment, economic activity, and social life on which contemporaries commented were overwhelmingly European, with one exception. That
was the domestic servant, the male African worker whose labor facilitated so many of the comforts of Lusaka's European residents.

Lusaka's colonial origin as a town planned to serve European needs
certainly helps to explain the characterization of its having been
"dumped" in the middle of the African bush. The "colonial city" is
one type in classification schemes that anthropologists and geogra-
phers have proposed in distinguishing different types of cities in
Africa, taking into account such features as the presence or absence of
preexisting urbanism, the extent of European demographic and
politico-economic dominance, and urban functions (e.g., O'Connor
1983; Southall 1961:6 ff.). In such classifications, colonial cities are
viewed as the products of European imperialism and are accorded piv-
otal roles in the establishment, systematization, and maintenance of
such rule. Their spatial layout and their built environment served the

interests of the colonizers, who shared both ideas and plans for how to inscribe European domination into the physical and social environment (King 1976).[3]

The history of Lusaka as a planned colonial city with a focus on layout, structure, and built form has been written many times (e.g., Collins 1986; Martin 1974; Rothman 1972; Thøgersen and Andersen 1983). The planning of Lusaka as a capital in the 1930s was inspired by the British garden-city ideal of interacting neighborhoods and communities laid out with wide-open spaces adorned with greenery and with large building plots for the Europeans. An architect from Britain had selected Lusaka as the site for the new capital and drawn up its initial plan, and a British architect who had been involved with the design of government buildings in Pretoria in South Africa and New Delhi in India was brought to Lusaka for the same purpose.

While the building of colonial Lusaka was planned along the lines of a European garden city, it was significantly adjusted to the racial underpinnings of colonial rule. The colonial administration did not expect Africans to live permanently in the city, but to stay there only for as long as they worked for Europeans. These workers were predominantly men. Until the post–World War II years, the colonial administration considered male African urban workers to be temporary and migrant, with real homes in the villages where wives farmed and cared for children and the elderly in their absence. As in the white settler colonies in South Africa and Southern Rhodesia, European employers were responsible for accommodating their African workers while they were employed in town. In this way, shelter was tied to the job, and a worker lost his dwelling space when he completed his work contract.

Given this view, it is not surprising that plans for African housing in the new capital were added as an afterthought and were put out of sight from the town center, at the extreme southwest corner of the city. The layout of Kabwata, the first planned African township, was copied after the African compounds in Bulawayo in Southern Rhodesia (Thøgersen and Andersen 1983:32–33). It consisted of round one-room brick huts without windows, surrounded by small garden plots; cooking took place outdoors, and there were communal bathing and sanitation facilities.

Such residential areas were then, as they still are today, called *compounds*, a common term throughout the southern African region, first

used for the housing institution that was adopted on the gold and dia-
mond mines in South Africa in the late 1880s (Rex 1974; Turrel 1984;
Welsh 1971:180–81). A pamphlet, privately published on the occasion
of the official opening of the capital, explained that the "miscellaneous
African population of the Capital has, for purposes of accommodation,
been divided into two classes, personal servants and others, and these
classes have been provided with separate compounds. . . . [Servants']
quarters are only provided for one unmarried boy on each plot. The
other servants live with their families at a distance in the Personal
Servants' Compound" (Bradley [1935] 1981:13). A special compound,
the governor's village, was laid out for African clerks, *capitaos* (super-
visors), and artisans where they could rent not only the usual round
huts but also two-room houses (Bradley [1935] 1981:16).

The colonial system of planning and administration designed for
the growing African urban population of Northern Rhodesia shows
both similarities to and differences from the South African government's policy of racially separate development. The similarities are
more obvious than the contrasts, although the latter have more relevance to the postcolonial situation. While Northern Rhodesia's colonial administration duplicated many measures of the South African
racial control apparatus regarding segregated labor and housing,
health and movement, and domestic arrangements, the two govern-
ments differed significantly in the scope and direction of their policies
for urban Africans (Harries-Jones 1977:140–44).

From Lusaka's beginnings as a planned capital, its development as
a colonial city was qualified by the economic circumstances under
which it grew and by its lackluster performance in the shifting
regional political economy. Plans for the capital's development were
curtailed first by the Great Depression and later by World War II. The
copperbelt towns formed the country's economic backbone, and
Kitwe, the country's hub, was both larger in size and more prosperous than Lusaka until the very eve of independence. The post–World
War II period saw an economic boom in the mining industry and
some new housing initiatives in Lusaka. Lusaka's status declined further during the period of the Central African Federation, 1953–1963,
when many government functions of Northern Rhodesia, Nyasaland
(now Malawi), and Southern Rhodesia were jointly administered
from Salisbury (now Harare), the capital of Southern Rhodesia. The
boom had climaxed by the time of the federation, and only just before

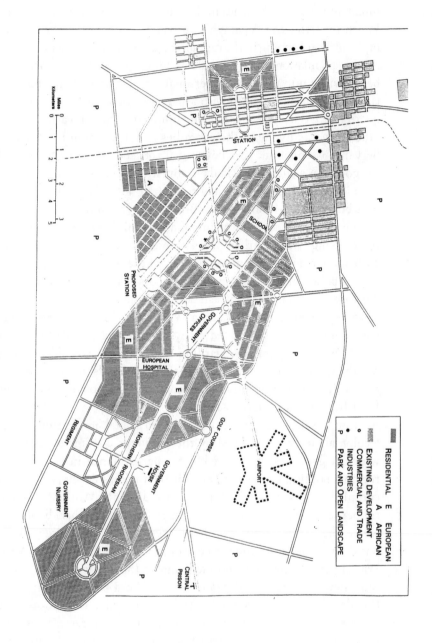

Lusaka Town Planning Scheme, 1954

RESIDENTIAL   E   EUROPEAN
  A   AFRICAN
EXISTING DEVELOPMENT
COMMERCIAL AND TRADE
INDUSTRIES
PARK AND OPEN LANDSCAPE

STATION

SCHOOL

PROPOSED
STATION

GOVERNMENT
OFFICES

EUROPEAN
HOSPITAL

REGIMENT

NORTHERN
RHODESIAN

GOVERNMENT
HOUSE

GOVERNMENT
NURSERY

GOLF COURSE

AIRPORT

CENTRAL
PRISON

Miles
0   1   2   3
Kilometers
0 1 2 3 4 5

independence did a rush of activity again take place in Lusaka's field of housing.

Throughout this period, Lusaka maintained the general structure of a colonial city. The European residential areas were divided into three subzones that varied in physical beauty and housed different income groups. Most of the Asiatic population, predominantly traders from different parts of the Indian subcontinent, lived on the premises of their businesses in the "second-class" trading area Luburma, next to Kabwata, the African compound; the small population of mixed descent, known as "colored" in this part of Africa, lived in an area segregated from the European "third-class area" by the railway line and the Great East Road. The majority of Lusaka's population, namely its African residents, was either tucked away in compounds beyond the varying splendors of the European first-, second-, and third-class residential areas or lived in these residential areas as domestic servants on the premises of their employers (Kay 1967:115).

The colonial government in Northern Rhodesia never went as far as the South African government in institutionalizing a migrant labor legislation that defined Africans as aliens within the urban areas. While the colonial administration in Northern Rhodesia also for a long time viewed African workers in the towns as temporary residents, it did not have sufficient resources either to repatriate men who remained in the cities once they completed work contracts or were laid off and lost their housing, or to send the women and children who kept arriving back to the villages. In fact, in the 1930s the mining companies had already begun to provide married housing both in Broken Hill and on the copperbelt. Similarly, in Lusaka most of the compounds built after the opening of the capital contained a proportion of married housing.

What is more, from the earliest years of Lusaka's existence, unauthorized dwellings shot up. Here lived wage-employed African men who found no employer-provided housing, self-employed workers, both women and men, and the women and children who were not supposed to be in town. Such settlements were areas where people took up residence without holding legal rights of tenure. Two types developed in Lusaka. There were unauthorized compounds where European and Indian landlords let Africans build in return for a monthly fee. Some of these had sprung from contractors' camps where employers allowed Africans to remain after completing work

contracts. Then there were areas where Africans began building without permission on European-occupied land or on Crown land. In common parlance, no distinction was made between them (Hansen
1982a:119); they both became known as *squatter compounds*, and
that is the term that I employ here.

In effect, squatter compounds and, as I discuss shortly, an urban
informal sector were part of the capital's development from the start.
Although some squatter settlements were demolished, they never
were as consistently razed in Lusaka as in South Africa (Stadler 1979).
While the authorities officially considered such settlements to be illegal, they tolerated them, for Lusaka never had sufficient housing
stock for its rapidly growing African population. Finally, in the late
1940s, at a time when South African urban influx controls had
become considerably strengthened as part of the institutionalization
of previous decades' de facto segregation by race into the system that
we have come to know as apartheid (Wilkinson 1983), Northern
Rhodesian authorities passed the 1948 African Urban Housing
Ordinance, which granted African workers urban residency status
and a house if they were married. This new policy, which was a
response to continued labor shortages throughout the post–World
War II years, was directed toward Africans who worked in the kinds
of employment that served European needs. Because the colony's
most profitable industry was on the copperbelt, it is not surprising
that African workers in the mining towns were the main beneficiaries
of the new policy (Thøgersen and Andersen 1983:87).

Already during World War II, the construction of Old Chilenje
and Kanyama was begun in Lusaka, and two new African suburbs
(New Chilenje in 1950 and Matero in 1951) followed after the passage of the new housing ordinance. These new suburbs included
schools, churches, welfare halls, recreational facilities, beer halls,
and stores. As in South Africa, beer hall profits were used to finance African welfare facilities. Additional African suburbs with
rental housing were planned at this time but postponed during
the economic slowdown from the mid- through late 1950s and
only revived prior to independence. Experiments were also made
with a small number of plots on which Africans could build their
own houses; the first, Maploto (meaning "plot"), in 1936, was
later absorbed into Old Chilenje, Chibolya was built in 1952 and
New Kanyama just before independence, in 1963. These develop-

ments not only gave Africans in Northern Rhodesia a much more legitimate urban stake than their counterparts in South Africa but also dramatically challenged the inherent limits on Lusaka's planning as a colonial city centered on administrative functions and European comforts.

Comparisons, Contrasts, Contexts: The Copperbelt and Lusaka

In contrast to Lusaka, the copperbelt towns were industrial centers whose raison d'être was mining, which was controlled by two private companies. Although these towns had both mine and municipal townships, the mining companies were the major landlord, owner of the ration store, distributor of health services, and supervisor of recreational facilities.[4] The exception was Ndola, the copperbelt's administrative center, which also had some manufacturing activities that serviced the mines. As a subtype of the colonial city, the mining towns on the copperbelt might be described as colonial company towns, or as Coketowns (Hannerz 1980:123).

Urban development on the copperbelt dates from the late 1920s, when large-scale commercial production of copper proved profitable. The rapid growth of towns in this region attracted the attention of anthropologists associated with the Rhodes-Livingstone Institute, who undertook pioneering research into the problems that arose from the involvement of Africans in industrial wage labor at a time when little urban research was conducted in the discipline. This research broke in many ways with conventional anthropology's bounded notion of culture by viewing African urban interaction as influenced by forces having to do with the needs and requirements of wage labor and the wider economy. Drawing on an impressive methodological repertoire and examining a range of concerns, these investigators produced a rich body of urban ethnography.[5]

The hallmarks of this work include Wilson's description of the emerging social and economic characteristics of African urban life in Broken Hill (1941 and 1942), Mitchell's large-scale social surveys on many aspects of urban social organization and labor circulation (1987) and his examination of urban expressions of ethnicity in Kalela, a popular dance (1956), and Epstein's study of the development of African politics in both mine and municipal townships

(1958). In his work on African urban courts (1953), Epstein hinted at tensions in the African urban domestic domain, as did Powdermaker (1962), who provided the only distinctly American contribution to the urban body of largely British-influenced anthropology associated with the Rhodes-Livingstone Institute. But while it was hinted at, the unfolding domestic domain of household, family, and gender relations claimed little substantive attention during the 1950s heyday of the Rhodes-Livingstone Institute. Only after almost thirty years did Epstein return to his research in Ndola from the mid-1950s, providing a richly textured retrospective analysis of gender relations within households (1981).

The ethnography and conceptualizations of urban life that resulted from this work have left an important mark on the anthropology and history of this region, if not of Africa. Not surprisingly, this work has inspired controversy, debate, and continuous reevaluation.[6] A main thrust of these discussions has been to highlight, from many different angles, that African responses to life in the copperbelt towns were immensely more complicated than the accounts of the anthropologists associated with the Rhodes-Livingstone Institute revealed (Ferguson 1990b; Macmillan 1993). Still, much of this criticism disguises the most innovative methodological aspects of this work. Among these aspects are the focus on case and situational analysis and explicit concerns with networks and linkages that produced an understanding of villages, mining compounds, and towns as connected, but uneasily so, into a broader socioeconomic field of interaction.

Polemics aside, the power of this rich body of colonial ethnography is not revealed in the perceptions of critics but rather in the inspiration the work provided for developing urban scholarship in new or different directions. I suggest that including nonmining towns such as Lusaka in the study of ongoing socioeconomic change helps to cast additional light on the development of urbanism as an African way of life during the late colonial period.

Northern Rhodesia's capital constitutes an immensely more varied setting than the mining towns in which to examine African urbanism in the making. Lusaka's demographic and labor history differs from that of the copperbelt in many ways. In addition to being an administrative center, Lusaka also assumed many distributive and service functions because of its location at a rail and road junction. Most of its industry was food processing and construction. But by far the most striking differences between the mining towns and the capital were Lusaka's growing squatter compounds and its developing informal economy, as well as its wage-labor force, in which domestic service and government work formed the two largest occupational sectors. These phenomena were present in the copperbelt towns on a smaller scale than in Lusaka, yet they were barely noticed. In short, when compared to Africans in the copperbelt, those in Lusaka enjoyed much more diversity, not only in occupations but also in social groupings and interactional arenas across neighborhoods.

Of all the towns in Northern Rhodesia, Lusaka had the greatest variety of African housing of almost every classification, controlled by several authorities and private employers. In the 1950s, there still were the old Kabwata town compound and the municipal townships built during the 1940s, as well as new African suburbs, private locations, and squatter compounds (Boswell 1969:249).[7] In Lusaka, a larger proportion of the African population lived in servants' quarters on their employers' premises than in any other town (Collins 1986:125). And of all the towns, Lusaka experienced the greatest proliferation of unauthorized compounds (Martin 1974:74).

The differences between the copperbelt towns and Lusaka during the late colonial period are important. We may signal them by viewing African miners in the company-controlled compounds and informal-sector workers in squatter settlements as emblematic of each setting. This allows us to shift the copperbelt research focus on urban adjustment, trade unions, and politics to the study of place as a lived experience. Changing the focus in this way, we may then raise questions about how living in Lusaka was shaped by such factors as gender, age, and cultural practices. Thus we do not take the city for granted as a mere setting and locale, but rather we ask what sort of town Lusaka was and how its colonial-built environment and its particular occupational structure mediated experiences that were central to its development into an African city.

Urbanism as an African Way of Life in Lusaka

Colonial Lusaka might well have been created for its European residents, but it was always, as table 1.1 indicates, an African city in terms of demographics. In fact, judging from the censuses, the category

TABLE 1.1. *Population Growth in Lusaka, 1921–1956*

RESIDENTS IN LUSAKA

		Europeans			Asians			Colored			Africans in Employment		
		Males	Females	Total	Males	Females	Total	Males	Females	Total	Males	Females	Total
1921	Lusaka	141	102	243	1		1	1		1	1,280		1,280
1931	Lusaka	250	183	433									
	Lusaka suburbs	18	19	37									
	Lusaka & Suburbs	268	202	470									
1946	Lusaka	1,171	1,444	2,615[a]	106	44	150	11	12	23	7,485	59	7,544
	Townships			1,254									
1951	Lusaka Townships	1,983	1,806	3,789	247	112	359	45	36	81	13,054	184	13,238
	Suburbs	419	448	867	4	2	6	1	1	2	1,475	43	1,518
	Total	2,402	2,254	4,656	251	114	365	46	37	83	14,529	227	14,756
1956	Lusaka Townships	3,950	3,550	7,500	620	430	1,050	80	90	170	19,914	295	20,209
	Suburbs	970	970	1,940	10	10	20	10	20	30	2,184	51	2,235
	Total	4,920	4,520	9,440	630	440	1,070	90	110	200	22,098	346	22,444

[a] When Polish refugees were excluded there were 1,254 European residents in 1946.

Source: Bettison 1959:8–9.

"Africans in employment" grew at a much higher rate than the resident European population.

Because urban census enumeration practices throughout the colonial period listed only African men in employment, they enhanced the fiction that the town's African population was overwhelmingly male.[8] A battery of legal ordinances on rural-urban migration, employment, and housing contributed further to the notion of African men as units of labor, without dependents, who would return to the countryside when no longer employed in the cities. These ordinances had developed in the early years of this century, modeled on similar measures in South Africa and Southern Rhodesia; they were formalized in the late 1920s when, in the view of those in power, the rapid development of the mining towns required more control over Africans in towns; and many of them were amended in the 1950s to reckon with ongoing socioeconomic and political developments that were gradually dislodging the racial underpinnings of colonial rule. Still, some of them were not repealed until immediately before independence.

According to these ordinances, Africans who resided in towns had to carry *situpas*, a local name for the identification cards or passes that employers had to endorse. When moving in the European areas of towns after nine o'clock at night, Africans had to carry night passes, which their employers issued. They were not allowed to conduct trade and business in the European areas, and beer brewing and distilling were illegal in the African residential areas controlled by the municipality. African visitors to town had to show permits, and the police were entitled to undertake night raids and to repatriate women and children who lived without legal male guardians. The penalties for noncompliance with these ordinances ranged from fines and imprisonment to repatriation to the countryside. In short, through the use of legal instruments, colonial power constructed the lives of its African subjects into the fiction of the temporary migrant who was single and male, wage-employed, and living in employer-provided housing for the duration of his temporary work sojourn in the city.

While the activities of Lusaka's African residents certainly were constrained by colonial rules and regulations, they did not resemble the fiction of the single, transient, male migrant worker whose rural family readily accepted the separation of kin. Government reports on urban living conditions in 1944 revealed some of the ways in which actual urban living arrangements differed from the official fiction. The urban African residents were estimated to be 23 percent women, 27 percent children, and 50 percent men. Of these 50 percent men, 40 percent were wage-employed, 2 percent self-employed, and 8 percent unemployed. They lived in abysmal housing conditions—for example, in municipal housing with 8.1 persons per unit, 7.3 persons in each room, and only 10.3 percent of the housing units had more than one room (Heisler 1974:92). This report demonstrates that in spite of being prohibited from leaving the rural areas, large numbers of women and children had already settled in towns. Finally, in the early 1950s, the colonial government abolished the urban influx controls.

To be sure, Lusaka was overwhelmingly an African city in demographic terms. More important for the purpose at hand, the capital's African livelihoods developed socioeconomic characteristics that were quite at variance with those the administration had intended. The fiction of the single male migrant worker who lived in town only for as long as he was employed did not reckon with a variety of phenomena that were among the unplanned results of the colonial regulatory framework, including the growth of squatter housing, the development of the informal sector, and the growing presence of women and children. These phenomena in part contributed to the rapid urbanization rate from the post–World War II years and onward, as a result both of natural increase among the urban African population and of ongoing rural-to-urban migration.

African Recollections of Colonial Lusaka

What were the effects of this rapid urbanization and its underlying demographics on the African men and women who made this colonial city their home? Who were they, and how did they experience life in the capital? Clearly, Lusaka's African residents could not always choose or design the institutions within which they lived. Their experiences of colonial power depended not only on the nature of that power but also on where they stood in relationship to it from within— that is to say, with their own backgrounds as men and women of particular ages and circumstances. Below, I offer two brief glimpses of how colonial Lusaka appeared to a man and a woman who have lived there since the last half of the 1930s, that is, during the time when the colonial administration held on to the fiction of the familyless, transient, male worker. Because we do not have any detailed ethnography of African township life in colonial Lusaka, I draw on a number of surveys from the 1950s in an effort to establish some background.

"It was nice in those days," said Mr. Zulu, a civil servant in his mid- to late fifties whom I called on in Lusaka in 1983 in order to inquire about pension regulations in domestic service. "Nice" must be understood against the backdrop of the early 1980s, which was a period of economic downturn that particularly affected the availability of basic consumer goods. Mr. Zulu had come to Lusaka with his Ngoni parents from the Eastern Province in the mid-1930s, and he recalled his life in Lusaka as a boy and a young man. They lived in "the lines," the messengers' compound that housed the African staff employed, like the senior Zulu, at the *boma*, the administrative headquarters of the territory. As noted previously, the *boma* was built on Cairo Road, Lusaka's main north-south thoroughfare, when the capital was moved from Livingstone. It was demolished around 1965 to make way for a state-run department store, Mwaizeni.

Lusaka was spread over a large area, and its street layout was designed with automobile transportation in mind. Most Africans walked. Describing Lusaka's geography, its private compounds (employer-provided), and its squatter settlements, Mr. Zulu spoke with excitement of how he and his young friends would walk from the messengers' compound, just south of the Kafue roundabout, into town. They would watch people coming and going at the train station, look at the shop windows in the "first-class" trading area and, in particular, they would admire "those big old cars with horns, some even had canvas roofs." To be sure, there were restrictions on where they could shop, but it was mainly, he explained, the butchers who insisted on serving African customers through a hatch rather than from the main shop. There were many things to buy, he said, all kinds of things. Good clothing, for example, was available, much cheaper than today. They could not walk in the European residential areas after nine o'clock at night without permission. But servants readily got "night passes" from their employers, and in the 1950s better-educated people like clerks and teachers got "exemption certificates" from the night pass ruling. He did not recall these restrictions as particularly tough, he said, "for we could move all over the African areas."

As he grew up, there were lots of activities to get involved in. They included interschool competitions, for instance in sports. On Sundays there was church, and after church there was the beer hall at Kabwata, the first African township planned along with the capital in the 1930s. Outside the beer hall there was "tribal" dancing, and in the welfare hall at Kabwata there were regular ballroom dance competitions between ballroom dance clubs from different towns. During World War II, the administration installed radio loudspeakers in the welfare halls for specially edited transmissions of war news. The welfare halls were also used to show films approved by the film censor board. "We enjoyed ourselves," said Mr. Zulu in the same breath as he noted that both "tribal" and ballroom dancing declined in popularity during the late 1950s "when politics took over."

Contrast this to the very different experiences of Mrs. Mubanga, who was born in Lusaka in 1935 to Bemba parents from Mpika in the Northern Province. Her father worked as a mechanic on a European farm near Chelston on the eastern fringe of Lusaka. As a child, she lived in the farm compound. Unlike Mr. Zulu, she never went to school, except as a young adult to attend domestic science courses at the Kabwata homecraft center. For some years, she worked as a helper to the European social workers in the welfare department, which was established in 1952. Some of these social workers taught African women in the municipal welfare center at Chilenje. She married a skilled carpenter who got housing from his employer. They lived in the contractors' compound until they built a house of their own in Libala, one of the peri-urban townships established by the municipality shortly after independence.

Over the years, Mrs. Mubanga made extremely good use of her acquired skills in domestic crafts by pursuing a variety of informal-sector activities. When I talked to her in 1992 at her secondhand clothing stand in Mtendere, all the children, except a married daughter whose husband was studying in Canada, had left home. Mrs. Mubanga and her daughter contributed to household income by selling secondhand clothing. Mrs. Mubanga, whom I first met in 1971, had begun this line of trade by purchasing used clothing directly at the doors of expatriate households. In 1992 both she and her daughter bought bales of used clothing imported from the West from a number of commercial importers who ship this merchandise into Zambia.

In these brief recollections, colonial Lusaka's built environment comes into view. We see the colonial institutions for supervision and socialization, such as the *boma*, the school, the welfare hall, the beer hall, and the domestic science training center. We also see Lusaka's segregated housing, such as the municipal townships, the messengers' compound where Mr. Zulu grew up, the new African suburbs, and their postcolonial successors like Libala. And we see the private employer–provided compound for peri-urban workers on farms where Mrs. Mubanga grew up and the contractors' compound where she went to live with her carpenter husband. Of Lusaka's total African population of 64,754 in 1957, 31,542 lived in municipal housing and 8,917 in private employer compounds. We hear in passing about servants domiciled in the European areas. Servants' quarters housed 11,934 of Lusaka's population in 1957. The rest of Lusaka's African population lived in eight squatter compounds, of which several have remained as part of the capital's physical and social landscape (Bettison 1959:20).

Fleshing out the social side of these recollections, we recall that Mr. Zulu and Mrs. Mubanga were born in the last half of the 1930s. This allows us to trace their backgrounds to the 17 percent of men and 23 percent of women over twenty years of age who, according to a 1957 survey of Lusaka's African population, had lived more than 90 percent of their lives in an urban area (Bettison 1959:8).

Mr. Zulu and Mrs. Mubanga come from two of the many ethnic groups represented in Lusaka, the Ngoni and the Bemba. Compared to that of the copperbelt towns, Lusaka's African population was always more heterogeneous in ethnic terms, including persons from nearly all of Zambia's more than seventy ethnic groups, as well as nonlocal Africans. In general, the largest part of Lusaka's population originates from the hinterland to the east of the city all the way to the border to Malawi, including persons from that country. The completion of the Great East Road in the late 1920s provided a major conveyor belt for rural-urban interaction (Hobson 1979:131). In 1957, Nsenga people from the Petauke district formed the largest group of Lusaka's population, followed by the Ngoni and Chewa, all from the Eastern Province. Bemba-speaking people from the region in which the copperbelt is situated formed the fourth-largest group (Bettison 1959:xvi).

Lusaka had an earlier established married population than the copperbelt towns did, and Mr. Zulu and Mrs. Mubanga come from such backgrounds. Mrs. Mubanga moved from the peri-urban farm compound where she grew up into Lusaka "through" her husband. The proportion of men who had their wives with them in Lusaka grew from 47.6 percent to 55.2 percent between 1954 and 1957 (Bettison 1959:xiii). Over that same period, the proportion of children of both sexes who lived with their parents in Lusaka grew from 76 percent to 90 percent. In addition, approximately one third of Lusaka's African households had live-in relatives, who were going to school, working elsewhere, looking for work or housing, doing household work, or combinations of these (Bettison 1959:32, 50). The extent to which such relatives in fact were tenants is difficult to assess, as subletting was illegal in the municipal townships.

A growing number of these relatives were children and young adults, especially boys, who worked with or without pay. According to the 1956 population census, three times as many juvenile boys as adult women were wage-employed in all economic sectors in Northern Rhodesia's towns (Hansen 1990:226). A limited system of compulsory education for children between the ages of twelve and sixteen had been introduced in some of the urban areas in the early 1940s, first in the copperbelt towns and later in Broken Hill and Livingstone. It did not include Lusaka, where the education of African children was sorely behind until schools were built in the new suburbs after the war (Rothman 1972:58–59, 71–73). As Mrs. Mubanga's story indicates, boys were more likely than girls to go to school. As a young adult, she attended classes, organized by the welfare department, in domestic science, including needlework, housewifery, mothercraft, and cooking. And in spite of her lack of formal education, she worked as a helper in the teaching of domestic crafts to women.

Mr. Zulu's father and Mrs. Mubanga's husband worked in two of the most important employment sectors in Lusaka: the senior Zulu as a messenger in government service and Mr. Mubanga as a carpenter in the rapidly expanding construction industry. But domestic service formed the single largest employment area for African men during most of Lusaka's history. From the initial planning of the city to the eve of independence, government employment and domestic service were the two largest wage-employment sectors for African men in Lusaka (Hansen 1989a:221–22). While the construction industry has affected the relative proportion of these two employment categories at times of economic growth, it has not transcended their importance on a permanent basis.

Housing and Gender

Because Africans were prohibited from trading in the municipal townships, and because housing was tied to employment, the squatter compounds provided particular opportunities for self-employment. First, a brief overview of the scene: According to the 1957 survey, some of Lusaka's male African residents were self-employed and half of them lived in the squatter compounds (Bettison 1959:84). There were also self-employed people in the African suburbs, for example in Chilenje in 1957, including one man who had been a migrant laborer in Southern Rhodesia beginning in 1929 and worked in the mines there until he came to Lusaka in 1946 and set himself up as a freelance photographer. Another self-employed man who had lived six years in Chilenje combined upholstery with coffin making (Butler 1958:444–45). Both men and women were involved in firewood collection in the peri-urban areas. And some women practiced horticulture, although the density of housing in squatter settlements and some of the older municipal compounds made it difficult to plant gardens on the plots (Bettison 1959:92).

Several contemporary observers emphasized the connection between squatter compounds and work. There is no doubt, according to another survey, that "the vendors of herbs and dried caterpillars, the indigent carpenter and shoe-maker, the wise woman and snuff-grinders, all have an established position in the urban African society, and that at present they operate almost exclusively in the unauthorized locations" (Armor 1958, as quoted in Heisler 1974:117). The squatter compounds had a generally older population than the other townships, with a smaller proportion of men and especially women fifteen to twenty-nine years of age, and significantly more women thirty to forty years of age than any of the other townships (Bettison 1959:38).

What accounts for the special connection between unauthorized housing and women? (Bettison 1959:38–39, 42, 79). Even though colonial employment statistics must be interpreted with caution, they clearly indicate that very few African women were wage-employed. Women and children under fourteen years of age could perform wage labor only with the consent of their guardian—that is, their father, mother's brother, or husband (Browne 1933:160).[9] And housing was tied to the job. The 1948 African Urban Housing Ordinance, which opened up the construction of married housing, did not grant women housing in their own right. A woman's rights to urban residence and to municipal housing reached her through her husband, and as proof of the status of the union, a marriage certificate had to be produced. Because of the prohibition on trade in the municipal townships, the squatter compounds provided space for self-constructed housing and small-scale trade, making them a major attraction for women who wanted to work.

The regulations on marriage registration in connection with housing appear to have been enforced more rigidly in Lusaka than on the copperbelt (Epstein 1981:282). Many single women and couples in informal conjugal unions found shelter in Lusaka's squatter areas. Here, residents provided their own amenities. Markets developed that provided the goods and services unavailable in the compounds controlled by the municipality. Chief among these activities was the sale of prepared food, home-brewed beer, and sex, which, given the skewed sex ratio, found a ready male clientele and provided some women with a livelihood.[10]

In both the African and the official views, the *shebeen*, the African beer garden run illegally by women, became associated with the squatter areas. In view of the fact that Lusaka's only legal beer hall until 1950, the one in Kabwata, sold a not very popular diluted brew in a dilapidated building where brick and cement fell into the beer, it is not surprising that drinking in the *shebeen* was a preferred alternative (Rothman 1972:248). Even when the municipalities established more beer halls in the new townships, illegal brewing continued to expand.

Women's role in Lusaka's beer trade deserves comment because it points up how the official notion of gender was challenged. The vast majority of Africans in Lusaka had incomes that were barely, if at all, adequate to meet their most basic needs (Bettison 1959:58).[11] One woman recalled that brewing was "the only way she could raise school fees for her children," and another explained, "This is how we clothed our children" (Ambler 1990:304). Women brewers fought back on several occasions when authorities used police to suppress their production. A dramatic incident took place in Lusaka in 1954 when at the end of May, some two thousand women demonstrated at the *boma* against the municipal beer monopoly. The brewing and selling of beer was one of the few means available to urban women to contribute to household income or support themselves if they were single heads of households. The demonstrating women's request to continue to brew beer is not the least bit surprising. They explained: "Our husbands get low wages and we have large families. On our income we must pay tax, rent, church fees, etc." (Rothman 1972:257).

While they remained largely excluded from wage labor, women began gradually to make their presence felt in market trading. A 1954 study of Lusaka's main African market shows that about one fifth of the vendors were women. They were not full-time, regular traders but mostly sold fruit and vegetables when in season and also prepared foodstuffs. Most of these women were married either to market traders and hawkers with irregular incomes or to "the lower paid sectors of the community" (Nyirenda 1957:37). Yet the proportion of market women who were single heads of households was higher than in the urban population at large (Nyirenda 1957:42).[12] A restudy of Lusaka's markets in 1959 showed that women's participation had increased to one third of the vendors (Miracle 1962). They still concentrated in the fruit and vegetable trades, and their earnings were small. Although women made up a slowly growing proportion of market traders, they remained at the least profitable end of the trade, and the markets in this part of Africa remained disproportionately male throughout the colonial period.

Because colonial census enumerators categorized "work" as wage labor, which was men's work, they ignored women's nonwaged activities. When such activities were noted, for instance in the 1957 Lusaka survey, they were characterized as "principally in kind, in [women's] capacity as housewives, by the provision of garden produce, firewood, etc. Some engage in trade on their own account, have illicit income from breweries or distillers, while others benefit from prostitution, casual affairs and in other ways" (Bettison 1959:84).

Although colonial Lusaka's built environment and institutions were part of both Mr. Zulu's and Mrs. Mubanga's recollections, Mrs. Mubanga's involvements come less clearly into view. To a large degree this difference reflects the unequal exposure of African women and men to the new urban opportunity structure. In effect, the colonial administration sought to shape its African subjects according to its own image of what urban African men's and women's lives ought to be like. The *boma*, the church, and the school construed African men and women as different persons with different capabilities: African men as low-skilled wage workers and African women as wives and mothers. The institutions that the colonial administration introduced to socialize Africans according to this gendered image extended into leisure activity: the municipal beer hall and sports activity for men, and the welfare department for women's domestic science training. The welfare halls in the authorized compounds were the sites for supervised entertainment, including "tribal" and ballroom dancing, approved movies, and propaganda films produced by the information department.

Mr. Zulu's and Mrs. Mubanga's recollections and the urban surveys of the 1950s testify to the gendered nature of Lusaka's built environment and its wage-labor institutions. The colonial administration limited women's access to wage labor, thus contributing to their economic dependence on men. But gender had a more complicated relationship to both wage labor and the household than the colonial construction of African women's and men's proper roles allowed for. Economic processes beyond the household prompted a large proportion of Lusaka's predominantly non-wage-employed women, including Mrs. Mubanga, to turn domestic skills into income-generating activity. In short, the colonial construction of African women's role did not reckon with how the new institutional forms were challenged and reworked in local relations between women and men, especially in the household setting, thus turning it into an arena influenced dramatically by developments beyond it.

Associational Activities

Because of the predominantly sociological and administrative concerns of this era's scholarship, little attention was paid to the cultural side of colonial Lusaka's African urbanism. We know that most compounds were heterogeneous in ethnic terms. There is no doubt that a range of associational interactions arose to meet some of the new needs of an urban population dependent on cash incomes and upholding a variety of links with their home areas as well as to satisfy their desires for enjoyment and good times.

There are hints of some of the African social and cultural institutions that arose in Lusaka, among them funeral associations, "homeboy" groups, ballroom dancing, charismatic churches, and a variety of ritual activity (Boswell 1969). By 1910, dancing and drinking societies were already active. Drumming clubs, known as *kasela* or *kalela* in the Soli and Bisa languages, got together to perform on Sunday evenings. Members paid dues in return for food and beer at "subscription" parties on Saturday nights and Sunday afternoons. Out of membership fees they also provided help in cases of illness and unemployment, and above all, they functioned as funeral associations (Rothman 1972:231–32). So did the ballroom dancing clubs, in which domestic servants were especially well known for their skills (Hansen 1989a:161–66).

A good deal of activity revolved around church, both established denominations and independent churches. Many Africans in Lusaka found the Watchtower movement attractive, and by the early 1930s, perhaps 75 percent of Lusaka's Africans were among its followers (Rothman 1972:340–44). Marrapodi/Mandevu, a squatter complex on the northern edge of Lusaka, became a refuge for a charismatic church, the Masowe Apostles, that originated in Southern Rhodesia and South Africa. Zairean and Southern Rhodesian members of the Maranke church, another charismatic group, settled there as well. Because of their beliefs, both groups refrained from wage labor, making their living from basket making, tinsmithing, and carpentry (Jules-Rosette 1975).

It is also very likely that a variety of ritual activity took place—for example, healing practices, possession rituals, and cults of affliction in which women were central actors. Such practices hint at unease on the part of some urban women who through ritual performance might have sought to relieve stresses brought about by the needs of urban everyday life (van Binsbergen 1981:235–65; Vail and White 1991:231–77).

As the colonial period wore on, activities such as ballroom dancing fell out of favor, Watchtower followers were harassed by authorities, and the social field became increasingly politicized. African party politics developed. In the late 1950s, the two major African political parties, the African National Congress (ANC) and the United National Independence Party (UNIP), had chapters in several Lusaka townships, including the squatter areas, and the parties appropriated many of the beer halls (Ambler 1990:310–11). With the 1963 demise of the federation and the coming of independence in 1964, the stage was set for a new relationship between Lusaka's African residents and their government.

Permanent Urbanization

The economic and political processes that were instrumental in the creation of towns such as Lusaka had profound ramifications on the viability of rural livelihoods, on their gender division of labor, on the social fabric of village life, and on rural-urban interaction. As noted previously, the colonial regulations that supplied migrant workers to European farms, businesses, mines, and private households in towns were oriented largely toward men. The administration was concerned to prevent the growth of an urban African proletariat who no longer had ties to the land, and it therefore considered the village and the tribe to be the reference point for migrants.

In the colonial scheme of things, it was very important to keep women back on the farm. The viability of village life depended on their work, for in this region's agricultural systems women played the major productive role. Their work not only subsidized the migrant workers' substandard wages and ensured the reproduction of a new generation of workers without cost to the administration, but it also maintained migrant workers' ties to kin and land. Despite the reserves policy, which reduced the available land for many African groups, and marketing policies that paid them less than the Europeans for their produce, farm output from African producers did not disappear entirely from the market (Muntemba 1977). As long as it remained profitable to participate in food production, many African women continued to depend on their fields for a living, supplemented by remittances from absentee husbands, brothers, and sons.

These circumstances changed once the slump of the early 1930s had ended. Many more men went on labor migration. By the mid-1930s, more than half of the able-bodied African male population was working for wages away from home, half of them abroad (mostly in Southern Rhodesia and South Africa) and the other half within Northern Rhodesia (Roberts 1976:171). Women, children, and old people on some of the reserves were unable to meet their own needs for food without permanent cash support from men. Several studies from the 1930s onward indicate a growing gap in food consumption between African rural and urban populations (Fetter 1984; Thomson 1954). More women and children migrated to towns, sometimes alone, or accompanied by husbands, fathers, or guardians. During

World War II, when Northern Rhodesia experienced extreme food scarcities, the government tried in vain to stem this influx, devising a variety of measures to get women back to the villages, where in its view they belonged as food producers.

Questions about the effects of these processes on rural livelihoods, on relationships between the sexes and the generations, on rural-urban interaction, and on town life have been extensively discussed.[13] In a recent criticism of the historiography of urbanization and migration to the copperbelt, Ferguson (1990b) has argued that much of this scholarship drew on Eurocentric assumptions that reduced the complexity of rural-urban links to a progressive stage-wise emergence of a stable, settled urban working class with few rural attachments. Taking Ferguson to task for his use of the historical sources, Macmillan (1993) has questioned this argument. Interpretive battles aside, Macmillan points out that in spite of complex, and changing, links between Zambia's rural and urban areas and despite regional shifts in the rate of migration to different cities, the urbanization process continues. In effect, he finds Ferguson's conceptual vision limiting in its denial of permanent urbanization and proletarianization on the part of large population segments from the post–World War II years onward.

To be sure, migration patterns in Northern Rhodesia changed after World War II. They changed especially in gender and age terms, factors that both Ferguson and Macmillan note but do not bring to bear on developing their different visions of urbanization (Ferguson 1990b:911–13; Macmillan 1993:685–88). Many more men and particularly women and children migrated than before. As noted earlier, this process was facilitated to some extent by changes in government policy concerning housing for married workers. But while this observation takes note of women, it does so largely in relation to marriage and housing. Such an account obscures the way gender relations interact with economic processes. Not all women, of course, migrated merely to follow their husbands. Single women, divorcées, and widows left the villages because they had limited access to the means of production and other resources and because towns provided more diverse income-earning opportunities than did the rural areas. And certainly some women must have longed to exchange rural drudgery for urban adventure. When we explain women's migration only as a consequence of their dependence on men, we ignore that it also was a response to the ongoing decline of economic opportunities in the countryside. And we omit the role of personal agency in decision making. In this way we miss entirely the cultural politics that shaped gender relations and were centrally involved in both prompting women's migration and influencing their subsequent urban experiences.

As indicated earlier, Lusaka experienced a substantive increase in the proportion of men who had wives and children with them from the post–World War II period onward. What is more, there were single female heads of households living in the squatter compounds, and the number of single women who conducted market trade grew. In Lusaka, in contrast to other towns, a larger proportion of the population lived in squatter compounds, where many, especially women, made a living from informal-sector activity. Barely hinting at African economic involvement and employer-provided housing outside the formal wage-labor nexus, the urban anthropology of the copperbelt towns in the 1950s took little notice of the social and economic forces and gender dynamics that have developed into the most widespread arrangements for living throughout postcolonial Zambia's urban areas.

2

A House of One's Own

A house of one's own is something special for persons with modest means, particularly in Zambia's urban areas, where colonial policy discouraged African owner-occupancy from developing. The exceptions to this were the small schemes of self-help housing both on the copperbelt and in Lusaka and the squatter settlements—particularly in Lusaka, which provided self-built shelter in a housing market that otherwise was wholly tied to employment.

Mtendere township, where Mrs. Mubanga has her used clothing stand, presents an excellent example for a discussion of the importance of housing and home ownership to urban arrangements for living in the wake of independence in 1964. The township was established as a site-and-service resettlement scheme on Lusaka's eastern outskirts in 1967 and incorporated into the city when the urban boundary was extended in 1970. The processes that led to the development and subsequent growth of a township like Mtendere offer evidence of highly self-conscious actions by urban low-income people who constitute "the common man" against the backdrop of a history mostly of government indifference.

This chapter presents an overview of the rapid urbanization and economic changes of the first decades after independence, with particular focus on the built environment and the low-income housing question in Lusaka. Concerns about what types of housing to plan for low-income people led to the creation of such townships as Mtendere, the haphazard development of which I trace in the rest of this chapter. The arrangements for living to which Mtendere is host are the subject of chapter 3.

Postcolonial Urbanization

Independence in 1964 triggered substantial growth of all of Zambia's urban areas, most spectacularly of Lusaka, the new nation's capital, whose population on the eve of independence was roughly similar in size to that of Kitwe on the copperbelt. As indicated in table 2.1, Lusaka soon outgrew Kitwe in size, replacing it as the country's hub. Favorable economic circumstances during the years immediately preceding independence and continuing through the 1960s turned the capital into an attractive destination for a growing number of migrants who anticipated increased work and housing opportunities in the wake of independence.

Good export earnings from copper after independence enabled the new government to shift the course of economic development to some degree. The economic links to white-dominated South Africa and Rhodesia were diminished, and Zambia initially went to great lengths in cutting her trade with those two countries.[1] Between 1968 and 1970 the hold of the two multinational companies on the mining industry was modified through a state-initiated partnership, made possible by economic reforms (Martin 1972). Local manufacturing had never been actively encouraged during the colonial period, save in products shielded against overseas competition because of perishability or simplicity, such as food processing, beer brewing, furniture making, and newspaper printing. Extending and diversifying local industry, the new government constructed a hydroelectric plant at Kafue, where it also built a chemical fertilizer, a cement plant, and a textile factory. The country itself now was to produce what previously had been imported. While some industries expanded rapidly in the 1960s, many former imports were not replaced by locally produced ones, and import substitution amounted largely to local assembly of foreign parts (Seidman 1974).

Lusaka hosted the economic boom following independence, as the new government set out to establish its headquarters. An international airport was built, and the capital soon featured the country's first university and a teaching hospital. More schools were built. As

TABLE 2.1 *Urban Population Growth in Zambia, 1963–1990*

URBAN AREAS WITH 50,000 INHABITANTS IN 1980

URBAN AREAS	POPULATION				AVERAGE ANNUAL GROWTH RATE (PERCENT)		
	1963	1969	1980	1990	1963–1969	1969–1980	1980–1990
Lusaka	123,146	262,425	535,830	982,362	13.4	6.5	6.1
Kitwe	123,027	199,798	266,286	338,207	8.4	2.6	2.4
Ndula	92,691	159,786	250,502	376,311	9.5	4.0	4.0
Mufulira	80,609	107,802	135,535	152,944	5.0	2.1	1.2
Chingola	59,517	103,292	130,875	167,954	9.6	2.1	2.5
Kabwe	39,522	65,974	136,006	166,519	8.9	6.6	2.0
Luanshya	75,332	96,282	110,907	146,275	4.2	1.3	2.8
Livingstone	33,026	45,243	63,275	82,218	5.4	3.0	2.6
Chililabombwe	34,165	44,862	54,737	76,848	4.6	2.1	3.4
Kalulushi	21,303	32,272	52,146	75,197	7.2	4.3	3.6
Large urban areas	682,338	1,117,736	1,736,099	2,564,835			
Towns 5,000 to 50,000 in 1980	32,682	74,380	522,401	720,931			
Total urban	715,020	1,192,116	2,258,500	3,285,766	8.9	5.8	3.7

Source: Compiled from Zambia Census, 1981b, 1990.

a result, the construction industry expanded, and employment opportunities increased in government service, as they did in transportation, communications, and commerce. Some light industry developed as well.

The number of African men in wage employment in Lusaka nearly doubled between the 1961 and 1969 censuses, from 24,942 to 49,010 (Wood 1986:175). Because of inconsistent enumeration procedures, neither the 1963 nor the 1969 census recorded the proportion of wage-employed women. A comparison of the 1956 and 1969 censuses reveals that there were approximately 62 men wage employees to every one woman in Lusaka in 1956 and 10 to one in 1969 (Fry 1979:57). Yet the apparent increase in the proportion of wage-employed women fades in the light of the now larger female urban population. Formerly skewed sex ratios evened out after independence as more women moved to towns. Lusaka's sex ratio changed from 123 men per 100 women in 1965 to 101 men per 100 women in 1980 (Jackman 1973:17; Republic of Zambia 1981a:6).

Since Lusaka is the political and administrative center of independent Zambia, economic developments there have served as a magnet for migrants from within and outside the country. The capital's population grew from 123,146 to 262,425 between the 1963 and 1969 censuses. By 1974, Lusaka's population stood at 421,000. It rose to 535,830 in 1980 and to 982,362 in 1990. While part of this increase reflects the extension of the city boundary in 1970, the major factors were natural increase and migration from the rural areas.

The Eastern Province continues to provide the largest proportion of persons not born in the Lusaka urban district, with around 36 percent of all migrants to Lusaka in both 1969 and 1980.[2] In recent years, in-migration from the Copperbelt Province has expanded from providing 7.6 percent of Lusaka's migrants in 1969 to 12 percent in 1980 (Wood 1986:167). International migration, principally from elsewhere in Africa, especially Zimbabwe and Malawi, grew numerically yet decreased proportionately from 16 percent to 7 percent of Lusaka's total population between 1969 and 1980. The largest non-African element of Lusaka's migrant population originates from the United Kingdom (Wood 1986:169). Lusaka is also home both to a longtime resident population from the Indian subcontinent, many of whom are involved in trade and commerce, and to expatriates from that region who are working in the capital on shorter contracts.[3]

Urban Planning and Low-Income Housing

Lusaka entered independence with a severe housing backlog, especially for the population with limited economic means. How and where was the capital's rapidly growing population to find shelter and how was the much-needed expansion of its housing supply to be financed?

At independence, the colonial labels for Lusaka's built environment were changed. The former European residential parts of the capital became known as low-density, the African municipal townships as medium-density, and the African squatter settlements as high-density housing areas. While this shift in terminology erased the former racial labels, it still contained a considerable degree of segregation, albeit now in socioeconomic terms (Kay 1967:118–32). As noted in the previous chapter, the linking of housing to employment, which was part of the colonial period's contract labor system, had already progressively eroded in Lusaka before independence, partly because of shortages of medium- and low-cost housing and partly because of the growth of a labor force that did not participate in the contract labor system: the informal sector. While employer-provided housing or subsidized rents continued to be standard procedures and many workers expected employment-dependent or -supported housing as part and parcel of working for wages, the massive increase of Lusaka's population in the wake of independence placed enormous pressures on the city's existing housing stock.

How was Lusaka to house its growing low-income population, who could not afford much in terms of cost? Bettison noted in his survey of Lusaka's African residential areas in the last half of the 1950s that the majority of workers earned too little to afford to pay economic rent, let alone to buy their own houses (1959:91–94).[4] And this was at a time when pay in most sectors save domestic service had changed from cash and rations in kind to an all-inclusive wage. Except for residents of squatter townships and the few self-help housing schemes that had encouraged owner-occupancy, most urban workers were tenants. In most of the copperbelt towns, the mining companies owned the larger part of the housing stock, but in Lusaka the government was the major landlord.

This is to say that having a house of one's own was possible largely for those who took up residency in the rapidly expanding squatter areas, where in fact the matter of ownership was an issue, since such

Lusaka on the Eve of Independence, 1963

Forest Reserve
Industrial
City Center
Government Precinct
European Housing
European Smallholdings
Coloured Quarter
Asian Quarter
Municipal African Townships
Other African Settlements

0 1 2
miles

areas were not authorized and their inhabitants had no legal tenure rights. Two developments in low-income housing, aimed at harness-ing the ability of squatters to house themselves, took place during the 1960s and 1970s in the effort to meet the rapidly increasing housing needs. One was a policy of establishing low-cost, serviced plots on which people could construct houses within a set of established spec-ifications. When this proved to be too costly, requiring higher and more stable income than most prospective residents could afford, housing policy shifted toward the upgrading of squatter areas.

While employment opportunities initially had kept pace with Lusaka's population growth, housing did not. Lusaka's squatter set-tlements proliferated as people in search of living space began more openly to defy landowners. In spite of the ongoing construction boom, the access to housing had hardly improved since the colonial period. High- and medium-cost dwellings, mostly for civil servants, accounted for most of the additions to the existing housing stock. In 1969, for example, the city council spent twice as much on civil ser-vice as on low-cost housing (Simmance 1974:506). Although the squatter settlements grew in all the major towns, Lusaka experienced by far the most extensive of such new developments.

Urban planning in the immediate wake of independence envi-sioned wholesale demolition of squatter settlements with subse-quent resettlement of their residents. Toward the end of chapter 1, I noted how UNIP had garnered political support from mass mobiliza-tion in these townships before independence. To be sure, urban housing and amenities were "inflammatory local issues bound up with expectations of rapidly improving standards" as the new gov-ernment attempted to move away from colonial housing policies (Harries-Jones 1977:140). In approaching the question of affordable housing, the Zambian government adopted an idea that at the time was popular in many other African countries (Skinner and Rodell 1983). To reduce the low-cost housing backlog, the Ministry of Local Government and Housing in 1965 instructed all local authorities to plan 30 percent of their housing as site-and-service schemes (Republic of Zambia 1965). Local councils were to provide services (plot pegging, water, sanitation, and roads), while residents were to build their own houses according to predesigned plans. Roof loans were available, and management fees and modest rates were charged for water and garbage collection.

Core house under construction in stage 1 of Kaunda Square
site-and-service scheme, 1972

View of core houses at Kaunda Square, stage 1

Such site-and-service schemes were developed from the copperbelt to Lusaka during the last half of the 1960s (Republic of Zambia 1966). The first scheme in Lusaka was planned within the squatter township Marrapodi/Mandevu to resettle some of its residents (Jules-Rosette 1981:22–26). Since it proved difficult to contain squatting and to relocate households within the area where they already lived, vacant land was selected for future schemes (Republic of Zambia 1967a). The city council opened the first of these, Mtendere, initially known as Chainama Hills site-and-service resettlement scheme, in 1967 on a farm outside the city boundary to resettle squatters from designated areas. But within one year its development was halted by instruction from the highest level within the central government. While scheduled for removal, the township was from then on supervised by an agency of the Ministry of Lands and Natural Resources called the Squatter Control Unit.

Lusaka's next site-and-service schemes were all situated on lands away from town (Doxiades Associates 1969). These schemes developed slowly, for several reasons. Their peripheral location made prospective residents reluctant to settle. Services were late in being installed, and predesigned plans, for instance that of Kaunda Square, stage 1, were very unpopular. The funds allocated to such schemes were in any case far too limited to provide site-and-service plots for all of Lusaka's squatters, who at the turn of the 1960s accounted for at least one third of the city's population. What is more, not all squatters could afford the costs required to participate. In effect, the building of a house in a site-and-service scheme became progressively difficult for low-income households, as costs rose much faster than incomes did.

While the government's formal stance on squatter demolition during the 1960s was ambiguous at best, it eventually accorded the squatters a new role. The sheer scale of demographic increase in Lusaka in the 1970s, which was reflected by the growth of squatter settlements (see table 2.2), made repressive responses to urbanization untenable. The course of events from that decade on created a variety of new dynamics.

On the political front, Zambia was declared a one-party participatory democracy at the end of 1972. The government of the Second Republic, its party UNIP, and the para-statal companies established during the economic reforms of the late 1960s soon faced pressing concerns resulting from an economic slowdown created by the decline of world market prices for copper and the oil crisis of the early 1970s.

TABLE 2.2. *Growth of Squatter Settlements in Lusaka, 1954–1980*

YEAR	SQUATTER POPULATION	TOTAL AFRICAN POPULATION	SQUATTERS AS PERCENTAGE OF TOTAL AFRICAN[a]	TOTAL LUSAKA	SQUATTERS AS PERCENTAGE OF TOTAL
1954	11,886	47,793	25		
1957	15,786	64,754	22		
1963	18,000	95,939	16	123,146	35
1969	91,804			262,425	35
1973	160,000			380,952	42
1980	269,000			538,469	50

Source: Adapted from Seymour, 1976:67–68; Martin, 1974:74; and Republic of Zambia, 1981b:8.

[a] The squatter percentage for 1980 is a conservative estimate, calculated from population growth rates between 1973 and 1980.

There was little money with which to finance development of any sort, much less housing. In Zambia's second national development plan, 1972–1976, the government acknowledged what many squatters had known since the colonial period: they were in town to stay. Local housing advocates for squatters played an important role in provoking this policy shift (van Velsen 1975). In their advocacy, they were greatly influenced by Turner (1965, 1972), who had observed how squatters allotted their own means to housing, developing and improving it according to their changing circumstances and needs. The government now recognized that demolition was no longer a practical solution, that squatter areas represented considerable investment on the part of their residents and required formal planning and services (Republic of Zambia 1971:262).

Because of accelerating rate arrears and tight budgets, local authorities were unable to undertake upgrading. The squatters' needs were not attended to until external funding enabled the government to develop plans to improve their situation. By then, development projects in rural and urban areas alike had become increasingly dependent on international grants and loans for their execution, and Zambia's foreign debt grew throughout the 1970s and afterward.

For the squatter upgrading project, arrangements were finalized with the World Bank for a loan in 1974. The World Bank was a patron of several urban shelter upgrading projects elsewhere, for example in Kenya and Côte d'Ivoire (Amis 1990:18–19). Begun in 1975, the Lusaka project aimed to provide services and improve housing in three of the capital's largest squatter complexes (George, Chawama, and Chaisa/Chipata). Additional plots were planned in overspill areas next to squatter settlements and in new site-and-service areas (Pasteur 1979:14).

Far-flung changes in land laws and property ownership were undertaken to facilitate this project, partly because of World Bank pressure. The Housing (Statutory and Improvement Areas) Act of 1974 enabled residents of site-and-service areas to obtain occupancy licenses of up to ninety-nine years, while those in upgraded and overspill areas could hold occupancy titles for a thirty-year period. By these rulings, plotholders in previously unauthorized areas became tenants of the state and were given some security against the threat of demolition for the first time in Zambia's urban history. The Land (Conversion of Titles) Act of 1975, among other provisions, vested all land in Zambia in the president, converted freehold into statutory leasehold titles for one hundred years, nationalized vacant land and undeveloped plots, and forbade the subdivision and sublease of land without the president's consent (Simons 1979:18–20). In effect, these changes established security of tenure for plots on which residents owned houses and enabled them legally to transfer the occupancy title to a new owner when selling the house.

The upgrading process was riddled with problems, some local and others extraneous. The discrepancies between the goals of the upgrading project and its outcomes are the subject of an extensive body of literature.[5] For the purpose at hand, it suffices to note that the upgrading scheme fell short of expectations and beyond the financial reach of many of those it was meant to help. Many planned services—such as clinics, primary schools, markets, and community centers—were not completed, and there were problems with the building of roads and the installation of water and sanitation (Republic of Zambia 1981a). Some findings indicate that several original participants who could not afford the costs, many of them single women and men who had been tenants before they were relocated, moved from the overspill and new site-and-service schemes back to squatter areas elsewhere. Because female heads of households tended to earn irregular incomes from self-employment, they in particular had difficulty meeting the required costs (Todd and Mulimbwa 1980:51; Rakodi 1988a:317).

In 1980 the squatter upgrading project was handed over to the district council. Uncompleted operations and those settlements not included in the 1974 World Bank project faced an uncertain future. By 1980, more people lived in squatter areas than in any other type of housing in Lusaka (Wood 1986:185). An upgrading project in one of Lusaka's oldest squatter settlements, Kalingalinga, was initiated in 1979 with funds from the West German government and phased out in 1986 (Maembe and Tomecko 1987:1). In this and later upgrading schemes, such as the Norwegian-supported upgrading of Bauleni, begun in 1991, policy has moved increasingly toward community participation in order to reduce dependency on external sources. Still, NGOs continue to play a central role in improving particular aspects of life in the squatter areas (e.g., economic promotion, health and nutrition training). As a result, there has been no comprehensive follow-up of the World Bank project and no significant allocation of resources to squatter upgrading (Rakodi 1990).

Meanwhile, housing access has become increasingly skewed if not regressive. In fact, housing subsidies increased both in absolute magnitude and as a proportion of income for the relatively wealthy Zambians who resided in high-cost urban employer-provided housing. By contrast, low-income urban households received rental allowances that were barely sufficient to pay for rents even in squatter settlements (Sanyal 1981:436). In the mid-1970s, the top 10 percent of Zambia's highest-income households received housing subsidies amounting to almost 50 percent of their remuneration, whereas the bottom 50 percent (those with low earnings) received housing subsidies that constituted only 10 percent of their incomes (Sanyal 1981:428). And in terms of government investment in the predominantly urban housing sector, a decade later 2 percent of the Zambian population enjoyed more than 50 percent of that investment, leaving less than 45 percent of it for the remaining 98 percent (*Times of Zambia* 1987). For the 50 percent of the Zambian population who live in rural areas, mostly in poverty, the government as landlord has little to offer except the incentive to migrate to the cities and find what shelter they can.

The chief observable change in urban planning policy since the early 1970s has been the encouragement of private home ownership through the sale at a price that is not subsidized of former rental houses and flats owned by the council and new construction of low-cost houses specifically for sale. Most Zambians cannot afford such housing; they compete for shelter in existing authorized and unauthorized areas as best they can. Lusaka's squatter areas doubled their share of the capital's residential space from 12 percent to 24 percent between 1969 and 1980, whereas site-and-service schemes increased their part only from 5 to 7 percent during that same period (Wood 1986:176). The 1980s and 1990s saw no development of a clear national housing policy, and apart from political exhortations, no steps have been taken to confront the increasing need for housing for the growing urban low-income populations. In effect, squatting continues (Mulwanda and Mutale 1994).

Throughout the 1980s, the government intermittently instructed district councils and local authorities throughout Zambia's urban areas to prevent structures from being built in existing squatter areas and to curtail new developments (Kasongo and Tipple 1990). Eviction and demolition continue to take place in Lusaka, particularly in old squatter settlements close to the city center, including Misisi and John Laing, to yield to commercial or industrial developments (*Weekly Post* 1992). Dilapidated houses in Lusaka's older authorized townships, such as Kabwata, Old Chilenje, and Matero, are also being razed (*Zambia Daily Mail* 1992). The Lusaka district council on its own does not have sufficient means to move such residents into council housing, resettle them on new plots, or upgrade the existing squatter areas.

In view of Lusaka's shortage of low-income housing, it is not in the least surprising that commercialization of the available supply is taking place, as owner-occupiers or even absentee landlords rent out rooms (Bamberger, Sanyal, and Valverde 1982; Rakodi 1988a:317; Schlyter 1991a:37). This process is clearly becoming more widespread in Lusaka, although it does not yet appear to be as extensive as it is, for example, in Nairobi in Kenya (Amis 1984) and in Harare in Zimbabwe (Potts 1991). While such subletting is illegal, the growing incidence of it across Lusaka's high-density housing areas demonstrates not only marked differentiation in housing access in general but also unequal distribution within specific residential areas.

Mtendere: A Township Called Peace

A house may become an asset, a workplace, and a source of income. Because a house of one's own in Zambia's rapidly growing cities is, above all, a stake in the city, shelter and space are objects of struggle. The struggle for the city, according to Cooper, is "cultural as much as political, and it goes on every day, as well as bursting forth when basic structures are at issue" (1983:34). From this perspective, the previous overview of the provision of housing for the low-income groups in Lusaka during the first decades after independence is more than a discussion of the difficulties inherent in urban planning in a poor country. For squatting was not so much a consequence of so-called excess numbers or of what some have called overurbanization (Gugler 1988) as it was—and continues to be—a product of an economy that rarely paid a living wage and often left people to create their own means of livelihood. As such, squatting constitutes a struggle over housing and urban space that involves social, economic, and political issues.

Such struggles were key to the establishment and subsequent development of Mtendere, the township that has been an important site for my research in Lusaka since the early 1970s. Throughout the township's existence, Mtendere residents have engaged in a two-pronged battle for tenure: tenure as a legal right to build and own a house (which I discuss below) and tenure as a socioeconomic foothold in the city (which I turn to in the next chapter). Yet in spite of—or perhaps because of—their struggles, long-term residents are very attached to their township and are so proud of it that they describe Mtendere as the nicest of Lusaka's compounds.

What eventually became known as Mtendere opened in 1967 as Chainama Hills site-and-service resettlement scheme.[6] Situated on Lusaka's eastern outskirts, ten kilometers from the city center on hills behind Chainama, the state mental hospital, the township was planned to accommodate residents from some of Lusaka's oldest squatter settlements. As a basic resettlement area on unoccupied land, the township was conceived with a view to housing people who could afford little in the way of construction and site-rental costs and therefore would have to be content with very minimum services, such as all-weather roads, communal water supply (one tap per twenty-five plots), and pit latrines (Republic of Zambia 1967b). The city council demarcated some three thousand plots on which residents were expected to build houses according to predesigned plans. Construction had to begin within a specified time, or the resident would lose his or her plot. Assisted by two German volunteers, the city council built four core houses to Zambia housing board design, which were to serve as both offices and demonstration houses. Roof loans were available, and the city council applied a sort of means test before permitting prospective residents to apply for plots (Republic of Zambia 1966). The plan also included space for commercial developments, a clinic, and a primary school in each of the township's four sections, and plots to house the associated staff (Republic of Zambia 1968).

The Chainama Hills site-and-service resettlement scheme was inaugurated in August 1967, and by the end of that year a total of 3,030 plots had been demarcated. While the city council records are somewhat ambiguous concerning which squatter settlements were targeted for resettlement at Chainama Hills, they leave no doubt that the majority of the new residents came from Kalingalinga, an adjacent squatter settlement that lacked most basic amenities. Earlier in 1967, a survey had been conducted in Kalingalinga to ascertain whether or not residents were economically able to participate. Many Kalingalinga residents were interested in moving to the new township, attracted by the prospects of water, good roads, schools, and a clinic (Republic of Zambia 1967c:24).

Lusaka, 1985

No matter how attractive it had appeared to prospective settlers, the new township developed very slowly. Some residents refused to start building until public transport was provided. No formal market had been mapped out. There were no signs of schools or a clinic. In June 1968, the Ministry of Local Government and Housing instructed the city council staff in charge of the Chainama Hills settlement to discontinue their work. The township's supervision was then taken over by the Squatter Control Unit of the Ministry of Lands and Natural Resources, which carried out this function until the end of 1971.

What prompted this change? While I have not seen any single authorized explanation, a variety of observations may be brought to bear on the fall from official grace of a carefully conceived resettlement scheme for people of few economic means that had been planned to avoid the problems associated with shelter provision in already built-up areas. Because of the nondelivery of promised services, the new residents were unwilling to pay their monthly plot rents; because households had widely different water needs, they were reluctant to pay identical water rates for the use of communal standpipes; and because the incomes of many households were low and/or unstable, few residents had applied for roof loans.

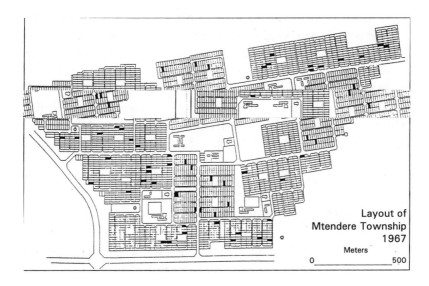

Layout of Mtendere Township, 1967

In addition to these economic problems, which were in no way unique to the Chainama Hills resettlement scheme, there also were political issues at stake. Those residents who had joined the new scheme from Kalingalinga had left behind them a squatter settlement in which the opposition party (the ANC) had a considerable base (Seymour 1976:115–16). It was predominantly UNIP supporters who moved to Chainama Hills, where they began establishing a party organization. There were rumors of plot allocations that did not follow city council procedures but were made as individual favors. Hints were dropped that some absentee landlords were persons of influence.

While the local UNIP supporters were putting their stamp on the running of the new township, its very location became an issue. The scatter of unfinished houses that straddled Chainama Hills was visually very prominent, and some considered it an eyesore. But the Chainama Hills scheme was not only located within full view of Lusaka's Great East Road, which led to the airport, it was also situated on land that was scheduled for a "superhighway" in the new Lusaka development plan designed in 1968 by the government's planning consultant, the Greek firm Doxiades Associates. In short, discussion was under way to discontinue the Chainama Hills scheme entirely and to move its residents to another location. But that never took place.

Although officially the Squatter Control Unit was in charge of the supervision of the township, in practice the local UNIP organization took control. Disliking the connotation of Chainama, the nearby state mental hospital, the UNIP members renamed their settlement Mtendere, which means "peace" in Nyanja, the lingua franca of Lusaka. This name condenses their story of leaving Kalingalinga, which they considered to be full of political strife and dangerous because of its widespread poverty, and moving to Mtendere, where they found a space for peaceful party-line association.

In legal and administrative terms, Mtendere was an unauthorized township during those years. In effect, Mtendere's initial settlement was completed by efficiently organized, planned squatting. The "illegality" of the settlement was an important source of the leadership power that evolved. The leader, a barely literate man from the Eastern Province, was one of the early UNIP sympathizers who had left Kalingalinga; he allocated plots in much the same way that rural headmen distributed land. Without permission, he transformed spaces designated for community services and commercial facilities into housing plots. He turned a blind eye to illegal practices such as beer brewing and distilling, and he allowed extensions of buildings and subletting to take place. Meanwhile, he set himself up with a grocery store, two taverns, and a second wife. In tribute to his patronage, when the UNIP structure was formally established in the township, Mtendere residents reelected him to the office of ward chair every three years until the dismantling of the one-party state at the end of the Second Republic in 1991. Like other townships, Mtendere constituted a ward. The ward was divided into four parts, each with a branch chair, below whom were section leaders, one for every twenty-five houses. This was the politico-administrative structure through which Mtendere township was managed when the city council again was charged with its supervision at the beginning of 1972.

Since the late 1970s, schools, clinics, formal markets, one tarred road, and fairly regular public transportation have been put into place in the township. In the mid-1980s, Mtendere was linked to Lusaka's electric circuit, although only a minority of residents can afford to pay connection charges and monthly rates. The population grew from 10,000 in 1971, to 22,000 in 1981, to an estimated 40,000 at the beginning of the 1990s (Republic of Zambia 1981b:22). Over the years, the areas around Mtendere have been absorbed by other developments: Chainama Hills Hospital; a large European-owned commercial farm; Kalikiliki, a small squatter settlement; Helen Kaunda, low-cost owner-occupied houses built by the city council during the late 1970s; and new low-density residential areas in the Ibex Hills. With the physical expansion of the township curtailed in this way, most of Mtendere's population growth has been accommodated on subdivided plots, in housing extensions, and in rented rooms. All of these practices are beyond the letter of the law.

From 1972 to 1991, during the time when UNIP was in charge of the township, two institutions played major parts in the lives of residents: the party and the churches. Aside from facilitating or obstructing particular kinds of economic activity, the party organization attended to many of the residents' concerns, including domestic trouble and strife among neighbors. Party representatives wrote letters to the local court at Chelston on behalf of residents who needed to summon adversaries to court when informal mediation failed. The party in turn pressed residents, particularly women, into service, such as lin-

ing the streets or going to the airport for the arrival of visiting dignitaries from abroad. But above all, the party involved itself in providing funeral support—in the night-long mourning that accompanies a
death, the transportation of mourners to the funeral site, and the provision of food afterward.

With respect to funerals, the party perhaps deliberately encroached on an activity that had long been the purview of the churches. Several of the many denominations to which Zambians claim allegiance are represented in Mtendere, some of them with church buildings. The church is a central influence that perhaps is more significant than the party in many people's lives, especially women's. The township also has a small mosque, built between 1972 and 1981 by migrants from Malawi for adherents of Islam, who constitute a tiny but slowly growing population segment.

The Nicest of Lusaka's Compounds

For most of the people who settled in Mtendere during the township's early years—who are the chief actors in this book—as well as for those who joined them over time, owning a house in a township such as this was a result of considerable mobility across Lusaka's low-income residential areas and occasionally domestic servants' quarters in the capital's high-income neighborhoods. When they moved to Mtendere in the late 1960s, few of them were newly arrived from the countryside;

Various stages of house construction in Mtendere

most already had considerable experience with the vagaries of the capital's economy and its depressed low-income housing market. Some had migration experiences from other southern African countries, and several had worked in towns elsewhere in Zambia.

There is no doubt that settling in Mtendere represented a considerable improvement in standard of living, especially for those residents who, from small beginnings and in very piecemeal fashion, consolidated their home ownership over the years. Did the changes in Mtendere's legal status from site-and-service scheme to squatter settlement and again to authorized township make any difference to its residents, who, after all, considered it their place to live? Did these shifts mean discontinuity in their everyday lives? From their perspective, there were no radical breaks. This is to say that the question of change was a question of urban administrative policies rather than of people's living arrangements. Consolidating a house of one's own was what mattered to residents, rather than the momentary preoccupations of policymakers.

The people who lived in Mtendere during the years of administrative shifts set out to build houses of greatly varying designs and standards, with very different completion stages. The question of the township's legal status did not concern them as much as did their continuous experience of inequality, which over the course of those years disadvantaged residents of compounds such as themselves in comparison with the *apamwamba* (Nyanja term meaning "those on the top"), who lived in *mayadi* ("the yards"), the former white residential areas.

When Mtendere residents compare their township with others, they use terms that derive from the colonial urban control apparatus that before independence invoked race to segregate housing, labor, health, and domestic arrangements. Back then, "the compound" referred to the racially segregated housing institution tied to employment. In postcolonial Zambia, the semantic field of the term *compound* encompasses all low-income areas. Within that broad field, urban residents make distinctions between shanty compounds, which are the squatter settlements, including those that have undergone some upgrading, and site-and-service compounds, such as Mtendere.

Long-term residents speak positively about Mtendere and express a confident sense of their compound as a peaceful place that does not exhibit quite the extent of trouble found in many others. In the mid-

1970s, their standard of house construction was higher than that in any of the unauthorized areas (Republic of Zambia 1975). It is not surprising that they consider Mtendere to be the nicest of Lusaka's compounds and themselves to be slightly better off in economic terms and by housing standards than residents elsewhere—most certainly those who live in shanty compounds like Kalingalinga—although not nearly as well situated as the black and white residents of *mayadi*, the high-cost residential areas next to them.

As time passed, there were long-term Mtendere residents who looked back on the township's early years with yearnings for a better day that they could not reclaim. But at the same time that old-timers speak proudly of their own achievements, their commentary offers important clues about their relationship to space and politics, and therefore to their state. The terms *compounds* and *yards* (*mayadi*), which they invoke for space, speak directly about their suspended beliefs in the much-hoped-for progression to freedom from economic want and most certainly about their disenchantment with the lack of opportunity during most of the years of Zambia's Second Republic.

As parents, the Mtendere residents I turn to next are well aware of the difficulties of establishing households in today's strained economy. They are concerned about their children, for whom the dream of a house of their own most likely will be replaced by accommodation in rented rooms. They know from their own experience that a house of one's own is an important hedge against socioeconomic adversity. In their experience, housing is much more than shelter. Its physical environment is often inseparable from a host of activities and social relations. But the way in which these low-income urban households use housing is significantly influenced by the changing economic activities of household members as well as by cultural notions that shape these members' access. As I demonstrate in subsequent chapters, although housing can support people's social and economic efforts, it can also complicate them, particularly when access depends on gender and women obtain it through men.

3 | Urban Arrangements for Living

The struggle for control of space that eventually gave house owners in Mtendere legal occupancy title involved not only housing but also work. As in colonial Lusaka, housing was an important asset in the efforts of low-income residents to establish a socioeconomic foothold in the city and improve the life situation for themselves and their children. I use the term *urban arrangements for living* in order to stress that housing and work together shape efforts to make a living, facilitating or constraining those efforts as the case may be. Mtendere residents' urban arrangements for living involved many types of household forms in pursuit of both economic and social ends. Household members did not necessarily always agree on what these ends were; over the course of the household development cycle, individual members gave priority to some, played down others, and put still others off altogether (Leeds 1974:75).[1]

In this chapter I first introduce some of the residents of Mtendere, describing who they were and how they had set themselves up with housing and work when I first met them in 1971. Drawing on several follow-up studies that I undertook during the 1980s, I then discuss how their urban arrangements for living were affected by the country's ongoing economic deterioration during that decade. Much of this discussion focuses on what has been called the *informal economy*, a term that I have used descriptively and without clarification. In this chapter's last section I characterize the domain of activity that makes up Lusaka's informal sector and examine its limited ability to generate economic resources, particularly for women. The reasons for that are not only, or exclusively, economic; I turn to the sociocultural factors that make household dynamics and gender relations important to economic pursuits in the next chapter.

Mtendere: Residents and Housing Biographies

When Agnes Siame and her husband, Kapansa, moved from Kalingalinga to Mtendere township in 1968, it was a real step up. Agnes was born in South Africa in the 1930s. There she met and married Kapansa, a migrant worker from Zambia's Southern Province. When I first met them and their six children in a small four-room house in Mtendere, they had lived in Lusaka for five years. Kapansa had left his job in South Africa when Zambia became independent. On their journey north, they stayed with some of his relatives in Rhodesia before traveling on to Lusaka in 1966. Kapansa worked as a security guard until his retirement in the first half of the 1980s. Agnes initially earned money from dressmaking at home, and throughout the 1980s she pursued a wide variety of trading activities, some from home, others from the market, and still others from across town and into the rural areas.

Over the course of those years, they extended the house with several rooms and a verandah. In order to earn money from subletting, they built two additional rooms, with a separate entrance. In the late 1980s, they installed electricity. Although all their children today are adults and have children of their own, Agnes and her husband rarely, if ever, live by themselves. Instead, their household expands or shrinks depending on the number of daughters and grandchildren who are living with them as a result of troubles in their own households. They have also hosted a stream of young country people who assisted with household tasks and Agnes's trade in return for food, clothing, and occasional spending money.

Many men of Kapansa's generation migrated, especially from Zambia's Eastern and Southern Provinces, to Rhodesia and South Africa in their search for work during the colonial period. Like Kapansa, many returned to Zambia around the time of independence, with wives they had married while abroad. This was the case in 18 percent of the one hundred households that made up my sample in

Mtendere in 1971.[2] One of them was the Mbebe household, which returned to Zambia after Pius Mbebe had worked for eighteen years in South Africa as a domestic servant. In the 1950s, he had married a South African woman, Margaret. Of their four children, only one daughter survived.

When I first met the Mbebes, they had recently arrived in Lusaka. They had spent only three months in Mtendere, where they lived in temporary housing, put together from wooden boards and plastic. They had first stayed for nine months with Pius's matrilineal relatives near Katete in the Eastern Province. While he was in South Africa, Pius did not actively maintain contact with his relatives, and neither he nor his wife felt at ease staying with them. They then went on to Lusaka in search of work, even though Pius already was fifty-five years old. As he did not find a formal job and he was tired of domestic service, he initially hawked *kapenta* (a small dried fish) and Margaret began sewing clothes for sale from home.

Over the course of the 1970s, the Mbebes built a house. Margaret taught her husband sewing and after a domestic service job in the mid-1970s, she felt too tired to work for money. When she died in the late 1980s, Pius remarried. His new wife, less than half his age, traded in the township's market. Because of a general lack of building materials, especially window frames, the house has never been completed. The daughter meanwhile married and later divorced in Ndola on the copperbelt.

In 1971 I also met other Mtendere residents of the generation of Mr. Zulu and Mrs. Mubanga, whom I introduced in chapter 1— namely persons who were born in town or had arrived there as children with their parents. Slightly younger than men like Kapansa and Pius, who had migrated to Rhodesia or South Africa, this particular segment of the population, with its urban background, illustrates the decline of external migration and the growing urban stabilization of the years just prior to and following independence. The housing profiles of these people share many aspects of the overall housing story of a place like Mtendere.

By and large, Mtendere residents put together their houses as best they could. Some improved the temporary shelters that they initially erected or, like the Mbebes, began building a house on the plot next to the shelter. Most construction was piecemeal, room by room. Many never completed the building process, because of the rapidly rising costs and growing scarcity of construction materials as well as tight household budgets throughout the 1980s. During this transformation process, many people continued to live in the house while adding rooms to it. They rarely undertook the actual building work themselves but hired self-employed builders, mostly from within the township. Since few loans from formal lending institutions were available to low-income people, the building process sometimes took years, and in some cases, such as that of the Mbebes, it never ended. But as households grew, some houses were transformed, expanded, and solidified. Through this process, houses acquired biographies that encompassed their residents' experiences. Such housing biographies contributed to the construction of the township's history and to the positive attachment of long-term residents to their compound.

When I began my research in Mtendere, I drew my initial household sample by stages of house completion to reflect the ongoing development of the township at the time. Of the total sample of one hundred households, thirty-three lived in completed houses, fifty in houses that were under construction, and seventeen in temporary structures where construction had not yet begun. Although some residents were employed as teachers, clerks, and nurses, the great majority were unskilled workers. Such employment meant low earnings. In respect to housing, low incomes meant that the prospects of completing a house were uncertain.

Although my sample survey of one hundred households cannot represent all of low-income Lusaka in a statistical sense, the range of activities it encompasses was found throughout such areas (cf. Jules-Rosette 1981; Todd and Shaw 1980). Like Lusaka in general, Mtendere township was very heterogeneous, with ethnic groups from the Eastern Province making up about half of my sample. As table 3.1 illustrates, members of ethnic groups in the Central and Southern Provinces formed the second largest, but much smaller, category, while very few members of the sample came from the Northern Province. Most of these groups are matrilineal. Some foreign nationals lived there as well, the majority of them from Malawi, followed by Zimbabwe and South Africa. In later years, some Zaireans moved in.

Only 9 percent of the persons in my sample had come to Mtendere directly from the rural areas. In fact, most of them were not recent urbanites, and as indicated earlier, 18 percent had work experiences from Rhodesia and South Africa. And 12 percent had lived in other

Different types of houses in Mtendere

TABLE 3.1 *Ethnic Background of Mtendre Sample, 1971*

SOCIAL TYPE	ETHNIC CATEGORY		NUMBER OF MALES	NUMBER OF FEMALES	REGION
Northern Matrilineal	Bemba type				
		Bemba	4	4	Northern Province
		Kunda		1	Eastern Province
	Lamba type				
		Lamba	1	1	Central and Western Province
Central Matrilineal	Tonga type				
		Tonga	4	4	Southern Province
	Lenje type				
		Lenje	1	2	Central Province
		Soli	6	5	
Bilateral	Lozi type				
		Lozi		1	Barotseland
Northern Patrilineal	Mambwe type				
		Mambwe	2	1	Northern Province and Tanzania
		Nyika	1	1	Tanzania
	Henga type				
		Henga	1	1	Northern Province
		Tumbuka	7	5	Tanzania and Malawi
		Lambya	1	1	
Eastern Matrilineal	Chewa type				
		Chewa	20	18	Eastern Province and Malawi
		Nsenga	18	20	
		Nyanja	8	5	Malawi
Southeastern Patrilineal	Zambezi type				
		Chikunda	2	5	Eastern Province and Mozambique
Southern Patrilineal (Shona)	Korekore type		1		Rhodesia
	Ndau	Shona	1		Rhodesia
		group	2	4	Rhodesia
Southern Patrilineal	Sotho type			2	South Africa
	Zulu type				
		Ndebele		2	Rhodesia
	Ngoni	group	17	15	Eastern Province and Malawi
Others	South African (colored)			2	South Africa
	Luo		1		Tanzania
	Scandinavian		1		Sweden
	Unidentified cohabitant		1		Zambia
Total			100	100	

These categories are drawn from Mitchell 1956:46–49.

urban areas within Zambia before coming to Lusaka. Twenty-five percent had lived in Lusaka for more than ten years, while the remainder had spent an average of seven years in the city. This is to say that the majority had arrived in Lusaka around the time of independence, in 1964.

The diverse backgrounds of Mtendere's residents were accentuated by interethnic marriages, which accounted for 35 percent of my sample population. More than half of all the husbands had come to Lusaka in the company of their wives; about half of the remaining husbands had married in Lusaka, where most of the interethnic marriages had been contracted. Two of the marriages in the sample were polygynous, and a few were remarriages after divorce or the death of a spouse. Two households were headed by women who received support for themselves and their children from male companions.

I deliberately focused my attention on married women who were adults at the time of independence. Their situation was different from that of the first post-independence cohort of better-educated, younger women who enjoyed more occupational mobility and marital choice (Schuster 1979). More than half of the women in my sample had never attended school, compared with 29 percent of their husbands. The women who had received some schooling had attended for an average of four years, compared with five for their husbands. With regard to age, while the women's average age was twenty-seven, more than one third were older than that. They had an average of four living children. More than half of the total sample population consisted of children under fourteen and slightly more than half of the children over the age of fourteen had left their parents' house at Mtendere. A quarter of all these households accommodated additional residents, mostly relatives who had come from the rural areas in search of jobs or children attending school. There were also rural visitors and, as indicated earlier, rural youth, whose presence in these households made distinctions between employment and kinship ambiguous.

Women, Men, and Work

Mtendere's "illegal" status in 1971 and its location on the outskirts of Lusaka might easily leave the impression that the township was a self-contained community. It certainly was poorly connected to the heart of the city on many counts and could be reached only by one access road that wound its way down the hills and through Kalingalinga and low-density residential areas before reaching the city's center. In 1971 the bus service was limited and irregular. There were still neither schools nor clinics, only one unfenced market, and not one single authorized butcher.

Yet the impression of Mtendere in 1971 as an enclave with little interaction with the city and its institutions is misleading. As table 3.2 indicates, a quarter of the husbands were wage-employed in construction and related industries, and approximately another quarter worked as domestic servants in expatriate and Zambian households in Lusaka's low-density areas (*mayadi*), or in food service in institutions like hotels, hospitals, and educational facilities. The remainder were either self-employed or low-level white-collar workers in public-sector offices and in some private firms. The fourteen men who were self-employed within Mtendere operated small market stalls, hawked clothes, food, or produce, repaired cars, or built houses. These men had a lower average monthly income than the amount estimated for expenditures on food in an urban budget survey of low-income households of similar size (Republic of Zambia 1969). About one third of the women were self-employed within the township, most of them conducting small-scale trade from their homes and yards. In short, Mtendere's residents depended on the wider urban setting and its resources, and in turn they contributed necessary services, which the economy at large did not always provide.

Because economic means were tight, the women I met wanted to contribute to the household economy. Many of them were less than a generation removed from rural backgrounds, where husband and wife had well-defined roles in household work and agricultural production. They were not used to depending on husbands for cash handouts to cover each and every household need. To be sure, they all liked the fact that their children had better opportunities to go to school in Lusaka. Some said that they liked not being under the supervision of the extended family. But they disliked that in the city everything had to be bought. Their typical comment was that many foodstuffs could be taken from their gardens in the village. Although some residents had small gardens on their plots and others planted on the outskirts of the township before the rainy season, they harvested vegetables (e.g., cabbage, onions, tomatoes, and maize) mainly for household consumption.

Women in Mtendere wanted more than anything else to feed their children adequately and to provide for their school needs. Even though elementary school in 1971 was free of charge, the children needed uniforms, shoes, and supplies. Most of the women lived in dwellings that were begun as one or two core rooms; they wanted their house to be

TABLE 3.2 *Men's Occupations, Mtendere Sample, 1971*

Occupation	Number	Percent	Category
Unemployed	4	4	Unemployed
Cleaner	3		
House servant	3		
Gardener	5		
Cook in private house	9		
Cook at institution	8	28	Domestic
Self-employed storekeeper	3		
Self-employed clothes seller	5		
Self-employed fish seller	1		
Self-employed soft drink seller	1		
Self-employed bricklayer	2		
Self-employed mechanic	2	14	Self-employed
Beer hand	2		
Lorry hand	1		
Fireman	1		
Post carrier	1		
Porter (airport)	2		
Messenger	2		
Worker for the municipality	3		
Shop assistant	1		
Security guard	5	18	Employed (unskilled)
Waiter	1		
Hospital attendant	2		
Driver	3		
Radio technician	1	7	Employed (skilled)
Painter	2		
Plumber	4		
Pipe layer	1		
Carpenter	3		Construction
Bricklayer	15	25	(skilled and unskilled)
Clerk	1		
Engineer	1	2	Clerical
Student	2	2	Student
Total	100	100	

comfortable for the size of the household and substantial enough to withstand heavy downpours during the rainy season and strong winds during the chilly winter. And some dreamed of better cooking facilities, upholstered furniture, new clothes for Christmas, and, as the years went on, electricity and television sets.

In fact, most of these women wanted to work in order to earn incomes. What could they do? If the lack of provision of urban low-income housing was a colonial legacy that had lingered after independence, so was the differential involvement of women and men in wage labor. In a market already oversupplied with male workers, these women's limited education decreased their wage-labor prospects even more. And in Zambia in general, few unskilled women get jobs that men can do. A few of the women had previous wage-labor experience from outside the country, for example, in tobacco and textile factories in Rhodesia. Five percent had at one time or another worked as domestic servants, a job they gladly left when they got married or because of a pregnancy. Low-income women take domestic service jobs only as a last resort, such as in situations of family crisis or because they have no means of support. Aside from supervision by another woman, which the women dislike, domestic service pays miserable wages, and women readily earn more from small-scale trade.

From the perspective of most Mtendere women in 1971, income-generating work was synonymous with trade. Around one third of them had devised ways of making money, many by working full-time from their homes, yards, or streets, selling home-brewed beer or *kachasu* (distilled alcohol), fruit, vegetables, dried fish, cooking oil, charcoal, kerosene, ready-made food, and secondhand clothing. Some undertook similar activities intermittently, and some, like Agnes, did such handwork as sewing, embroidery, knitting, and crocheting.

The small scale of women's enterprises was a result of the limited economic resources with which they were able to work. The decisions that guide allocation of women's and men's economic means are a subject on which I shall say more in the next chapter. Briefly explained, some women drew their start-up capital for trade from the small household allowance they received from husbands, whereas others borrowed from relatives or occasionally from friends. As the types of their trading activities demonstrate, women's lack of capital tended to confine them to small-scale retail trading. Because of their limited stock and tiny bulk, their profits were small. And their low earnings in turn limited their access to sources of supply. Except for charcoal and secondhand clothing, the women purchased their resources from markets or wholesalers in the city, reaching the downtown by public transportation or "private" (i.e., illegal) taxis that they shared with others. They purchased charcoal from persons who burned it in the countryside, and in their search for secondhand clothing they called on residents in *mayadi*, principally expatriates. Of all these activities, the brewing of beer, distilling of alcohol, and sale of secondhand clothing were the most profitable in 1971.

Earnings from small-scale trade went largely, in the women's words, "into the pot." This is to say that women traders spent most of their earnings on daily consumption. Aside from that, their income helped to cover children's school expenses. Once household needs had been met, parts of the profits of some women in the more lucrative trades were spent on construction of the house or the purchase of furniture. Most women encountered incidental, but frequent, additional expenditures because of the arrival of relatives from the rural areas, and finally, some women from time to time sent money to relatives in the countryside. Spending their earnings from trade in these ways meant, of course, that few women ever established a nest egg from which to expand their trade or shift to another enterprise. What is more, these practices blurred distinctions between business and household, thus hiding the economic dimensions of women's work.

Household Continuity in a Declining Economy

As time passed, there was both continuity and change in Mtendere. On my return in 1981, I found that some of the long-promised services, such as schools and clinics, had been established during the intervening years. The market had been formalized and fenced in, and several rows of shops and stalls had been built in the marketplace. There were now regular butcheries in the township and many more bars and taverns. I identified ninety of the original one hundred plots on which I had interviewed ten years previously and found forty-six households living in the very same place.[3] I also traced the whereabouts of twenty-two households who had moved to other parts of Lusaka or to other towns and a mere handful who had moved to the rural areas. The households whose movements I was unable to trace included ones in which a spouse had died or a divorce had taken place;

I was told that some of their houses had been sold, but I found no further information about the former inhabitants. And former residents who had moved over the intervening decade and whom I did succeed in tracing often were renting their houses to nonrelated persons and having a relative collect the rent. In a few cases, relatives lived in the previous residents' house.

The persons I traced in 1981 represented a cross section of the original sample in terms of age, averaging thirty-seven years, with fifteen of them being forty-five years of age or older. Most of the women had remained married to the same husbands, while two more women than in 1971 now lived as single heads of households. The major marital change had been the addition of spouses. In 1981, there were ten instances of polygyny, as compared to two in 1971.[4] Most of the men who had taken second wives were unskilled workers; several held office in the local UNIP branch.

In the intervening decade, the households still resident in Mtendere had not shrunk in size but had grown in diverse ways, and many were overwhelmed by dependents. More children had been born, while others had left home. There were relatives living in about one third of these forty-six houses, including married offspring with children and spouses, unmarried daughters with children, householders' younger siblings (sometimes with dependents), and even a few aged parents brought to town from the countryside. One or more children lived at home after failing grade seven in slightly fewer than one fourth of the households. In some households, relatives depended on members for food and occasional financial handouts; in other cases, it was a relative who contributed cash or services to the household.

During the ten-year interval between my first two studies, Zambia's economy had declined and overall wage employment had stagnated. Only the public sector continued to provide jobs. In about half of the households in Mtendere, the husbands worked for the same type of employers as they had in 1971. These were predominantly public-sector employers, but included also a few long-established private firms in Lusaka. In most of the remaining cases, husbands did the same types of jobs as in 1971 but had different employers. The shift had taken place from private-sector to public-sector employment. The principal type of occupational change was from wage employment to self-employment—for instance, bricklayers who set themselves up in the township or men who, after holding many jobs, established themselves in trade.

Such self-employment was not necessarily the result of unemployment but was rather a conscious decision by men who knew that their formal job skills were unlikely to increase their incomes.

As in 1971, the incomes of most Mtendere residents barely covered the needs of their expanding urban households. Fluctuations in the availability of basic consumer goods because of import restrictions and currency devaluations had prompted frequent scarcities and

Woman informal trader operating from her yard, selling beans

fueled inflation. The retail distribution system had deteriorated badly, foreclosing some trading avenues while opening up others. In 1981, only eight wives made no money in their own right. And eight other women were now wage-employed, working as domestic servants, hospital attendants, or janitors. The rest were involved in trade, seven in the township's market, the others from their homes, yards, and streets, offering a limited and rather uniform variety of goods for sale. In fact, they traded much the same items as in 1971, though more women had begun to knit and crochet in the meantime. Depending on product availability, some women also sold such goods as salt, sugar, rice, cooking oil, soap, detergent, and candles, which frequently were scarce. Others would occasionally sell items brought to town by rural relatives, mostly dried fish, vegetables, and fruit. Rural visitors would return to villages with such scarce items as cooking oil, soap, and detergent, and some took new and used clothing to the countryside to sell on commission for their urban relatives.

In addition to these trading activities, which were common in the township, some women had expanded their range of trading activity to include items of apparel, the most popular of which were shoes, hand-

Woman informal trader operating from her yard, selling *munkoyo* (a homemade, slightly fermented beverage)

bags, clothing, and watches. Particularly enterprising women obtained such items on shopping trips that they undertook in groups of two or three to neighboring countries to buy the commodities, including food staples, that were in short supply or of poor quality in Zambia. This type of long-distance "suitcase" trade had developed when the border to the south had been reopened after Zimbabwe gained independence in 1980, but it also included Botswana, Swaziland, Malawi, and Zaire.

Undertaking such journeys successfully required considerable practical knowledge and depended a good deal on diverse networks of support. Women had to be familiar with travel as well as with ways to avoid customs inspection. And they had to be able to commit time, which prevented them from doing their usual tasks. Capital, in the form of foreign exchange, was a must, as was a social network that provided information about where to shop and where to sleep. While the "suitcase" trade was commonly known and everybody aspired to own some of the goods these traders brought into the township, it was conducted only on an off-and-on basis by a changing group of women in my sample who could mobilize the necessary know-how and capital through their networks. Overall, it was a risky but profitable business in which the possibility of official harassment was balanced against the prospects of rapid gain. In 1981 such "suitcase" goods could be resold with as much as 200 percent profit.

When I returned for the third time, in 1984, I traced thirty-four of the original households. The twelve households that had dissolved between 1981 and 1984 did so because of, in order of occurrence, transfers to other towns, return to the villages, and death. Relatives lived on a few of the original plots. I was unable to trace the whereabouts of three households that were polygynous in 1981. Among the reasons given for their dissolution was divorce. Of the thirty-four households that had remained in Mtendere, six were polygynous in 1984. In one of the previous polygynous households, a co-wife had left in 1981. Three households were now headed by women. The reasons for female headship included the death of a husband in one case and divorce in another. And in the third case, the husband had returned to his village, leaving the wife, who was unwilling to accompany him, in Lusaka. The rest of the women lived with the same spouses.

The gradual dissolution process touched additional households between 1984 and 1985. The sample now comprised twenty-nine households. Three, including one that was polygynous, had moved to other townships in Lusaka, one of those to a peri-urban rural settlement. One householder had died. In all cases relatives now resided on the plots. Between 1984 and 1985, one woman had divorced her husband, and she now headed a large household of unmarried daughters and their children. Two other households were headed by women. They were not divorcées or widows but had refused to accompany their husbands, who had retired to the rural areas. The rest of the women lived with the same husbands as in 1971.

While more women were contributing to household incomes without being wage-employed, their husbands had not experienced major employment changes during those years. A couple of husbands retired from the labor force and were supported by their wives and/or adult children. The remainder kept working in low-income jobs, mostly in the public sector, in the types of activities that have been Lusaka's mainstay regardless of economic ups and downs: service, distribution, and administration. A few more men took up self-employment in the township, and some pursued sideline activities while holding on to their formal jobs. The economic activities that the women pursued in 1984 and 1985 were also largely the same as in 1981. The brewers and distillers in this group persisted in their activities. And a small group of women, almost the same number as in 1981, earned no income. A few more had begun to trade, and some of the previous traders from homes and yards now operated from the township's market. Between 1984 and 1985, a second market opened in Mtendere. A couple of domestic servants had become janitors in institutions. But long-distance "suitcase" trade had almost ceased in 1984 because of import restrictions and drastic cuts in foreign exchange allowances. In 1985, a revival was taking place, now with a change in regional focus. That year, some women from Mtendere traveled to areas immediately beyond the borders of Malawi and Zaire where, unlike in Zimbabwe and the south, local traders still accepted Zambian currency. The women traders brought back printed cloth and items of clothing and apparel from Zaire, and from Malawi they returned with rice, a commodity of which there then was a shortage in Zambia.[5]

Informal-Sector Dynamics

Since the early 1970s, the urban informal-sector concept has been a subject of voluminous debate and extensive research that has tended to cluster around two particular Western policy interventions aimed at increasing economic growth in developing countries (Roitman 1990; Sanyal 1991).[6]

Briefly, the first cluster of work on this subject was influenced by Keith Hart's research among migrants in Accra, Ghana, which coined the term *informal sector* for self-employment, legitimate and illegal, as opposed to regularized wage labor (1973). International development agencies were at this time concerned about the failure of large-scale industrialization efforts to improve economic growth in Africa. Hart's concept was quickly absorbed into International Labour Organisation (ILO) policies directed toward satisfying basic needs by helping people help themselves and thus harnessing informal income opportunities (Sethuraman 1981). In Zambia, the idea of the informal sector was introduced by Jolly, coauthor of an ILO report that emphasized its role in reducing unemployment and argued for an end to harassment of informal activities (International Labour Organisation 1977:129–38).[7]

The second cluster of work on the informal sector has appeared in the wake of the International Monetary Fund's structural adjustment programs, particularly from the last half of the 1980s on. Many of the policy measures (e.g., removal of subsidies on food, fertilizer, and housing, and introduction of user fees in schools and hospitals) advocated by the IMF and the World Bank to transform Africa's centralized economies into market economies have adverse effects on already vulnerable groups. Today, international development organizations, including the United States Agency for International Development (AID), national development agencies of many other countries, and NGOs are paying renewed attention to the informal sector and its potential to put people to work productively (Becker, Hamer, and Morrison 1994:158–69).[8]

Whether such a potential in fact exists requires understanding of the nature both of the activities in question and of the social relations on which they draw. How the informal sector is defined or characterized has obvious policy implications for how target groups are identified, as well as for where and which kind of intervention is planned. Social scientists have discussed this question extensively, debating, for example, whether the separation between the formal and informal sectors may be accounted for by Hart's straightforward distinction between wage employment and self-employment, or

whether a continuum of work situations ranging from casual work
to wage labor is at issue (Bromley and Gerry 1979). The problems of
operational definitions have been far from resolved, and terminology such as *petty commodity production, upper and lower circuits,
black or parallel markets,* and *second economies* suggests the
quandary (e.g., Armstrong and McGee 1985; Lemarchand 1988;
MacGaffey 1983, 1991; Mingione 1991; Moser 1978; Peattie 1987).
Some researchers avoid such discussions entirely by using descriptive terms like "micro-enterprises" (Liedholm and Mead 1987). But
the activities encompassed by such terms draw on widely different
resource access, require different inputs, and, above all, involve the
young and the old and women and men differently. And all these factors change over time in their interaction with economic and policy
developments in the economy at large. Unless the economic and
social nature of such activities is accounted for in more specific
terms, development assistance risks being selective and restrictive
and thus jeopardizing the very goal of expanding employment generation that it set out to pursue.

Because the extensive discussion about the informal sector has
failed to produce an agreed-upon definition, it is important that I clar-
ify my own usage of this term. In this book I use the term *informal
sector* as a general shorthand for small-scale activities entailing self-
employment, such as those I described for Mtendere in the previous
section. But in order to specify this term in the Zambian context, we
must account for the nature of the activities that it encompasses in
terms of their social, political, and historical background. That background makes a separation of informal and formal activities problematic because of the way in which both colonial and postcolonial
economic policies created a cheap labor economy and constrained the
activities of small-scale producers and traders by a host of restrictive
regulations. In effect, ever since the colonial period, both informal and
formal activities have been part of the overall system of production,
distribution, and exchange. This means that the relationship of urban
informal activities to the entire economic system in a country like
Zambia is likely to be structured differently from seemingly similar
activities in, for example, Accra, Ghana, or Nairobi, Kenya.

The previous discussion of the urban arrangements for living that
Mtendere residents set up for themselves during the economic
decline of the 1970s and 1980s demonstrates the growing importance

of what may be called an urban informal sector in providing work, housing, and a variety of services. But nowhere are distinctions between a so-called formal sector and an informal sector more imprecise than in this set of observations. The economic activities that Mtendere residents pursued involved several socioeconomic strata and forms of work that were all part of the Zambian economy. In effect, the relative welfare of particular households depended on both formal and informal activities. Women small-scale traders, for example, depended on formal wholesalers in the city for a substantial proportion of their goods, and many used the public transportation system to carry their goods. Those who traveled on the long-distance "suitcase" trade depended on the cooperation of bank and customs staff and on lorry drivers. And some had connections to people of influence. The list could go on. Informal work, in short, is not confined to a distinct sector of the economy but encompasses a heterogeneous set of activities undertaken by a diverse set of actors throughout the economy.

What is more, Zambia's informal sector is not primarily urban. The activities I have described have no specific territorial locus but are conducted in private and in public, in cities and in the countryside, as we saw in the exchange of "urban" goods such as clothing for "rural" produce and in the circulation of people between cities and villages. The chief commonality among all these activities in Zambia is that they are not legally established. But aside from occasional raids, mostly of women street vendors, the state does not have the necessary resources to regulate them.

Although the urban informal sector in Zambia is not a new phenomenon, the forces that have fueled its postcolonial growth, and particularly its significance in low-income residential areas such as Mtendere, are recent. We saw in the discussion on colonial Lusaka how the regulatory framework on employment, housing, wages and rations, and trade left sufficient scope for self-employment to provide both goods and services to Lusaka's rapidly growing African population. African women, who were barely represented among the wage-employed, began to put their stamp on these activities, especially small-scale trade and personalized services. Insofar as these activities were outside the scope of colonial law, they were illegal, one of the attributes often associated with the informal sector. But while such informal activities were unauthorized products of the colonial economy and its peculiar sociopolitical framework, they were closely linked to the formal economy because of the widespread need for cash income. The recent economic processes that have contributed to vastly increased informal-sector activities in the postcolonial era have expanded their scope across the economy from top to bottom. It is largely because of this expanded scope that the informal sector today differs from that of the colonial period.

Young men informal hawkers operating a roulette game

Young men informal hawkers selling cigarettes

Some observers of Lusaka's markets over time have noticed their limited specialization. Norwood found the nature of industrial endeavors in Zambia "retarded" in comparison to similar activities in Malawi (1975). And the diverse work in recycling scraps into functional household items that takes place in Kenya, for example, is hardly found in Zambia. Kenneth King has noted that markets in Lusaka sold many more mass-produced goods from foreign countries than did markets in the towns of East Africa. In 1975, for example, Lusaka's Luburma (Kamwala) market had some twenty to thirty foreign lines as compared with only two to four local Zambian products (1977:203). By and large, Lusaka's markets have not expanded because of diversification in the division of labor. Instead, the increase has occurred chiefly in the form of duplication of existing activities. In short, markets with so many similar products offer at best a "conserved," or "frozen," level of technological development (Jules-Rosette 1979:225).

Mtendere's economic expansion in the postcolonial era took the form of the multiplication of many small enterprises—shops, market stalls, street stands, and yard- and home-based activities. These activities involved increasing numbers of women who entered at the very bottom of the range. If small-scale urban trade during the colonial period was very much a man's world, it has increasingly become associated with women during the postcolonial period. In the view of most Mtendere women, income-generating work means trade. Several other studies of Lusaka's low-income areas show that the proportion of women in market trade has increased considerably since the late colonial period (Bardouille 1981; Schuster 1982; Todd, Mulenga, and Mubanga 1979:iii–iv). This means not that more women are becoming better off economically but that market trading is one of the very few income-generating options available to them. These studies and my own observations in Mtendere's main market in 1981 indicate that in trades in which both women and men operate, men consistently sold more. Women clustered in the least profitable trades, vegetable and fruit vending, and their profits were low. Most of these profits in all likelihood went "into the pot" instead of being reinvested in the expansion of enterprises.

The combined effect of state regulations concerning health, location, building, and licensing on small-scale production and trade in Zambia's urban areas has been to concentrate informal activity in

homes, yards, and streets, and in public places away from the direct
gaze of authorities. While many of these places, especially streets and
public areas, are cleared of illegal vendors from time to time, the state
is unable to enforce its own regulations. This incapacity or ineffective-
ness opens a range of opportunities that women traders have grasped.
Their small-scale trade and marketing are facilitated by state ineffec-
tiveness, and they persist in spite of the state's attempt to intrude. In a
conceptual sense, women who pursue such activities do not disengage
from the state or operate outside of it, as some have suggested (Parpart
and Staudt 1989). Such suggestions must be demonstrated empirically
and specified in relation to their changing local politico-economic and
sociocultural contexts (Hansen 1980, 1989b). Mtendere women's trading activities are not the remnants of traditional practices carried into
the city on which they fall back, pulling away from the state, when
times are tough. Instead they are the products of an economy that is
managed, however imperfectly, by the state, and they are clearly oriented toward living within that economy rather than outside of it.

Local specifications such as these cast questionable light on the
enthusiasm of international development agencies about the informal
sector's capacity to absorb ever more people. Zambia's informal sector
has been noted not for its diversification of small-scale manufacturing
activities but rather for its overwhelming focus on distribution
through trade. Lusaka's bottom rung of the informal trading economy
is already crowded by women who buy in order to resell, offering a
limited and rather uniform range of articles for sale. This informal
sector, so closely linked to and dependent on the formal sector, is
unlikely to absorb all newcomers, including those who are laid off
because of IMF-imposed retrenchment programs and young school
leavers who do not find formal jobs. What is more, with more people
crowding the informal sector, including more men who are laid off
from wage labor, women are likely to be displaced from the most
lucrative of the activities in which they now engage. This is because
Zambian society privileges men over women in both households and
the economy. As I discuss in chapter 4, legal control of trade and marketing and fluctuations in the availability of goods are not the whole
explanation for why women traders from Mtendere operated on such
a small scale. To qualify this explanation, we must take a closer look at
women's household situation, specifically their changing relationship
to husbands and children as the household development cycle unfolds.

According to a 1986 labor market survey in Zambia, more women than men worked in the informal sector: 42 percent of all women compared to 40 percent of all men in the rural areas, and 9 percent of all women compared to 6 percent of all men in the urban areas (Republic of Zambia 1991:27). While this survey is likely to underestimate the extent of women's urban informal-sector work by viewing it as household supplementation, there is no doubt that the participation of urban women in the informal sector has increased considerably during recent years. My long-term observations in Mtendere clearly demonstrate not only that the number of women involved in informal-sector work grew but also that the households that remained in the township through the 1980s weathered the overall economic deterioration in no small degree because of women's work efforts. In spite of a restrictive regulatory framework, occasional harassment by police and party youth, and frequent maligning in the press, women's small-scale work efforts often contributed the economic margin that made a difference to their households' ability to survive.

Through their informal-sector work, many women also added value to the house. Their earnings from trade contributed, in cases such as Agnes's, to the extension of the house and the addition of rooms to sublet. Incomes from subletting helped to tide many households over during the economic deterioration of the 1980s. Almost all the households that remained part of my sample over those years undertook some subletting, many of them building special rooms for that purpose. And for the many women who traded from homes and yards, the house was their place of income-generating work. Part of their earnings from trade helped to finance improvements of the house. Here we see the blending of space for working with that for living, which is another way of highlighting what this chapter has intended to demonstrate, namely that housing and work together influence people's urban arrangements for living.

4 | On the Home Front

A house of one's own provides much more than shelter. As a low-income housing area, Mtendere facilitated arrangements for living in many ways. As indicated in previous chapters, a house was often an economic asset for the residents who remained in the township during the 1980s because it offered rental space and served as a place of income-generating work for many women. Above all, houses hosted social relations embedded in cultural practices that significantly influenced the activities of residents.

The need to shore up sagging household income was not the only source of women's economic activities during the progressive economic decline in Zambia that began in the early 1970s. Explaining the initiatives of women during that time solely as reactive responses to the worsening economic circumstances in the society around them hides both their agency and the cultural politics that shaped gender relations within households and the wider society. The home front stands between the individual and the wider society as a site where women and men negotiate efforts to make a living in accommodation to, or in struggle with, normative cultural practices. We have already seen how urban arrangements for living often stretched across the threshold of the house, where in turn, as I demonstrate in this chapter, social organizational practices at times subsumed some of them. With this in mind, it becomes difficult to uphold rigid analytical distinctions between household and market, domestic and public, when accounting for the sources and nature of women's work.

This chapter concerns gendered experiences within households and the normative background that filters women's economic activities in homes, streets, and markets. I begin by discussing some important social organizational dynamics that shape access to, control over, and legitimation of resources within households. Although the claims women can make on resources are culturally constructed, they impose their own interpretation of the situation in a number of ways, which become particularly evident as the developmental cycle of households unfolds. These observations have implications for interaction beyond work in settings that also channel resources, including the neighborhood, church, and a variety of associations. I conclude by explaining the limited role of ethnicity in township interaction.

Households and Gender

Throughout this book, I have used the term *household* to refer to a site of interaction rather than to any empirically observable entity or conceptual unity. Household members come and go, they draw on kin-based resources and on non-kin networks, they interact with different material and personal interests, and as I discuss shortly, they do not always agree on the terms that should structure their relationships.

Households, their different forms, and their changing roles over the course of the developmental cycle of domestic groups have held center stage in anthropological work on social organization (Fortes 1949, 1958; Goody 1958). What households are, or rather what they are not, has been a subject of much discussion, contributing to breaking down any unitary conceptions of joint utility functions by demonstrating the proliferation of household forms that have assumed diverse and changing functions at different times and different places (e.g., Netting, Wilk, and Arnould 1984; Smith, Wallerstein, and Evers 1984; Smith and Wallerstein 1992; Wilk 1989). This massing of evidence is important to the study of gender relations because it has questioned the universality of distinctions between domestic and public and demonstrated the variability across time and space in women's work within and beyond households (e.g., Comaroff 1987; Folbre 1986; Guyer and Peters 1987; Peters 1983).

Jane Guyer advises us not to spend our time debating the status of households as units of analysis or devising typologies of their forms, but to ask questions about their resources. Otherwise, she warns, "it is difficult to locate their importance in the wider systems to which they now belong and to theorize the dynamics of change" (1981:123). As Fredrik Barth recognized long ago, change is more easily examined if one looks at social behavior as "allocations of time and resources" (1967:661). Like Barth, Berry (1989) and Guyer have argued that such resources are not only material but also jural and cultural. Because social organizational practices such as kinship and marriage structure productive relationships and identify the rights and obligations of household members, they constitute the framework within which gender roles and relations are constructed. Such jural and cultural practices "do not change imperceptibly through culture change, nor rapidly through rational choice; they are typically to be struggled over, sometimes with painful and contradictory results" (Guyer 1981:101). Rather than explaining changes in gender roles and relations as simple and unidirectional in terms of either economics or culture, this approach highlights their interaction. While Guyer does not specify an analytical strategy, she offers a perspective, inviting us to use households as entry points to processual analysis of the ways in which different resources both shape and are shaped by social organizational practices and external relations.

Such a perspective moves the study of gender relations far beyond earlier efforts to restore women to view.[1] In the case of my observations in Mtendere, this change in focus makes gender relations, not simply women, and the cultural practices that shape them central to my account of income-generating work among low-income people, its nature, and its changes. A focus on households, used descriptively, allows close scrutiny of the nature of gender relations and of the cultural and economic factors that help to bring about changes in them. Such an analysis helps us to make women's and men's private troubles public, and it demonstrates in more ways than one what the classical political economists recognized long ago, namely that households are at the heart of the economy. But instead of presuming them to be a haven in a heartless world, we should always raise questions about gender relations within households and accord women an active role in shaping and changing them.

The Household Development Cycle and
Diverging Gender Interests

Within most households in both urban and rural Zambia, women and men of different class backgrounds are grappling with questions about how conjugal life should be structured. Gender relations in Zambia share many similarities with those elsewhere in Africa: cultural norms and assumptions support male authority and power, regardless of whether descent is traced patrilineally or matrilineally (as in most societies in Zambia). A woman's access to productive resources is mediated through a man: her father, husband, uncle, or brother. On a husband's death, property devolves on his descendants, not his wife. A critical issue in Zambia in this regard is the dissolution of property in matrilineal descent systems. When a husband dies, his matrilineal relatives may descend on the urban household, grabbing all it contains and sometimes claiming the house itself, thus ignoring that household property is a product of the work of both spouses. In spite of the introduction of a new Intestate Succession Act in 1989, allowing widows and children some access to resources, there is sufficient evidence that prevailing ideology often makes the new act ineffective in practice.[2] The fact that such practices continue reminds the urban wife that she should not expect security for her old age.

Divorce does not alleviate this grim situation. Once a marriage has been dissolved, women need not expect to receive property or maintenance for themselves and their children, since customary divorce law, which persists unreformed, imposes no such obligations on husbands. Even while women are married, men's attentions are uncertain. A husband's earnings are not household income in the sense that they go into a common purse to which wives have equal access. And unlike husbands in some West African countries, Zambian husbands are not obligated by custom to give their wives a household allowance. But while wives have no claims on husbands' earnings, husbands make culturally legitimated claims on their wives' time, work, and in some cases, even their earnings. Whether husbands give their wives anything is influenced not so much by the size of their income as by their personal inclination.

During my first period of research in Mtendere, I carried out a household budget survey to explore how money was allocated between spouses. In 1971, half of the wives received a monthly allowance from their husbands, out of which they were to provide the household with food and themselves and the children with clothing. In 20 percent of my sample of one hundred households, women received a tiny allowance, while their husbands purchased staples and clothing. And 5 percent of the women received no allowance whatsoever, whereas 18 percent were fully in charge of their husbands' pay (Hansen 1975:786–88).[3] This budget allocation system between spouses meant not only that most women had few means to invest in business but also, and more important, that only a portion of a man's disposable means reached his own household; some of it might be spent on entertainment, including "a wife on the side," and drinking. Because many wives were aware neither of the full amount of their husbands' earnings nor of exactly how they spent the portion not allotted to household use, suspicions about the husbands' activities when they were off work and not at home readily arose. As in the past, the conjugal domain is fraught with tensions, in part because of the persistence of marriage practices permitting polygyny and the existence of a sexual double standard that condones men's extramarital relationships while blaming women for sexual promiscuity (Epstein 1981; Powdermaker 1962).

In low-income households in townships like Mtendere, women's economic initiatives are confronting male authoritarian cultural practices based on widespread norms and assumptions in society at large about male dominance and female subordination. This cultural bedrock prompts a conflictual negotiation process in which women at various stages of their married lives over the course of the household development cycle seek to fulfill expected roles as wives and mothers, yet pursue actions that make them economically independent of men at other stages. Moore and Vaughan's observation from the rural Northern Province applies equally well to Mtendere households. They suggest that "the cooperation implied in conjugality and evidenced in the sexual division of labor is something to which individuals aspire, but it is often a feature of a particular stage in the developmental cycle of the household rather than a fact of life or of social organization" (1994:225). Over the stages of the household development cycle, women and men in Mtendere hold different and changing views about who should engage in work and how to spend earnings. In short, they use money and networks for different ends.

As women grow older, once the needs of their young children are met, they become more concerned to benefit in their own right from economic activity than women at other life stages or in different marital situations. When Mrs. Simpemba's husband married a second wife in 1975, she began to be slighted in terms of household allowance. When I first met her in 1971, she was twenty-four years old, had four children, and sold kerosene, eggs, cooking oil, and *kapenta* in front of the house. The two wives, who now had to live under the same roof, did not get along at all; when I spoke to her in 1981, the senior Mrs. Simpemba felt that she was being mistreated. The junior wife had given birth to several children, whereas she had had only one child since the husband took a second wife. Allegations of witchcraft were made between the co-wives and Mrs. Simpemba went to complain about her co-wife to the UNIP representatives of the township, hoping that she would receive a sympathetic hearing and that they would intercede on her behalf with her husband. Since several of the township UNIP representatives were themselves polygynous, it is not surprising that they did not heed her complaint.

The predominant view of gender relations was decidedly negative against the senior Mrs. Simpemba. Concerned that the needs of her five children were being neglected because of the husband's diminished support, she subsequently sent the oldest daughter to a rural boarding school, using money from her earnings to help pay for school uniforms, shoes, and other necessities. She had given up trading from her front yard in the late 1970s. Too many women were trading, she complained when we spoke in 1981, and because many basic commodities were scarce, she did not regard the small and uncertain earnings worth the trouble of traveling downtown to look for goods to resell in the township. To support her children she had taken a job as a nanny in a Zambian household some eight months previously (Hansen 1987:15–16). The circumstances that prompted this decision demonstrate the observation I made earlier that women consider domestic service a last resort and largely take such jobs in times of family crisis or when they have no other means of support. Like many wives seeking work away from home, Mrs. Simpemba first had to get her husband's permission. She had compromised with her husband, who agreed with her plan on the condition that she spend part of her earnings on household needs. The rest she could spend on her own children.

Cultural and economic factors interacted in complex ways in shaping women's activities. Mrs. Simpemba's economic initiatives may at first glance be interpreted as a reaction to the depressed economic situation in the society at large, which was placing additional hardships on the already vulnerable household of which she was a member. Although many husbands in Mtendere, including Mr. Simpemba, still were employed, wages had not increased at a rate to keep pace with inflation. The extension of most households by more children and live-in relations meant that many women were contributing increasingly to household income. But while women's economic responsibilities were growing, their resource base was shrinking. As the value of wage-employed husbands' earnings declined because of accelerating inflation, so did women's household allowances. Like Mrs. Simpemba, some of these wives became co-wives in polygynous marriages over the years, in most cases against their wishes. Adding up all of these factors, one would think that they adequately explain why many more women were busy with income-generating work in order to contribute to shrinking household economies.

Perhaps the economic nature of women's activities hides their cultural side, but evidence for this dimension is not difficult to find. In the women's words, most of their earnings went "into the pot," which is to say that they were spent immediately on household consumption instead of being set aside for enterprise expansion or diversification. This was not only because of the general economic hardship that made the feeding of household members a day-to-day battle but also because of cultural dynamics that shape gender relations within households. Because they did not have any cultural claim on part of their husbands' earnings, married women did not expect much constancy in their husbands' contribution. Like Mrs. Simpemba, many women in Mtendere took matters into their own hands, seeking through income-generating activity to ensure at least that there was food in the pot and that their children's school needs were met. In short, what appears to be a reaction to a depressed economic situation was also a result of women's active resolve.

This is not the whole story, however. Through interviews of supporting household samples in 1981 and 1983, I gained insights into how more recently established households were reacting to the general economic downturn. Marriage was the chief means of economic support, however uncertain, for most newly married women, as it was for many mothers with small children. Some husbands forbade young wives to pursue income-generating activity, and some women did not consider trade a possible "work" option. All my observations over the years in Mtendere point to age as the most significant factor in shaping women's work entry, as do other studies of the urban informal sector in Zambia (Bardouille 1981; International Labour Organisation 1986:59–61; Jules-Rosette 1979; Todd and Shaw 1980).

Married women who pursued income-generating activity in Mtendere tended overwhelmingly to be close to the end of, or beyond, their childbearing years. The informal sector, in other words, is not "the natural resort of recent migrants to the city" (Sanyal 1991:40). Because of their age, many of these women had considerable urban experience and knew their way around wholesalers, state shops, and middlemen; they also knew how to deal with police and party youth who might harass them. And age meant that child care was no longer a critical issue. Most of these women had teenage children who could look after younger siblings, and many of these households hosted a turnover of young people from the villages whose responsibilities blurred the line between being "kept" relatives and poorly paid workers. Another conspicuous category of traders and vendors was women who were single heads of households—widows, divorcées, or unmarried mothers—for whom an income in their own right was a must. While contributing to the pot, most women's income-generating work now had another dimension. They were increasingly concerned to make money that they controlled themselves.

This concern must be seen in the light of cultural norms and practices that shape gender relations within households in Zambia. Women's chief complaint was that their spouses did not support them and the children adequately. A wife expects her husband to "keep" her and her children, by providing them with shelter, clothing, and a household allowance, yet she is well aware that cultural norms do not obligate him to do so. In short, wives do not anticipate their husbands' undivided attention, either economically or sexually. This does not mean that all conjugal relations are characterized only by discord; certainly among some of the households that remained in Mtendere spouses cooperated, especially with regard to the task of raising young children. Yet the gender division of labor and responsibility diverged considerably as the children grew up, as did women's and men's involvements beyond the home.

The growing need to make ends meet easily placed additional pressure on already tense conjugal relations. Salome Nyirenda, one of the beer brewers who remained part of my sample throughout the years, put this squarely when suggesting that male/female relations were changing for the worse as the economy deteriorated. She explained: "Men cannot be relied on anyway. They spend their time and attention elsewhere than on their own wives and children." Extrapolating from the experience of her divorced daughter, who had moved in with two children in the late 1970s, she argued that "as soon as they see someone they like, men drop their own wives" (Hansen 1984:236).

Regardless of age, women in Mtendere knew not to expect much from men. Younger women's sexual vulnerability was heightened because they were poor. Their economic dependence and worries about husbands' lack of attention gave them little control over the conjugal relationship. But older women were less subservient to the will of men. When in the mid-1980s the senior Mrs. Simpemba no longer was willing to tolerate her husband's neglect, his favoritism of the junior wife and her children, and the co-wife's hostility, she left their Lusaka home and joined rural relatives.

Older women in Mtendere who took less dramatic action than Mrs. Simpemba devised ways to divert part of their earnings from trade or wage labor to personal use. Some of them asked relatives to manage their specially earmarked funds, investing them, for example, in cattle kept by rural matrilineal relatives or running market stalls registered in the name of a relative. Other women pooled part of their earnings with a female friend every month in *chilimba*, a rotating credit arrangement between two trusted partners who reallocated funds among themselves for special purposes (Hansen 1985). They made such transactions without their husbands' knowledge and for the purpose of creating something of their own on which they could fall back if a husband's support ceased, or in case of his death and the arrival of his greedy relatives.

Housing and Gender

Household resources in Mtendere were clearly struggled over, at times—as Guyer suggested—with painful and contradictory results. While a house of one's own facilitates urban arrangements for living in important ways, it might also be a major factor of gender inequality when women obtain their access to it through men. This is the case in Zambia, where housing and housing allowances are allotted to men; wives get access to housing through husbands; and employed women who are single heads of households have no claim to housing in their own right. Similar observations apply to women's access to land, credit, and building materials (Hansen 1992). Because the statutory rules introduced after independence in 1964 have not specifically prohibited such practices, they continue to shape urban gender inequality. In this way, hierarchical power relations in interpersonal gender relationships extend beyond the household to reinforce gender inequality in society at large. The construction of gender that results from this is based on assumptions, widespread across all levels of Zambian society, that view women as dependent on men.

The consequences of this gender construction are evident in many domains of life. They are grimly demonstrated, for example, in the property snatching that takes place after a husband's death, even since the passage of the new Intestate Succession Act of 1989.[4] In spite of women's own construction of informal-sector trade as "work," the surrounding society tends to view such activity as supplementation of household income. So do the matrilineal relatives of deceased husbands, who invoke "custom" to their advantage when they legitimate their right to household estate by referring to their payment of bridewealth when the marriage was initially contracted. Since few widows in Zambia today agree to become the wife (to be "inherited") of one of the deceased husband's male relatives, as might have been the case in the past, in-laws expect that a widow will remarry and thus enter into a new property arrangement to which they will have no claims. Viewing the deceased husband as the breadwinner, they consider the wife's contributions—for instance, improvements or extensions of the house—as enhancing the estate of the deceased rather than as a product of the wife's own work efforts. In effect, the declining economy, which has turned many women into important contributors to household welfare in the face of men's shrinking incomes from wage employment, has aggravated the built-in tensions in the conjugal domain without transforming rights and claims in a manner that rewards women for their work efforts in their own right.

In one such case in Mtendere in 1988, the widow had been left with the house, eating implements, and cooking utensils for herself and the children. Although she knew, as did everyone in the township, of cases in which the deceased husband's relatives had evicted widows and children from the family house, she was bitter about the in-laws' grabbing the furniture and the bedding. She had adult employed daughters who were helping out, yet how was she to manage with the children still attending school? While fairly similar observations have been made in patrilineal societies—for example, in Kenya and Zimbabwe—a widow in a matrilineal system is particularly vulnerable because she is in charge of the children (e.g., Ncube 1987; Nelson 1978/79).

Why do widows not remonstrate? Some do, and their ability to do so is affected by the extent and diversity of the resources they command. These resources include not only their economic means but also their security of tenure in the house. Above all, resources also include their urban experience and the kinds of social networks they have established as a result of lengthy urban residence. Long-term full-time traders, for example, who had been used to operating independently of their husbands, rarely agreed to be "inherited" by one of the husband's relatives upon his death. Mrs. Banda, whose husband passed away in the mid-1980s, refused this practice. "Over my dead body," she said adamantly when I returned to her home in 1988 after the husband's death and inquired into her actions. She pointed out that she had paid for the construction of the house and had always been in charge of the household economy through her good profits from beer brewing.

Unless she has adult children who are working or relatives from her own matriline to call on for support, an urban widow with small children might easily be left to her own devices, once the husband's relatives have taken what they consider their customary right. Yet many widows seek to keep up some semblance of good relations with their deceased husbands' relatives. They are concerned about their own and their children's future welfare. Women, including widows, who have few economic means and little education consider marriage a means of economic support, although they are well aware that many men are unreliable and that well-paying jobs even for men are few and far between. In order to remarry, widows in several ethnic groups within this region must undergo a cleansing ritual conducted by their deceased husband's relatives, and some do not interfere with grabbing relatives for fear that they might not perform the ceremony. Finally, there is also the ever-present fear of witchcraft accusations from the family of the deceased, which makes some widows reluctant to instigate action against in-laws.

Houses in townships like Mtendere are important economic assets for low-income urban residents. While they shelter the material circumstances of urban lives and facilitate many women's income-generating activity, the chief beneficiaries of house ownership are men. Land record cards and occupancy titles usually contain men's names, regardless of the extent to which their wives' work efforts directly or indirectly contribute to construction, maintenance, and improvement of a house. It is also men who are the primary actors in the buying and selling of houses.

As I noted in chapter 3, houses were rarely sold in the households that dissolved in Mtendere over the course of my study. The majority of these houses were rented out, and a relative was put in charge of rent collection. In the view of retirees, and of senior relations of deceased householders, who like the older generation almost everywhere often claimed that as the young were irresponsible, it made little sense to pass a house on to a young son or daughter. And it made no economic sense at all to sell a house in town. Because urban housing is in short supply and prices are skyrocketing, absentee ownership is an important hedge against inflation. Retaining the house in town also provided those who moved to the village a place of return in case rural life proved unbearable. Indeed, between 1972 and 1981, I saw former Mtendere residents return to the township from the village precisely for that reason.

An interesting exception to the reluctance to sell is the case of Katherine, the oldest daughter of the senior Mrs. Simpemba, who with her husband and their two young children rented her father's house in Mtendere when he and his junior wife left Lusaka in 1986. Mr. Simpemba had retired from long-term employment as a bricklayer in a government department and went with his junior wife to the rural area near Mbala, a small administrative center in Zambia's Northern Province. They are Mambwe by ethnic background, one of the few patrilineal groups among Zambia's predominantly matrilineal societies. Katherine herself had married an Nsenga man after he acknowledged being the father of her first child. He "keeps me well," she told me in 1988. Her husband worked as a computer programmer in one of Lusaka's major banks and gave her a household allowance that was sufficient to cover the children's and her own daily needs. Nursing a three-month-old baby, she spoke enthusiastically about her plans to take a dressmaking course. She wanted to become independent, she explained, so as never to repeat her mother's experience of dependency as a co-wife in a polygynous marriage.

On my return in 1989, the senior Mrs. Simpemba, Katherine's mother, had died, and Katherine and her husband had bought the house from her father, paying in installments. They made some extra money by renting out two rooms. Katherine had still not enrolled in the dressmaking course, though her enthusiasm had not declined. She now spoke of wanting to work in a garment factory. Her skills in knitting were well known in the neighborhood, and she occasionally took orders to produce items of knitwear for sale. Yet although Katherine had ten years of schooling, her wage-employment prospects were not much better than her mother's had been in the early 1970s, because of the economic stagnation of the intervening decade and a half. When Katherine and her husband bought her father's house in Mtendere in 1989, her parents' household development cycle had come full circle, but with a number of twists, which I discuss in chapter 6, that point to the divergent gender and generational interests within postcolonial low-income urban households in Zambia.

Gender Axes of Sociality

The built-in tensions both in gender relationships and in women's and men's individual efforts at defining themselves as spouses, parents, and workers are difficult to contain in Lusaka's depressed economy. Women and men grapple with these tensions within households, at places of work, and in neighborhoods, and they have implications for social interaction and leisure activity in general.

In many Mtendere households, wives were expected to handle the pressures of maintaining the household, searching for scarce foods, and queueing up for necessities without the help of husbands. In most of these households, men still ate separately from women and children, and they spent their time where and with whom they liked, unquestioned but certainly not unnoticed by their wives. Husband, wife, and children might attend church together, but by and large the social interactional networks of spouses did not overlap. Across all class levels in Zambia social interaction away from work tended to be rigidly segregated by gender.

Women's social interactional sphere included female residents from the township and beyond it, to whom they turned for a variety of purposes. Many of their needs prompted contacts with neighbors, church friends, and relatives. Interaction within the immediate neighborhood ranged from the lending and borrowing of common household items like charcoal or salt to watching the house and keeping the key while a neighbor went downtown to shop. Neighbors' children were called on freely to run errands. Much casual conversation took place across yards, in streets, and by the communal water standpipes, revolving around two main issues: the availability and prices of common consumer goods and the activities of neighbors, for example, a trip "outside" (the term used for traveling across the border and to other countries) or domestic strife. Neighborly interaction did not result in strong emotional attachments but largely produced attitudes of noninterference. Because many activities—for instance, cooking, laundry, hair braiding, and napping—took place in yards within full view of neighbors and passersby, residents were concerned about the impression their activities made on others. Everyone was wary of rumors. Suspicions easily arose over the source of property acquisitions, and, in particular, residents who were somewhat better off by township standards feared their neighbors' jealousy and envy. Those who were less well off in turn described their better-heeled neighbors who kept to themselves as "proud."

Interaction with women from other neighborhoods within the township often included church members. Many Mtendere residents claimed church membership, and some women took church-sponsored activity very seriously. Church involvement in Mtendere includes membership in African independent and charismatic churches, some of which engage in healing rituals. While such churches draw an important allegiance from residents, their activities are less noticeable on the township scene than those of the conventional churches. The major established churches in Zambia, for instance, the Catholic and Anglican churches, have well-organized networks of women's and youth groups in Mtendere who hold Bible study, choir activity, and skills training (handicrafts, nutrition, adult literacy), among others. Some residents also called on church elders and fellow church members for advice when they encountered problems at home. While women who were actively involved with church functions had the opportunity to interact with male church elders, in general women were more devoted participants in church services and church-organized activity than were men. Church involvement brought women into contact with residents

Women neighbors with their children at bath time

Mrs. Sakala doing laundry

across town who played various roles in their resource networks, expanding their contacts and information sources.

Each church has a mutual support system to ease the burden of funeral expenditures on an individual household. On the occasion of a death, women canvassed fellow church members for donations in cash and in kind, largely mealie meal, the main ingredient in *nshima*, the standard meal of maize porridge. And during the activities that accompanied the funeral, women church members participated in preparing and serving food to the mourners. As mentioned in chapter 2, UNIP's party organization in the township sought to increase its involvement in township life by performing similar support services.

In addition to churches, the department of community development and an intermittent presence of NGOs introduced skills-training programs and support services particularly directed at women in Mtendere over the years. As elsewhere in Zambian townships, the community development section of the district council established women's clubs, where domestic science training was offered, especially in handicrafts (e.g., knitting, crocheting, embroidery). NGOs provided training in tailoring. At one time, a production unit in Mtendere made uniforms for all the township's schools. Such activities have never claimed a big following, for two main reasons. Skills-training courses easily interfere with women's time commitments to home and trade, and they depend on inputs that are too costly for many women (Hansen 1982b). The tailoring project lapsed once the sewing machines were stolen.

Beer halls and taverns provided recreational facilities that were highly gender-segregated. Townships like Mtendere were known in other parts of Lusaka as having quite a number of drinking places, serving bottled beer, and *chibuku*, a less costly opaque beer with less alcohol content than bottled beer. If beer was unavailable downtown, in fact, it might be found in Mtendere. There were different kinds of home-brewed beer for sale as well, and *kachasu*, a distilled alcohol with a potent reputation. Because home brewing and distilling were illegal, they took place in homes and yards. While all these drinking places had male clients around the clock, drinking peaked in the evenings, often resulting in rowdy scenes. In general, the volume of drinking and the type of drink were influenced by the monthly pay cycle, but they also fluctuated according to the availability of bottled beer and *chibuku* from the national brewing company. Women who were concerned about their reputations did not usually frequent public drinking places unaccompanied. They might buy a pint of *chibuku* to consume at home or stop briefly into a nearby *shebeen* for a tot of beer or *kachasu*. Their visits to beer halls and taverns were spoken of immediately, as were the lunchtime calls at a local tavern that my assistant and I made for a while during the summer of 1981.

Everyday life in Mtendere was affected by the coming and going of people and events. The demands of everyday life and the routines of neighborly, church, and organized-group activity might be interrupted by any of a variety of happenings, such as the arrival of visiting relatives or participation in special events. Many Mtendere residents had relatives within the township itself and/or elsewhere in Lusaka, and there was ongoing interaction between urban and rural kin, including frequent circulation of children. Many Sundays were spent in the company of Lusaka kin. Some visits took place because of the need for an informal family forum to discuss a problematic issue within the household, for example, an unmarried daughter's pregnancy, marriage negotiations, funeral arrangements, or financial matters. Customary patterns of hospitality require the preparation and serving of food to visitors. Depending on the length of the visitors' journey and the means available, such food may be either a full meal consisting of *nshima* and relish (vegetable and/or meat sauce) or, at the least, a cooked snack such as bread and fried eggs. A wife who slights this duty leaves a poor impression. When visitors arrived, Mtendere wives left their market stands to attend to the needs of the guests, who at the end of their stay were escorted to the bus stop and often given transportation money for their return trip.

Although some members of my household sample had not been back to their region of origin since they first left it, many Mtendere residents maintained diverse relations with rural kin. The exception to this was residents of different national origin who were not married to Zambians. Of my initial sample, 43 percent of the households had gone to the rural area within the preceding year for many different purposes and occasions, including funerals. One woman returned to her parents' village near Chipata in the Eastern Province each time she had a child. A couple of women went to the rural areas during the rainy season to help with farm work. Over the years, as Lusaka's economy deteriorated, the involvement of some Mtendere residents with the countryside increased and diversified. These interactions were not always mediated by kinship but took the form of trips by women traders, who exchanged goods from town that were not easily available in the villages for rural produce. Such exchanges included commodities that frequently were scarce in the 1980s, for example, tea, sugar, salt, detergent, bar soap, and bread. In the 1990s, second-hand clothing became a very popular exchange item in this urban-rural trade. Last, but not least, the declining resource base in the urban setting made some better-off Mtendere residents speak of peri-urban farming, and some began planning land acquisitions in the Chongwe area, not far from Lusaka.

Celebrating Womanhood

Special occasions bring women together at rigidly sex-segregated events that celebrate womanhood. In some but certainly not all of the households in Mtendere a daughter's coming-of-age was marked in ways that retain some aspects of a previous era's initiation rites (Richards 1982).[5] Throughout my years in Mtendere, I have attended several events of this nature. In Zambia, such events are organized for individual girls rather than for a cohort of girls. The seclusion of the novice tends to take place during school holidays when it interferes least with her school attendance. In some cases it lasts up to a month, during which the young woman is instructed by a senior woman counselor (*banachimbusa* in Bemba), who advises her about her duties toward her husband and teaches her how to give him sexual satisfaction. She is taught how to perform particular dances and how to interpret the meanings of drawings her instructor traces on the walls or the floor. And she is told not to complain about her husband but to keep "things of the house" private.[6]

For a week or more after Esther's coming-out in 1984, neighbors and friends of her mother called on her parents' house every after-noon to see her demonstrate her dancing skills to the accompaniment of drumming by two senior women. Women in the audience danced as well and threw money at the new initiate, her instructor, and the musicians. On such occasions, the participants drink beer, and the noise of the party and the music draw attention in the neighborhood. In households whose residents were devoted Christians, a truncated version of this celebration took place. In the words of my companion at one such event, there is less "lewd" dancing and soft drinks take the place of beer. I have also visited Christian homes where a girl's initiation was observed during the school year. In such cases the girl attended school as usual, but for a specified period of time she returned straight home from school and remained inside afterward.

Esther's parents were Kunda and her instructor Nsenga. I attended other celebrations where the novice, her instructor, and the drummers were all from different ethnic groups. When attending such events, participants described them by several terms: *namwali, mwali, moye,* and *chisungu,* as though they all were synonymous. In the past, these were regional terms, designating the young novice in several of Zambia's languages: *namwali* or *mwali* in Yao and Chewa, as well as in Luvale and Chokwe, and *chisungu* in Bemba (Drourega 1927; Mair 1951; White 1953). In effect, to the extent that residents in places like Mtendere refer to fairly similar urban initiation ceremonies by a variety of names, it seems that regional distinctions have largely eroded in the urban setting.

Only in 1971 did I ever witness the *njau* dance performed in connection with a coming-out celebration in Mtendere. The *njau* is a male dance form distinctive to the Eastern Province and the Chewa speakers of Malawi. In the past, young boys performed the *njau* at the major transition rites, including female initiations. They learned the skills of *njau* performance art as part of their own initiation into a boys' secret society. The role of women in the *njau* was strictly accessory to that of men: they brought food and prepared it. In the performance I saw, adult women in the audience joked at the young male dancers while children repeated song lines. I learned of weekend performances of *njau* in the township on a couple of other occasions during my 1971–1972 study, but since that time I have never seen a locally organized *njau* performance (as opposed to a "staged" performance by the national dance troupe at a public function). Perhaps this performance art has lost some of its salience as a result of Mtendere's growing ethnic heterogeneity as well as of hostility on the part of some churches (Schoffeleers and Linden 1972).

Over the years of my comings and goings in Mtendere, another all-female event has become increasingly popular. This is the bridal shower, locally called a "kitchen party," which I never came across in the early 1970s. But by the mid-1980s, some Mtendere women were speaking of staging and attending kitchen parties, sometimes in the township but more frequently in "the yards," that is, the high-income residential areas. Although only some women can afford the cost of staging such an event, most of them have attended several such parties. Through friends and relatives they are all part of networks that cross townships, occupational groups, and class distinctions.

Kitchen parties are all-female events at which relatives and friends, including expatriates, come together with presents to help a bride-to-be with kitchen utensils for her new home. A wide range of women is invited, including friends of friends. Some of these parties are quite large, between one hundred and two hundred persons; they tend to take place outdoors, in a spacious garden, on Saturday afternoons toward the end of the month, when wage-employed workers have received their paychecks. They are modeled on a loose version of initiation ceremonies, and feature as party manager a senior woman marriage instructor who, before the party, has taught the bride-to-be how to behave toward her husband, both sexually and interpersonally. The party gets going after the bride-to-be has demonstrated her dancing skills, especially how "to dance in bed." Subsequent events include individual performances, as each guest who cares to or can be cajoled into dancing steps into the center, commenting on the present she has brought "for the kitchen" in terms of its importance to the marital relationship.

Regardless of the ethnic background of the bride-to-be, the senior woman marriage instructor and the female drummers tend in Lusaka to have Eastern Province origins. The drummers are mostly recruited from the low-income townships. While some of the dances and songs performed at kitchen parties may derive from another era, these events are characterized by their ethnic and socioeconomic heterogeneity, and above all by their preoccupation with male-female relations and heterosexual norms. Ample food is served and, except in some Christian homes, such events feature a good deal of drinking, especially of beer but also, in wealthier homes, of wine and alcohol-spiced punches. Kitchen parties are one of the few events that bring women together in Zambia to share stories about their joys, successes, troubles, and tribulations as well as information with which they assist one another. Given the male authoritarian atmosphere that characterizes sociality across all class levels in Zambia, it comes as no surprise that men view kitchen parties as events where married women get drunk and indulge in social evils, such as exposing unmarried women to offensive songs about sex and gossip about extramarital relationships.[7]

Urban Life and Ethnicity

What role did ethnicity play in the social interaction of Mtendere residents? The urban initiation rites and kitchen parties just described are not specific to any single ethnic group. Their participants are heterogeneous in terms of ethnic background (and class background in the case of the kitchen party). These celebrations speak less to ethnic distinctiveness than to notions about gender that are shared by Zambia's many ethnic groups, regardless of whether they are matrilineal or patrilineal. In effect, we may describe them as thoroughly "Zambian" rituals. I develop this point further in chapter 6.

Throughout this book I have specified Mtendere residents' background in regional rather than in distinctly ethnic terms. In my view and in the view of many observers of Zambia's urban scene during the late colonial period, ethnicity is not a very salient factor in shaping the nature of urban interaction (Gluckman 1961). Most urban residential areas, including Mtendere, are very heterogeneous in ethnic terms, although for historical reasons some, for example Lusaka's Marrapodi-Mandevu township, contain population clusters of particular groups (Jules-Rosette 1981). The ethnic heterogeneity of Zambia's urban settings is accentuated by the widespread practice of interethnic marriage. The ethnic mix of a particular township is always in flux because of population turnover and changing migration patterns. In the wake of the decline of mining employment in the copperbelt towns, more people from the north are moving to Lusaka, where in the early 1990s more Bemba, the dominant language of the north, was spoken than ever before. This is evidenced in Mtendere, where a study from 1991 noticed a much larger proportion of Bemba speakers than I did in 1971, when my sample included only four Bemba households (Weinberger 1991).

Outside of Mtendere residents' non–ethnically marked worlds of work and leisure, I have observed invocations of ethnicity in only a few contexts, although of course there may be others. One such context concerns a grouping with diverse southern African backgrounds, including Sotho, Tswana, Zulu, and "coloreds," who pooled money to help relieve funeral expenditures. This pooling sometimes took place at parties organized along the lines of the "subscription party" of the colonial period. A member hosts the party in her home, gets female friends to help with cooking, and charges a fee for a dinner plate. The participants refer to one another by the English gender-inflected term "home-boys." I was told that residents from Malawi organized similar groups. As I see it, these are regional associations, rather than distinctly marked ethnic groups.

When in the late 1980s the Mtendere home-boys considered establishing themselves formally, they encountered problems with the registrar of societies. At issue was membership, which for a formally registered society had to be opened to Zambians. Since their goal was to cater to the special needs of persons originating outside of the country, in southern Africa, the requirements associated with formal registration defeated their purpose.

Some Mtendere residents from Malawi and the former Rhodesia occasionally invoked ethnicity when complaining of how they felt slighted in formal employment as a result of ongoing Zambianization, that is, the effort to privilege the employment of nationals. During the federal period, 1953–1963, when labor moved more freely across borders, Malawians and Rhodesians, who at that time were considerably better educated than Zambians, were employed at the lower clerical ranks in government institutions. Such jobs had largely been taken over by Zambians in the early 1970s (Matejko 1976). One Rhodesian resident in my sample had worked on one of the government-controlled newspapers. When he was dismissed, he set himself up as a storekeeper in Mtendere. As in the case of the home-boys, ethnicity in this instance was less about primordial sentiments than about the politics of regionalism.

There is also national political culture to consider. When assessing the role of ethnicity as a resource or liability to economic efforts, neighborhood, and leisure interaction in Mtendere, we must not lose sight of the fact that my observations between 1971 and the late 1980s were undertaken during a period when official political ideology sought to create "One Zambia, One Nation" out of the country's many regional groups. According to a colonial handbook, republished by the government printer shortly after independence, Zambia contained seventy-three tribes (Brelsford 1965).[8] Did Mtendere residents downplay ethnicity? I do not think so. They had no hesitation about speaking of which chief's area they or their parents originated from—for example, Chief Chikuni's area—which in local parlance amounts to identifying a tribe. And they readily pinpointed categorical differences between groups when joking about the Lozi as fish eaters and

the Chewa as eaters of rodents. These examples illustrate how categorical indicators of group relations draw on ethnic and regional char-
acterizations with overlapping meanings, much as Mitchell observed
on the copperbelt during the late colonial period (1956).

Regional categorical ethnicity of this kind had little salience in the
everyday life of residents in Mtendere. When they compared themselves to other urban Zambians, they spoke not about ethnic differences but about inequity in opportunity and power. In their description
of themselves, they had appropriated the generic term "the common
man" from party and media discourse but assigned it meanings that
derived from the difference they perceived between themselves and the
apamwamba, who lived in *mayadi* (the yards). We recall that the
Nyanja term *apamwamba* means, literally, "those on the top." In the
class terms of postcolonial Zambia, we might say that *apamwamba* has
replaced the colonial period's term *wazungu*, which applied to those
who used to live in the yards—the Europeans or whites in general.

These terms are not so much ethnic as they are economic, for they
speak about differences in opportunity and power. Consider the following characterization that Agnes Siame made after one of her first
long-distance "suitcase" trading trips across the border into Zaire in
the mid-1980s. "The *wazungus* in Zaire," she said, "are *mwenye*
[Indian]." In the copperbelt region, specific economic opportunities
have opened up and disappeared, attracting changing groups of
"aliens," who have been described differently over time by members
of their host society. Prostitutes from the Belgian Congo were usually
called "Kasai" women during the colonial period. Since independence,
the copperbelt region has seen the making and scapegoating of
"Zaireans," "Senegalese," and "West Africans." These ethnicities are
the products of recent political and economic events and have little to
do with primordial feelings. Instead, their boundaries have been constructed through cross-border interactions that involve both legal
issues and power relations.

In the kinds of socioeconomic interactions I have observed in
Mtendere over the years, gender has played a much larger part than
ethnicity in shaping opportunity. At the level of organized group
activity in Zambia, gender has occasionally been a rallying point in
women's demonstrations both during the colonial period and after
independence. In July 1981, for example, more than three thousand
wives of miners demonstrated in support of their striking husbands

in Chililabombwe, one of the copperbelt towns. The demonstration was triggered by the withdrawal of credit for mealie meal, the main staple, in the company store. Booing two company managing directors who urged them to persuade their husbands to resume work, the women argued that they had been cheated for a long time and were no longer prepared to have sex in order to buy mealie meal (Hansen 1984:237; *Times of Zambia* 1981). Yet ethnicity has to my knowledge not played a corresponding part in public confrontations.[9]

As indicated by the incidents described above, ethnicity is just one among many relationships in terms of which people construe their actions. Ethnicity interacts with a host of other relations, including social organizational practices such as kinship and marriage, class, and race. Ethnicity may also be constructed with reference to gender. Recently, it has been common within the social sciences to speak of the intersection of such relationships (Moore 1988:186–98). This formulation warns us against singling out any one of these relationships as the determining one. My observations in Mtendere demonstrate complex interactions among and between these relationships that draw on all of them, but variously. This means that they are subject to change and that the relative salience of ethnicity in everyday interaction may shift. The safest conclusion about dynamics on the home front is then perhaps to emphasize what this chapter has been concerned with showing, namely that we cannot understand how social organizational relationships, class, and race—and possibly ethnicity—interact without reference to gender. The home front stands between the individual and the wider society. As I discuss in the next chapter, when the problems that converge on individuals because of this intersection become persistent, people may resort to the courts to find a solution.

5 | Private Troubles and Public Issues

U rban arrangements for living among Mtendere residents were affected by pervasive problems, both private and public. In the course of my long-term research on household dynamics and urban arrangements for living in Mtendere, I decided in 1988 to spend some of my time in the local court at Chelston where Mtendere residents took their civil cases. As the postcolonial successors of the late colonial period's urban native courts, today's urban local courts adjudicate disputes that fall within what continues to be called "customary law." I was particularly intrigued by the insistence among Mtendere women that "one shouldn't wash one's dirty laundry in public," when in fact they brought cases concerning conjugal disputes and personal insult/defamation of character to court much more readily than men did. Exploring why women considered the local court a strategic place to air such disputes, I examine in this chapter how gender relations were negotiated in local court and what this tells us about the relationship between "custom" and postcolonial Zambian society.

The codification of customary law in colonial Central Africa was shaped both by European notions about Africans and by the concerns of Africans, especially chiefs and male elders (Chanock 1985). As such, customary law is less a factual legacy of tradition than it is a dynamic historical product, "which at once shapes and is shaped by economic, political, and social processes" over time (Roberts and Mann 1991:8). While the colonial era's customary law often supported ruling class (European) and African elite (male) interests, both the urban native courts of the past and the local courts of today were and are flexible in their arbitration and judgment of dispute cases, reckoning with the political and economic circumstances in the wider society. Thus there are both constraining and enabling aspects of law (Starr and Collier 1989:12). As I demonstrate with material drawn from local court cases, certain aspects of customary law appear to persist. On closer scrutiny, they are far from "customary" but represent instead reconstituted notions of custom, which today's urban justices invoke in their arbitration. What is more, these same justices are also creating "custom" out of practices that were not so recognized in the past. In short, this chapter is a discussion of the ongoing creation of custom and of the court as a resource that urban women use in struggles over poverty, work, autonomy, and above all, gender identity in postcolonial Lusaka.

The case method of legal presentation that Epstein pioneered in his work on the copperbelt in the 1950s offers a compelling framework for analyzing situations that produce conflict as well as for exploring the place of legal bodies in the broader structure of power of a particular society (1953:4). Describing a number of cases pertaining to the two seemingly disparate categories of conjugal problems and of personal insult and defamation of character, I identify issues that are central to both. These issues expose questions about what kinds of persons women and men want to be that are at odds with the roles that the wider society accords them. The issues are also indicative of conflicts that stem from the increased significance that property and individual personhood are assuming in today's society in the face of the declining significance of social relations based on broader kin groups (Chanock 1991).

Drawing on my prior understanding of ongoing social relationships within the setting in which disputes arose, I begin by discussing some of the mediation practices that Mtendere township residents made use of without involving the court. Then I follow some residents to the local court, briefly outlining court procedures and presenting cases, first in the category of conjugal problems and second, in that of personal insult and defamation of character. My description of cases is primarily concerned with indicating, by way of example, the tenor of the discussion and the nature of the arguments. In the subsequent section, I tease out a body of shared ideas from these two categories of cases and identify some of the criteria that the local court uses in issuing judgments. My concluding comments concern the powers of custom and court to redefine female and male against a backdrop of socioeconomic change.

Dispute Mediation Practices in Mtendere

When Mtendere residents took problems to court, they did so because of *mavuto* (singular *vuto*), which in the Nyanja language means "persistent trouble." Not all disputes turned into *mavuto*, for third-party resolution through court is considered a last resort (Himonga 1985:200–201). As the case material I am about to present illustrates, the parties involved had a variety of options: problems might have been handled in informal family forums before reaching court; if one or more of the parties to a dispute was an active church member, the problem might have been brought before church elders; depending on the issue at stake, an employer, social welfare officers (of the Ministry of Labor and Social Services), or the police might have been called on; above all, representatives of the township's UNIP organization might have been consulted in a process through which disputes moved from the section to the branch chairman. When problems persisted unresolved in spite of such mediation efforts, they became *mavuto*. In such instances, the party representative encouraged the complaining party to issue a court summons against the offenders. To this end, the person lodging the complaint was supplied with a letter to present to the clerk in the local court where the summons was issued.

To be sure, Mtendere residents preferred to solve their disputes without involving the local court. Almost without exception, the very frequent incidents of premarital pregnancy first prompted attempts at informal solution between the parties concerned. Once parents realized that a daughter was pregnant, they sought to make her reveal the identity of the man who was responsible. If she named the man, her parents then sent a middleman to the parents of the man involved to inform them of the event and suggest the amount of "damages" to be paid to the young woman's parents.[1] A middleman is a person who can be trusted, for example, a relative, friend, or fellow church member. In the case of the first pregnancy of Esther, the young woman whose *moyo* I attended in 1984, the young man's parents agreed to pay the requested sum, yet they never completed their obligation.

Esther's parents did not do much about it, as she got pregnant by another man who seemed more prepared to fulfill his obligation and accept responsibility.

But quarrels easily arose over "damages," and some young men denied their involvement. When Agnes Siame's son made a neighbor's daughter pregnant in the mid-1980s, Agnes, her husband, and a businessman friend of theirs discussed the matter of damages with the girl's parents. The son admitted that he had been involved with the girl, who still attended school, but explained that it was "an accident." The girl's parents stipulated the amount of damages, but before Agnes's party even had time to return with a response, they were served with a court summons to Chelston local court. In the court proceeding, Agnes's son acknowledged that he was responsible for making the girl pregnant. His parents explained that they had not declined to pay damages but rather that the girl's parents had not given them any time to discuss the size of damage payment they had demanded. In the end, the court insisted on an amount that was lower than that requested by the girl's parents.

The local court is a potential forum of reconciliation not only between parents who are troubled by the behavior of the young but also between husbands and wives. Yet local means were always tried first. Agnes's two eldest daughters had frequent problems with their husbands. When their problems became intolerable, they moved in with Agnes and Kapansa, who over the years undertook numerous visits, pleading with in-laws and asking church members and other friends to mediate. One of these young women experienced mistreatment bordering on violence by her husband, rather than economic neglect. In many other households, husbands sought to get their way with what they considered to be recalcitrant wives, and wives complained about their husbands' treatment of them. In a past era, such complaints would have been dealt with by relatives. When a husband's beatings reached an unacceptable level, a woman from the Eastern Province would seek protection from her husband's elder brothers, in special cases from her husband's paternal aunt or sisters. Only in extreme cases did a woman turn to her own father or other senior relatives. If she was so badly beaten that she could not carry out her daily activities, a woman would return with her children to her own relatives (Phiri 1993:16). In the Southern Province, a woman might very well first turn to kin.[2]

In cities like Lusaka today, such support structures are not readily available, and many women's economic dependency prevents them from leaving abusive or neglectful husbands. In all my years in Mtendere, Anna Njovu was always thoroughly dominated by her husband, who worked as a "lorry boy" for the district council. They were both Ngoni, members of a patrilineal society in the Eastern Province. Mr. Njovu did not allow his wife to trade, and he gave her a miserable allowance. At some point between 1972 and 1981, he took a second wife. And in 1976, he brought his mother, who was in her seventies, from the Eastern Province to live with them in Lusaka. Both she and Anna complained to the UNIP branch that he was not keeping them properly. The old woman, for example, had not been given one single dress during the four or five years she had lived in her son's house. Soon after the husband married his second wife, Anna went to stay with her parents near Chipata. But Mr. Njovu went to court to complain about his wife's desertion. The court judged in his favor, and he subsequently brought Anna back to town. By 1984 he had divorced the junior wife on account of her ill health. He still neglected the remainder of his household, and the Anglican Church assisted Anna and her five children with food and clothing.

Last but not least, in Mtendere's crowded neighborhoods, where household interaction rarely was private, tensions of various kinds arose. Because residents were extremely concerned to uphold respect for themselves and members of their households, seemingly minor matters such as who had been seen with whom or who said what to whom readily caused gossip. The common view was that "things of the house" ought to remain private; women should not complain about their husbands' behavior, nor should husbands entertain drinking mates with tales about domestic matters. Such preoccupations lent themselves to idle talk, if not malicious gossip. Both faulty and true interpretations of the motives and actions of other residents gave rise to shouting matches, some of which ended up in court.

Conflict Resolution and Local Court

Local courts are the lowest judicial bodies in Zambia's legal hierarchy. Their jurisdiction pertains to civil disputes under customary law, including such issues as marital and property claims. Appeals lie with subordinate courts, from which they may be advanced to the high court, and then the supreme court (Himonga 1987:58). Local courts are supervised by a presiding justice, who in some courts sits with a number of court justices. They are not trained lawyers, and their chief qualification seems to be their knowledge of customary law (Himonga 1985:226–27). During my observations at the Chelston local court, one of five such institutions in Lusaka, the presiding justice worked alone, assisted by a court clerk.

The procedures at this urban local court had much in common with those that Epstein described on the copperbelt in the 1950s: the facts of the issue are presented to the court by way of statement, each party—plaintiff (PL) and defendant (DF)—first speaking without interruptions from the presiding justice (PJ) (1953:7–8). The justice in turn questions and probes in an attempt to discover the cause of the problem.[3] He sometimes cross-examines the parties, including codefendants (CO-DF), and occasionally calls witnesses (WI) on the part of either party (WI-PL, or WI-DF). Then the justice sums up the matter and issues a judgment.

Today's court proceedings are conducted in the vernacular, which in the case of the Chelston local court was Nyanja. Translation was provided if one of the parties involved in a case did not speak Nyanja. For example, one case I observed was accompanied by translation from Nyanja into Tonga. The court clerk writes the record of cases in English, which contains many Zambian-English colloquialisms. In this chapter's presentation I have retained the court clerk's rendition of cases, adding occasional clarifications.

There were four broad categories of disputes among the wide range of matters that Mtendere residents took to their local court when other mediation efforts had proved futile.[4] Almost half of the cases revolved around conjugal problems (e.g., marital disputes, divorce, chase [away] from home/desertion/neglect and cruelty, adultery, premarital pregnancy, and appointment of an administrator). I have included premarital pregnancy cases in this broad category because they revolve around the problems of establishing conjugal unions. The second-largest category consisted of complaints about defamation of character, insult, and witchcraft accusations (and combinations of these). Complaints about debt and theft constituted the third-largest category, followed by a miscellany of disputes involving, for instance, tearing of clothes; refusal to return borrowed items; reten-

tion of blue book, national registration card, or land record card; out-
standing rent payment; and contempt of court.

Conjugal Cases

Striking gender distinctions are evident in the broad category of
cases involving conjugal problems.[5] By and large, women took men
to court for marital problems, for chasing them away from home, and
for divorce. Men took women to court for deserting the home, and
they took other men to court for committing adultery with their
spouses. As the following cases demonstrate, the outcome depends to
a large extent on the status of the conjugal union, which in the judgment of the presiding justice hinges on whether or not bridewealth
was transferred. In the records of the clerk at the Chelston local
court, bridewealth was rendered as "dowry." I have retained this
usage in order to indicate the reworking of a "traditional" concept.
The word *lobola* occurs occasionally for bridewealth, as do other vernacular terms for specific transactions that were, and sometimes still
are, part of marriage contracts.

In *Zulu v. Mbewe* (no. 754 of 1987), Mrs. Zulu sought a divorce
from her husband, Mr. Mbewe. They had been married, with a dowry
of K130, since 1982[6]; they had one child. The plaintiff (PL), Mrs. Zulu,
recounted:

> The defendant [DF] married me in 1982. That same month,
> September 1982, he chased me [away from home] saying I am
> barren. After a few days I was sent back to him. In October 1982
> he chased me again but the church elders advised him to talk to
> me and he agreed.
>
> I stayed with him for a few months and I conceived from him.
> Later after giving birth, he again chased me [away from home]
> when the baby was one month old. I was sent back to him but
> he said he doesn't want me and he sent me to . . . where his par-
> ents are. He was giving me mealie meal in a newspaper, and he
> was not buying me clothes.
>
> On 17/7/85 I went to my parents in Mtendere compound. He
> came and produced money as a sign of divorce. In April 1987
> again he chased me but he was advised by church elders to take
> me back. He refused and sent me to his relatives at . . . but I was

sent back to him but still he refused and I went to my relatives. Then I decided to cut [issue] him a [court] summons.

The presiding justice (PJ) then engaged the parties in a discussion:

DF. How many times have I taken you to church elders for reconciliation?

PL. Six times.

DF. Were you cooking and washing for me?

PL. Yes.

PJ. Did [DF] start to chase you [away from home] a long time ago?

PL. Yes.

PJ. Why are you forcing yourself to go back to his house?

PL. It is because I am pregnant.

DF. I deny to reconciliate with the [PL] because she does not follow my instructions in the house. She does not wash for me and she does not cook. I have taken her before church elders six times but she would not change for the better. I then gave her K10 as a token of divorce.

PL. Do you think I am a liar?

DF. Yes.

PL. Do you want me to give birth to children without keeping them?

DF. No.

PL. Who sleeps with me?

DF. It is me.

PL. Why don't you want me?

DF. It is because you don't want to listen to my instructions.

PJ. Is the pregnancy yours?

DF. It is mine.

PJ. Why can't you keep her till she gives birth?

DF. It is because one [i.e., the child] may die in the future.

PJ. In accordance to your custom, is it lawful to divorce a pregnant woman?

DF. Yes.

A witness (WI) from Mtendere entered in support of the PL.:

The plaintiff is my sister. I suppose the marriage has come to an end. Since they married, troubles have not ceased. The same year he married [PL], he started chasing her [away from home].

The church elders have tried their level best to reconcile the couple but [with] no change.

On 17/11/85 we held a discussion with [DF]'s mother and in her presence [DF] vowed to say he has lost love for [PL]. On 4/8/86 [DF furnished] K2 [a payment DF was asked to pay?] in presence of church elders. Later he produced K10 and gave it to [PL] and told her to go to the law [to court].

This case demonstrates the failure both of church elders and relatives to mediate a difficult marriage situation. In summarizing, the justice argued that since the DF had already agreed to divorce his pregnant wife, he must compensate K400 to assist her in preparing for the child's birth.

Aside from the special issue surrounding a wife's pregnancy in this case, court instructions for men to pay compensation to estranged wives were common in other divorce cases, provided that the spouses had been married "with dowry." Just how the court defines marriage was at issue in several of the following cases.

The *Banda v. Mutale* (no. 770 of 1987) case was brought to court by Mrs. Banda, who wanted to divorce Mr. Mutale because he "chased her [drove her from home] constantly." They had been married since 1976, without dowry, and they had four children. Mrs. Banda (PL) explained:

> PL. [DF] chased me [away] from the house on 11/7/87. This was not his first time to chase me [away from home]. He has chased me thrice since we married. At one time when he chased me he followed me and asked me to rejoin him. My parents told me to join him.
>
> One day during his absence about four people came to demand their monies [payments the husband owed them?]. I refunded the whole money totalling K300 when he was out at Lundazi. Later he went to Mansa and told me I should be keeping K100 each month. So when he came back in June he found me with K600 which he demanded me to give him and I did. Due to our troubles I reported at [DF]'s place of work and his boss advised me to sue him.

The justice sought to identify the problem:

> PJ. Where do you come from?

PL. Petauke.

PJ. Is there no dowry?

PL. It is not marriage.

DF. I started the friendship with [PL] in 1979 and asked her whether she has relatives in Mtendere; she told me she doesn't have. But she told me that she had an uncle in Mandevu [a low-income township in Lusaka] and that she will one day take me there.

One day a certain relative of [PL] came to the house, and since I did not know her I was shocked. When I came from Mansa it is true I found [PL] has kept K650 and I asked her to give me [the money] so that I can go and shop for the children at home. In June 1987 when I came asking [PL] to stop the child from sucking milk because the child has grown up. But my wife refused. She was even refusing me to have sexual intercourse with her. I have accepted the marriage to end because she does not listen to my advice.

PL. Was I not merely following by saying that I don't want to produce?

DF. It was not a joke.

PL. Do I refuse you in bed?

DF. Yes.

PJ. Do you accept to divorce even now?

DF. Yes.

PL. I want [DF] to give me property for the services I have rendered for him. [DF] also took my children.

DF. This time I took the children and I want my money which she refused.

When trying to ascertain the status of this union, the justice first inquired about the couple's regional background, probably in order to identify their ethnic group, and then went on to elicit information about whether or not relevant relatives had acknowledged the relationship as a marriage. He summed up: "This court dissolves the friendship because no dowry was paid to make the marriage legal. In this regard, no divorce certificate will be issued. In addition, [PL] cannot claim property which she bought before [DF] proposed to her and [DF] cannot take the children because no custom was followed in the sense that no dowry was paid."

The critical issue of childbearing in relation to marriage from men's perspective is also evident in the next case. In *Mushanga v. Phiri* (no. 631 of 1987), Mr. Mushanga (PL) took his wife to court to request divorce, claiming that she caused "a lot of dispute in the house." The court record described them as married in 1982, with no dowry, and no children. The justice probed into the matter and learned that a damage fee (and not dowry) of K15 had been paid at the beginning of the relationship.

> PL. In 1982 the [DF] became my girlfriend and I was told I had [im]pregnated her. But it was not true and I was charged K60 out of which K15 was paid. We looked for medicines [to facilitate conception] but all in vain. This is why I don't want her because we have no children.
>
> PJ. How long have you been in friendship?
>
> PL. Since 1982 up to date.
>
> DF. My brother asked [PL] how many witchdoctors we have gone to. The [PL] told him and my brother decided that we should stop looking for medicines.
>
> PJ. Is this a proper marriage?
>
> DF. It is just friendship.

A witness for the DF next argued that "the parties should separate because they were not properly married." Asked by the justice whether he agreed that "this was a mere friendship," the DF's witness answered in the affirmative. The justice then issued the judgment that the friendship should be dissolved because "no dowry was paid."

In this, and several other "divorce cases," the compensations paid to women depended on the status of the union—whether or not the parties had been properly married, i.e., with dowry. This meaning of "proper marriage" also entered into the court's decisions concerning compensation after adultery, as the following case illustrates.

In *Chirwa v. Poloti* (no. 378 of 1987), Mr. Chirwa claimed that Mr. Poloti had abducted his wife. Mr. Chirwa (PL) had been married to his wife since 1963, with no dowry, and they had several children.

> PL. I sued [DF] because he committed adultery with codefendant [CO-DF]. She had missed from the house and when I looked for her, I found her in the house of the [DF]. The [DF] threatened to hit me with a hammer.

PJ. Is [CO-DF] your wife?

PL. She is my wife.

PJ. Did you pay dowry?

PL. No.

PJ. Is she your proper wife then?

PL. She is just a friend.

DF. When I met [CO-DF] she told me that she was not married. So I took her to my house.

PJ. Did she tell you that she was not married?

DF. That is what she told me.

PJ (to DF). Is [CO-DF] your wife?

DF. She is my wife.

PJ. Did you pay dowry?

DF. No.

PJ. Is [CO-DF] your wife then?

DF. She is my girlfriend.

CO-DF. The reason I gave in to [DF] is that the [PL] doesn't support me. The [PL] doesn't stay at home.

PJ. Did [DF] pay dowry?

CO-DF. No.

The justice dismissed this case "due to the fact that [PL] and [DF] are just boyfriends to [CO-DF]. No dowry was paid from either side." It contrasts to other adultery cases where husbands were awarded compensation from men who had engaged in sex with their "properly married wives."

Marriage rather than friendship—that is, being properly married with dowry—is increasingly difficult in today's strained economy, as the *Mbewe v. Phiri* case (no. 694 of 1987) illustrates. Mrs. Mbewe (PL) took Mr. Phiri to court because he had deserted their home; she wanted reconciliation. They were married in 1963, had four children, and only part of the agreed-upon dowry had been paid.

PL. I married [DF] in 1963 and he has four children with me. When we went home [to the rural area] we stayed on the farm. He left me in 1985 at the farm, but he came [to Lusaka] for good. So I came to sue the [DF] for reconciliation.

DF. In August 1985, the [PL] went home to see her parents but when she arrived at home her grandmother wrote to say that [PL] will not come back until I pay lobola. So I came home and

I was charged to pay four heads of cattle. I told them I would
pay in money but they wanted the animals. So I came here [to
Lusaka] in March to work so that I can raise money to buy
animals to pay.

Asked by the justice about why he had not paid yet, the defendant
explained that he still was looking for money to buy cattle. When
cross-examined by the justice, the DF explained:

I am prepared to get her but the problem is accommodation
because I am occupying a one-roomed house. At present I am
not working, so I cannot promise [her accommodation]. I still
want my wife, but the problem is that her parents who charged
me animals will think that I have disobeyed their order.

PL. I am going home so when he finds a house he will write me.

In this case, the justice argued that PL "did not desert her but her parents said he should take her after paying four animals lobola." And
the justice advised: "The court cannot force them to marry, but [DF]
should show love to his wife by making sure that he finds accommodation for her."

The case just presented indicates that the local court does reckon
with some of the difficulties that hard economic times pose for
"observing custom." This court also, as the next case shows, makes
distinctions between persons who are less well off and those who have
better means. *Mwila v. Sinyinda* (no. 171 of 1988) is just one of the
many cases involving partners who in the court's view were not properly married. As we saw above, in most such cases women did not get
compensation from husbands once their marriages were dissolved.
But Mr. Sinyinda was a chief accountant for a well-known firm and
therefore much better able than most urban men to compensate his
estranged wife. They had been married since 1969 and had one child.
As Mrs. Mwila (PL) explained:

I married [DF] in 1969 after divorcing my first husband. I also
told him that I was once married and I had one child. He
accepted to keep me and my child. He paid K4 dowry to my
brother because I was once married. . . . The cause of breakage of
marriage is because [DF] sent me home and maintained another
woman. Later he was accusing me of trying to [be]witch him

. . . and he wrote me a separation letter. Since 1980 the [DF] never bothered to support me and my child.

Seeking to ascertain the facts, the justice asked about the chief reason for termination of the marriage.

DF. No support.
PJ. Since when has he not been supporting you?
PL. Since 1980.
PL. I have built a house at Kaunda Square [a low-income township in Lusaka] which he promised that he would build for me. But since he has not built me a house, I would be glad if the same house could be surrendered to me.

In the judgment of this case, Mr. Sinyinda was instructed to pay compensation of K1500 to his wife for the house he was expected to build but for whose construction she had been responsible.

Insult and Defamation of Character

As mentioned at the outset, personal insult cases predominantly involved women. They all revolved around issues that women consider crucial to their definition of themselves. The insult case of *Zulu v. Sakala* (no. 426 of 1987) was brought to court by Mrs. Zulu (PL), who wanted compensation from Mrs. Sakala (DF).

PL. In April 1987 the [DF] came to my house and accused me of committing adultery with her husband. She started insulting me.
PJ. Is this true?
DF. It is very true.
PJ. Did [DF] find you with her husband?
PL. No.
DF. When I came home from work, I used to meet my husband with the [PL]. When I complained to my husband, he gave me a nasty answer. This annoyed me and I went to insult [PL].
PJ. Were you right to go and insult [PL]?
DF. I was wrong.
WI-PL (witness for the plaintiff). The [PL] is my neighbour and whenever [DF] sees me with [PL], she [DF] suspects me of being a boyfriend to [PL].

In the view of the justice, the DF had admitted that she insulted PL, and he charged her to pay K180 compensation to PL.

In *Mbewe v. Metson* (no. 237 of 1988), Mrs. Mbewe (PL) argued that Mr. Metson (DF) falsely accused her of telling that his wife "bitched" about with other men. Mrs. Mbewe wanted compensation.

> PL. It was one day when [DF] came to ask for money from me. I told him I had no money but when leaving he banged the door. I then went to tell his wife that her husband came to ask for money. Later . . . I saw the [DF] and when he asked me, I told him. But when I bent down to pick up a stick he threw a bottle at me. When I asked him why he did that, he started shouting at me that I am a bitch. When I heard those words I left. The following day I went to his house . . . and he apologized. But another day he accused me of having told him to say that his wife moves about with other men and that he has frequently been beating his wife.
>
> The DF then asked PL: So did you say you beat your wife because I told that your wife bitches a lot. I did not tell you such words. I did say that if you are mad, then I will take you to Chainama [the nearby state mental hospital].
>
> DF. It was early February 1988 one day I was coming from work. I met [PL] by her home and I asked her whether *munkoyo* [a lightly fermented homemade beverage] was there and she told me it was there. Then she added words saying that my wife bitches about with other men. So I waited for my wife until she came home. I asked her where she was and she said at church. On 21/2/88 again [PL] was calling her bitch. . . . She shouted at me saying have you divorced your wife because of me. When I heard such words I told her that I wanted to wait for her husband so that we can solve the matter. Then the other day I sent for [PL] to come to my house for a discussion. When she came, instead of listening to what she was called for, she uttered words directed to me that "if you are mad then I should take a wheelbarrow and take you to Chainama."

After some cross-examination and questioning of witnesses, the justice concluded: "[DF] has failed to produce proof as to whether it is true that [PL] told him to say that his wife bitches with other men.

This proves to this court that by merely defaming [PL]'s character as such he [DF] must compensate [PL] the sum of K80."

"Bitching" and "moving about" are serious issues, as demonstrated in the *Nfonse v. Sitali* case (no. 204 of 1988), which involved witchcraft allegations as well. Ms. Nfonse (PL) explained how Mrs. Sitali had invoked witchcraft against her and that she had called her a "bitch" in a letter.

> PL. On 18/2/88 I received a letter from her labelling me a bitch and that I am an AIDS carrier. She also bewitched me. Lastly she threatened that she will do bad whenever she will meet me.
>
> DF. I wrote [PL] an insults letter because whenever she went to Kabwe and came back she used to convey greetings from Kabwe to me. [PL] is my friend but to my surprise when I went to Kabwe I caught a letter which [PL] wrote to the girl-friend of my husband and addressed it as Mrs. Sitali. So I got angry and wrote [PL] an insulting letter.

The court record contained the letter exhibit:

> Stupid Beatrice, . . . You were just fooling me coming to my house when you know the secret of Sitali, he is married to your friend [the letter writer]. . . . You are the one making me suffering. Why can't you look for your own husbands who are not married so that you also experience how it pains when you hear that your husband is moving with another woman . . . *ma hule imwe* [you bitch],[7] you even wanted to beat another woman because of your friends' husbands. You AIDS carrier, you even came saying Sitali wanted money from the bank when you know it was going to your fellow bitch. You idiots, why *mukonda ku sokweza ma nyumba banzanu* [why do you like to break your friends' houses]?

Strong allegations to be sure. In the judgment, the DF was reprimanded that she was wrong to insult PL in such a way. The justice instructed her to compensate the PL K120 for the insults.

Mavuto: Persistent Trouble

Raising touchy questions about gender relations and sexuality, the complaints in these cases expose complicated issues concerning power, autonomy, and gender identity in postcolonial Zambia. Outside the areas of male control over women as wives or daughters, Zambian society offers little legitimation for single lifestyles but tends overwhelmingly to view unmarried adult women as loose, prostitutes, or bitches, as in the records of the Chelston local court. These cases also prompt questions, to which I return shortly, about the local court as a forum for untangling such matters, and about whether, and if so how, the court is able to effect changes in gender relations.

The two categories of cases described above touch on thorny problems in Zambia's strained economy. Specifically, these cases expose charged issues that arise over tensions both between male authority and female dependence in private households and between women in the wider social arena. As the *Zulu v. Mbewe, Banda v. Mutale*, and *Mushanga v. Phiri* cases demonstrate, men expect women to follow their instructions to provide unpaid domestic services: to cook, clean, and supply sex on demand. In turn, women expect men to "keep" them and their children, which, as I have noted earlier, means providing them with shelter, food, and clothes. Mrs. Zulu conveyed her husband's utter lack of concern when she explained his tardiness with household money by describing how he brought her "mealie meal in a newspaper" (i.e., in a scrap of paper rather than a standard bag) and "not buying her clothes."

Having sex and having children are central to men's identity as household heads and persons in control, as illustrated in both *Banda v. Mutale* and *Mushanga v. Phiri*. Women also need children to legitimate their part in the conjugal relationship, and women occasionally sue men for divorce because they do not allow them to seek "traditional" advice and remedies to facilitate conception. The ability to control their own sexuality is an important way for women to achieve their identity as responsible adults. Some of these women fear that childlessness might cause them to lose their spouses' attention and support and/or that their spouses would take second wives or girlfriends.

Husbands took men to court for committing adultery with their wives, but wives did not take husbands to court for committing adultery with other women. Himonga relates the incident of a wife who complained of her husband's affairs to an informal forum of elders, only to be told that she could not stop a man from going out with other women if he wanted to because that was "the nature of men"

(1985:204). In cases not included here, where husbands took wives to court for deserting the home, the language of accusation often turned such wives into "bitches." As noted earlier, customary law approves polygyny and society at large does not object to men's extramarital relations. But wives do—and vehemently so, as we have seen. It is not surprising, then, that charges that women brought to court due to marital problems, on claims of lack of support, such as the *Mwila v. Sinyinda* case, often had the figure of the other woman, or girlfriends, looming in the background. Suing husbands in such cases, women drew public attention to men's failure as household heads.

The insult and defamation cases illustrate vividly how suspicious women are of each other. The emphatic way they defined themselves as their husbands' wives through categorical statements about other women who moved about, moved with, or "bitched," displays their anxiety about their own status as married wives. The troubled voice of Mrs. Sitali in *Nfonse v. Sitali* speaks with an immediacy and directness when she tells "how it pains to hear that [one's] husband is moving with another woman."

If the conjugal relationship is so tense, why then do women such as those in the insult and defamation cases so passionately demonstrate their status as wives? Airing their anger in public over what appears to be petty interpersonal squabbles, such women express their concerns over the potential for sexual misconduct. At the heart of their disagreement are gender constructions, both female and male, that are heavily charged by notions of sexuality, and more narrowly so for women than for men. The amount of compensation that the defendants in some of these cases were asked to pay indicates that the charges indeed were considered to be very grave ones.

The issues at stake in insult and defamation cases, I suggest, are about personal identity—that is to say, what it means to be a woman and a man in conjugal relations, and about what sorts of persons women and men are supposed to be in the wider Zambian setting. The two, of course, are intertwined, and the cases I have discussed reveal striking insights into economic and social relations in urban Zambia that put strains both on friendship between wives and husbands and between neighbors. Thus, many of these cases have to do with publicly asserting that the plaintiff is someone's wife, in effect evoking sexuality as a key dimension of women's identity. For being married is a more respectful status for an adult woman in Zambia than being single. A single lifestyle easily translates into "bitching," as we saw in Mrs. Sitali's allegations against Ms. Nfonse. But beyond that, the sexual slurs with which they charge each other barely mask the insidious battle that men's unreliability and tight economic circumstances help to provoke between women.

No Dowry, No Custom

The judgments issued in local court are informed by notions of gender that define women and men as different persons vis-à-vis the law: men have authority and thus rights and claims, whereas women merely are dependent. This difference is well expressed in the words of Agnes Siame's eldest daughter. At age twenty-seven, when she had experienced too many troubles with her husband, she finally took him to court for divorce. "I hope they [the court] will grant me freedom," she said, "[but] I don't think I stand any chance because according to our Zambian law a woman should not say, I don't want marriage, but a man has got all the right to say I don't want my wife."[8]

In the court's application of customary law, marriage has been redefined from being a series of processes involving a variety of transfers of wealth (Richards 1940) into one event that hinges on whether or not bridewealth was paid, or as this court renders it, whether the parties were "married with dowry." Epstein made similar observations in the 1950s when he argued that "in insisting on bridewealth as a criterion of a valid marriage, the urban courts were following, as much as creating, Copperbelt practice" (1981:279). In divorce cases that Mtendere women brought to local court, judgments tended to favor husbands if they did not agree to divorce women they had married with dowry. Having paid dowry, "men own women," according to popular male sentiments (*Times of Zambia* 1992a, 1992b). But if men agree to divorce, and dowry has been transferred, the presiding justice in this and other local courts tends to obligate men to pay some support to women and their children (Himonga 1987:66). In the view of this local court, such women had been properly married, that is, with dowry. This contrasts to divorce cases in which the parties were not married with dowry. As the cases I have presented illustrate, the court considers such unions to be not marriages but "mere friendships." In spite of the length of some of these unions and the number of children born, the court views such wives as girlfriends. Save under exceptional circumstances, such as in the *Mwila v. Sinyinda* case, the female party receives nothing from the male upon dissolution of the union. And in cases of adultery, husbands receive compensation from men who have had intercourse with their wives only if they themselves were married with dowry.

Keller's research in the local court in Mazabuka, a provincial town in the Southern Province, in the mid-1970s offers striking parallels. Her specific concern was with "marriage by elopement," a nontraditional method for establishing a potential marital union that had become common in the Gwembe Valley since the 1950s and exceedingly frequent by the time of her research. She describes marriage by elopement as a Tonga way of marrying of which non-Tonga were generally contemptuous (1979:581). The local court practice in Mazabuka of awarding compensation to the father or guardian of an eloped woman was not carried out in the Chelston local court during the period of my research. But the practices of calling noncontractual unions "mere friendships" and describing the women as "girlfriends" in spite of the length of cohabitation were evident in both courts. In both instances, the women were assigned a status—girlfriend—that attracted little respect from others, given the thin line between girlfriends and prostitutes in the popular view. In turn, the ability of such women to fulfill themselves and gain respect from others as "properly married" wives was probably reduced.

In short, there are certain advantages for both women and men, though for different reasons, to being married properly. Perhaps women's knowledge that the court might judge in their favor and award compensation, provided they were properly married and the husband agreed to the divorce, was one reason why, when troubles (*mavuto*) with husbands became persistent, they decided to wash their dirty laundry in public and brought divorce cases to court much more frequently than men.

In Lusaka in general, judgments in favor of women are more likely to be issued in local courts than in informal family forums and in the superior courts (Himonga 1985:249, 286). In *Zulu v. Mbewe* we saw Mrs. Zulu suing her husband for divorce in the hope of getting maintenance even after her mother and church elders had accepted divorce. And perhaps the fact that divorce settlements in women's favor indeed are made encourages the many women who are not "properly married" to go to court, hoping to be granted support or maintenance.

The *Banda v. Mutale* case shows Mrs. Banda, who had been married for twelve years, without dowry, and had four children by her husband, demanding to "obtain property for the services [she had] rendered." Her claim to property was not approved, yet she kept the children. This case demonstrates Mrs. Banda's attempts both to define a conjugal relationship and to contest it.

But pressures on the job and housing markets make it increasingly difficult to be properly married, that is, to pay the dowry, in Lusaka's strained economy. In the *Mbewe v. Phiri* case Mrs. Mbewe's rural relatives would not allow her to join her husband, Mr. Phiri, in Lusaka until he had paid up in cattle. But Mr. Phiri had a hard time finding a job, and he lived in a one-room dwelling, so how could he at once accommodate his wife and four children and afford to buy four heads of cattle? A large number of cases of divorce, marital problems, chase away from home, and neglect involved women and men who had lived together and had children, who described themselves as married but in the view of the court were categorized as living "in friendship." Here, as in some other parts of southern Africa (Comaroff 1980), the gender politics of everyday life give rise to considerably more ambiguity than does the local court over the meaning of marriage.

The tensions that are inherent in women's and men's aspirations for proper marriage and individual autonomy are difficult to contain in Zambia's strained economy. I noted in an earlier chapter how women's own designs on life become increasingly evident as they grew older. As illustrated in Agnes Siame's eldest daughter's experience, one aspect of this design is gaining freedom from unsupportive or philandering husbands. The cases discussed here show that while the local court sought to uphold a notion of what proper marriages ought to be like, that is, with dowry, it was simultaneously revising it in women's favor along lines that are more congruent with economic needs. Upholding a reconstituted notion of custom, the local court also exercised some freedom in the way it adjudicated disputes that contemporary socioeconomic contingencies aggravate. Other local courts have been known to award judgment in the interest of equity rather than through static interpretations of custom (Colson 1980:366). In effect, the local court is an arena where changes may be expressed, negotiated, and at times, legitimated (Comaroff and Roberts 1977:122). This is so in divorce cases where estranged but "properly married" wives have no customary claim on support from husbands but often are granted such support by the court. While the overall emphasis in the court's decision is biased in favor of men, the evidence I have presented here indicates that this bias contains space for contests that may turn out to women's benefit.

Custom, Court, and Gender Politics

When Mtendere residents explained their own behavior and attitudes regarding marriage in the courtroom, concepts like kinship and descent lost some of their jural meanings. Responding to queries from the presiding justice, women and men from Mtendere talked about lack of support and loss of love in terms that have much more resonance with their experiences of hard economic times and troubles on the home front than with kinship rules and descent obligations. Their kin-inflected language drew its everyday meaning from ongoing social interaction, distinguishing between in-laws and one's own relatives and making available to women and men differently constituted resource networks.

The court's usage of kinship language includes fragments of rights and claims distinctions that are informed by reconstituted notions of "custom." The two most important notions in relationship to the cases described here are dowry and support, the application of neither of which in the court's adjudication was "traditional." As I have shown, *dowry* refers to a reconstructed marriage practice in which the transfer of bridewealth has been transformed from a process into an event. And *support* applies to divorce cases in which "properly married" men are charged with noncustomary obligations.

In sum, the court's administering of customary law is flexible. Its decisions concerning proper marriages—that is, with dowry—which tended to privilege men's rights over women's also encompassed judgments that in divorce cases benefited women. The local court is thus much more than merely an instrument for upholding the status quo. It is also a forum in which women and men are both contesting and redefining conjugal arrangements and where "properly married" women in their attempt to redraw restrictive gender lines are getting a small measure of court approval in divorce settlements. While social interactional practices still leave much to be desired from women's perspective, this legal flexibility opens up the opportunity for Zambians to further redefine gender relations in terms of rights and claims rather than in terms of male authority and female dependence. A case in point is the 1989 enactment of the Intestate Succession Act, which stipulates the rights of widows and children to specified parts of a deceased's estate, although property grabbing has not ceased entirely (Coldham 1989).[9] Perhaps local court practices and women's own contests inside and outside of court may also become instrumental in enacting reforms of Zambia's customary divorce laws so as to entitle women to compensation for long-rendered services.[10]

6

City Limits?

As the Zambian economy continued to deteriorate between the late 1980s and early 1990s, the private issues and public troubles that preoccupied Mtendere residents became increasingly divergent in gender and generational terms at the same time as inequality within the nation at large became more pronounced. While the desire for a better life has materialized for some of the long-term house-owning residents who remained in Mtendere, the emancipatory vision that most parents held for their children has in many cases not come true. The children who now are adults in the households I began studying in 1971 have been differently exposed to influences from our late-twentieth-century world, which is very unlike the one into which their parents grew into young adulthood. They take less pride in their parents' consolidation of home ownership in the township and are more painfully and impatiently aware of their inequitable global position as citizens of a developing country. Their frame of reference is not defined exclusively in Mtendere, limited by Lusaka, or confined to their country. Instead, it engages a broader world of possibilities into which only a few have been able to tap.

Political and economic developments in Zambia during the 1980s did not bring about economic recovery. The foreign trade deficit grew, the debt burden increased, and foreign exchange shortages constrained local production. The availability of basic services in towns declined, the infrastructure was not maintained, consumer goods were scarce and, when available, beyond the means of many township dwellers. Formal-sector employment declined from 23 percent to 9 percent of the total labor force between 1980 and 1991 (Economist Intelligence Unit 1992:18). These figures hide large gender and class discrepancies. A 1986 labor force survey showed 4 percent of all women and 25 percent of all men in formal-sector employment, two thirds of them in urban areas (Republic of Zambia 1991:27). And in 1990, the average formal-sector wage in real terms was only 40 percent of its 1983 level (Economist Intelligence Unit 1992:19). The human and social costs that this progressive decline helped to set into motion were becoming all too familiar in low-income townships like Mtendere: rising unemployment, illness because of poor health and inadequate nutrition, epidemics like cholera and AIDS, death, divorce, and premarital pregnancies that forced many parents to accommodate more than one generation in the home.

During my last two periods of field research in Mtendere, in 1988 and 1989, I extended my concern with long-term residents' social and cultural responses in the face of their country's economic decline, by focusing on their children. In effect, this shift brought about a convergence of my interests in household formation and dissolution, and I observed some of these developments come full circle during short visits in 1992 and 1993. In this chapter, I examine the practices that members of my sample households organized around both of these processes, as the parents I began interviewing in 1971 approached the end of their household development cycle and their children reached marriageable age. I begin by describing the different decisions of senior female and male householders regarding retirement to the countryside. Then I discuss the diverging generational experiences and interests that postcolonial economic developments have provoked between Mtendere parents and their children. As I explain next, the younger generation's disenchantment with the suspension of economic progress speaks to deeply felt tensions between local issues and global influences. These tensions in turn are informing the construction of notions of what being Zambian means today as well as the creation of what I referred to in chapter 4 as thoroughly Zambian rituals, among others. This disenchantment also, as I point out at the chapter's end, produced discord between township residents and the local party organization, the people and the state, which were instrumental in the eventual dismantling of the UNIP government in 1991.

These processes further substantiate what I have argued throughout this study, namely that Mtendere was never a self-contained community. Thus this chapter describes ongoing changes in the township, demonstrating how the activities in which residents were involved not only brought them into more complex contact with the world outside but also filtered the experiences of their local world.

Return Migration?

Between the mid-1980s and 1990 the Zambian government and its party UNIP attempted to solve some of the country's economic problems, especially formal-sector unemployment and the rapid decline in urban real income, through the creation of agricultural resettlement programs directed toward youth and the unemployed. When long-term residents of Mtendere considered exhortations by representatives of their one-party state to "go back to the land" they shook their heads—not with disbelief, for they had heard this before, but with disenchantment. While back-to-the-land campaigns took place during the colonial period and calls to return to the countryside to feed the nation were made on and off in public policy speeches over the more than twenty-year period during which I have been an observer of urban life in Zambia, the volume and frequency of such efforts increased after the mid-1980s, when government revenues from mining exports had been low for many years.

From 1975 to 1981, Mtendere parents saw daughters and sons called up in a compulsory national service program in rural camps in order to acquire agricultural skills. The project was eventually discontinued, yet similar ideas were resuscitated in slightly altered forms as rural reconstruction centers during the mid-1980s and as rural resettlement centers for unemployed youth who were to be made into good farmers in the late 1980s. Some of these reconstruction centers, such as Kambilombilo on the copperbelt, lacked most of the basics: land had not been surveyed; shelter had not been constructed; few tools were available; there was no transportation; and the water and food situation was completely inadequate (International Labour Organisation 1986:99–111). No wonder that many youth deserted, returning to the hard but much more challenging work of getting by in Lusaka in exchange for rural loafing at the resettlement center at Kanakantampa, for example, not far from the capital.[1]

Good farming in Zambia in the 1980s meant cash cropping, especially of hybrid maize (Sano 1990; Wood 1990). And many urban residents, including people in Mtendere, were well aware of the almost
unbelievable chaos in their country's maize marketing system, created by deteriorating roads, lack of vehicles, and shortages of grain
bags, as well as low producer prices. They knew that an agricultural
policy that emphasized export crops and commercial farming had
brought little prosperity to the majority of Zambia's rural producers,
most of whose standards of living had steadily declined between the
mid-1970s and late 1980s, in terms of such indicators as income from
cash crops, food self-sufficiency, nutritional status, and child mortal-
ity (Colson and Scudder 1988; Freund 1986; Geisler 1992; Moore and
Vaughan 1987; Stromgaard 1985).

From the perspective of longtime residents in Mtendere, the decision to move to the countryside was a difficult one. Their unease differed in gender and generational terms. The cultural idioms in which
they expressed their anxieties were glosses for their economic concerns, which they readily identified: "There is nothing there." Aside
from the fact that several of these Mtendere residents had grown up
in the city, that few had maintained access to land and even fewer had
participated in agricultural production in any regular way, their
explanation captures the lack of consumer goods and basic services
that made rural living conditions in many parts of the country worse
in the 1980s than in the first decade after independence.

Much has been written in colonial urban scholarship, especially
on the mining towns, about the attachments of urban-located
Africans to their rural areas of origin (Mitchell 1959, 1987; Powdermaker 1962; Wilson 1941 and 1942). Some postcolonial scholarship
has pursued this issue, asking: "Do you intend to return to the rural
area?" (Bates 1976:182–87). I also asked this question during my
first period of research in Mtendere. But when I returned, I noticed
that people's actions did not always reflect the intentions they had
suggested previously. This observation made me reshape my
approach to ask questions about whether Mtendere residents held,
or had rights to, land and/or cattle in rural areas; how often they
went there; what their relationship was to local residents; why they
went there; how long their visit was; who, if anyone, accompanied
them; and when they last were there. Their answers to such questions informed me directly about the nature of relationships

between town and country rather than conjecturally about their intentions to return.

Because I kept returning to these households, I am able to flesh out the question about the move to the countryside in more concrete terms. The gender frictions that shaped decisions of whether or not to leave the city were interwoven with the different reactions of Mtendere women and men to the prospects of moving to the countryside. Consider the Phiri household, who moved back to the village in the Eastern Province after my first study in 1971 but then returned to Mtendere. In 1975 Mr. Phiri, a plumber, sold his house and moved his household to the rural area. By 1981 they were back in Lusaka and have remained in Mtendere since then, living in rented housing. In the village, Mrs. Phiri told me, her husband "lost all his money on beer." Her explanation was a gloss for the claims that rural relatives placed on the former townsman's resources. A stingy returnee is an easy target for witchcraft accusations, and in the view of many townspeople, rural life holds few attractions.

This view was shared but expressed differently by some of the female heads among my sample households. Among them were two women who had become female heads of households between the time of my 1984 and 1985 studies. They were not divorcées or widows but had refused to accompany their husbands into rural retirement. To explain this, they referred to the customary expectation that on his return to the village a man will be encouraged by local elders to take a second wife. These women, who had spent most of their adult years in town, claimed to know nothing about rural farmwork. Rural life is hard, they said, not being keen on the drudgery of collecting firewood and water and stamping grain. Last, but certainly not least, they wanted no part in a plural marriage. Instead, they chose to remain in town, supporting themselves from small-scale trade and incidental contributions from adult children.

Some of the women in my sample households who became widows were also unwilling to move to the country. Not wanting to be inherited by a relative of the deceased husband, they chose to remain in town as single heads of households. Among them were the successful beer brewers and *kachasu* distillers in my sample, who largely through their own work efforts had managed to send children to school and at times on to further education. Fearing that a move to the village might strip away the degree of urban autonomy they had laboriously carved out for themselves in the economic sphere and in relationship to men, these and many other women clearly preferred town over country. Finally, single heads of households with few resources, such as never-married women, often lacked the means to leave the city.

To leave or not to leave Lusaka remains a vexing question that continues to preoccupy Mtendere residents who are approaching the end of their household development cycle. In 1988, Mrs. Sakala informed me that her husband, who had retired from his job as a waiter a few years earlier, recently had gone to the rural area to prepare for their return. In her words, "preparing" meant securing use rights to land, and this he had managed because a relative had passed away. They could not afford to live in town, she said. Of their eight children, four lived at home, two still attending school and two unmarried sons working, one as a clerk and the other as a painter. She complained of her sons' lack of assistance. "They are wasting their money," she said, "playing around." She herself did not particularly want to move to the village, but since her husband did, she would follow him. But if he passed away, she argued, she certainly would return to town. Mr. Sakala's preparations did not have immediate results, for in 1989 I found them still in Mtendere. They had been troubled in many ways. Mr. Sakala had been ill with a stomach disease, a married daughter and her baby had died from AIDS, and a son who had helped to support the household had lost his job. Mrs. Sakala had "no idea" of when, or if, the move might take place. They remained in Mtendere as of 1992.

Uncertainties affected the Lungu household in another way. Mr. Lungu told me in 1988 that he was preparing for a move to his home village with his two wives. He had retired from his job as a porter at the airport the previous year. Except for the youngest son, still unmarried, who had taken over his father's job at the airport, the Lungus' six adult children lived and worked elsewhere in Lusaka. Over the years, Mr. Lungu had purchased twelve head of cattle in the rural area. During the course of my research in Mtendere, he had extended the house with a wing of rental rooms. One wife worked a stall in the market, while the other took charge of things at home. At some point in his life, he had acquired sewing skills and bought a sewing machine, and he made some money on the side by sewing clothes for sale. In 1985 he constructed a brick oven in the yard, in which one of the wives baked buns for sale. The oven had fallen into disuse by 1988, when flour had become chronically scarce. By then, the junior wife had taken up tailoring.

The rural return that Mr. Lungu envisioned was not a life of farming. A married daughter who made good money from her small tailoring shop had bought him a welding machine. He spoke of hiring someone to work the welding machine, and the sewing machine, in the market of Chipata, a small provincial town near his village. He did not intend to sell the house in Mtendere or to pass it on to the children but to use it for rent and as a place of security in case village life did not work out. In fact, he planned to lease the house to the airline and have the rent paid directly into his bank account. Mr. Lungu also spoke of taking some grandchildren along in order to help their parents reduce the cost of maintaining them in Lusaka. On my return to Mtendere in 1989, Mr. Lungu and his two wives were still there. He was hedging and uneasy about the return and altogether less confident about his plans to retire to the village than he had been the previous year. Yet by 1992 he and his two wives had indeed left Mtendere.

Diverging Generational Interests

Of Zambia's total population of 7.8 million in 1990, 49 percent were children under the age of fifteen years (Republic of Zambia 1990). These are the children who grew up after the end of the economic growth period that followed independence. Their experiences are likely to diverge considerably from not only those of their parents but also those of their older siblings. Mtendere parents' hopes for a better future for their children have in many cases not materialized. But a blanket generalization describing the opportunities of the second generation as worse than those of their parents' generation would mask the complexity of the situation. For the generation of most of these parents, who grew up during the colonial period, education was a privilege, and more so for girls than for boys because the establishment of schools for girls lagged far behind that of boys. Schooling during the colonial period served as an important channel for socioeconomic advancement. The newly independent government placed a strong emphasis on extending educational facilities, and immediately after independence great strides were made in providing health services, urban infrastructure, and transportation. Educational and health services were free, and mealie meal was subsidized. To be sure, many low-income urban households in townships like Mtendere enjoyed better living standards than urban households during the colonial period.

Anticipating that education might help their children progress, Mtendere parents, especially mothers, went to great lengths to ensure that children went to school, girls and boys equally, at least at the primary levels (Serpell 1993). But in the mid-1970s, the expansion came to a halt, and the economy has never fully recovered. This shift has produced a marked difference in the opportunity structure that the children of the Mtendere parents in my sample have been able to enter. Through the early 1970s, young people who completed secondary school were almost certain to obtain jobs because of the Zambianization of both the public and the private sectors. Some went on to university, some traveled abroad on training programs, and some achieved positions of prominence. Among the daughters, some might be characterized in fairly similar terms as the "new women of Lusaka" so intimately portrayed in Schuster's study of the women who began erasing the colonial period's predominance of men in white-collar jobs and contributing to an increase in the number of women employed in the professions as they moved into junior positions in administrative offices (1979). The force of Schuster's colorful description of these women's fast lifestyle, revolving around sex, drink, money, clothes, and status, hinges on presenting them as a transitional generation, caught, as it were, between tradition and modernity and satisfied with neither.

But if the first postindependence cohort of young women who had benefited from improved access to education and employment was transitional, the young people who came after them are even more so. Their transitionality is not so much a product of tensions between tradition and modernity as it is a result of a rapidly deteriorating economy in which job prospects have declined dramatically. Today's young adult women share few of the economic opportunities that their older sisters had access to. If the younger siblings reached secondary school at all, they were taught in poorly equipped classrooms by teachers who sometimes added to their meager wages by holding private classes or doing additional jobs on the side. Teachers' dedication and morale had declined as a result of deteriorating educational facilities, insufficient housing, and shrinking wages, and there were frequent strikes.

Children hawking vegetables in the street

Older sister watching younger siblings

Students who did complete secondary school during the 1980s encountered a contracted formal-sector job market and found their school-leaving certificates of limited value. Not only did those years see an overall decline in educational spending, but in an effort to improve its fiscal operation, in the late 1980s the government introduced school fees and examination charges. Meanwhile, the educational system declined so badly that parents who had the means to do so made their children repeat classes and retake final examinations to improve their grades. Many students with poorer parents dropped out of school before finishing. "Private schools" run by persons with entrepreneurial skills arose to cater to the still widespread belief in education as an avenue for advancement. In the late 1980s, about 150,000 young adults were leaving the school system each year, placing enormous pressure on the formal sector, which employed only 359,620 persons in 1989 (Banda 1990:18). Yet, as parents knew only too well from their own experiences, real wages had eroded so much that being employed was no guarantee of earning a living wage.

Because the children born to Mtendere householders spanned a range of years, many parents had at least one young adult who had benefited from the immediate postindependence boom in education and held a formal job in a field like nursing, teaching, accounting, or white-collar work in general. In effect, these households had become very heterogeneous in socioeconomic terms. Aside from accommodating a shifting retinue of dependent relatives and young children still attending school, members of such households included a wife who more frequently than not conducted informal-sector work; a husband in poorly paid wage employment or, if unemployed, in informal-sector work, or both; an adult son or daughter in wage work; and teenagers "just sitting," which in local parlance means having completed, or dropped out of, school and not earning money. Last but not least, when adult children who were working no longer lived at home, they often remained part of the household's resource base, providing intermittent support, as I noted in the case of widows who chose to remain in town and in Mr. Lungu's retirement story.

Young persons "sitting" at home might do odd jobs, for example, assisting mothers in their businesses or helping out around the house; some young men were trading on their own intermittently, for example selling *michanga* (cigarettes by the stick) or doing piece-work. But according to many mothers, they mostly were wandering around, up to nothing but mischief. Young adults of both sexes discussed among themselves and with their parents the "use" of attending skills-training programs set up by the district council and NGOs, particularly carpentry for young men, and homecraft/dressmaking for young women (Hoppers 1985). Young people with more advanced skills also entertained hopes of attending "private courses" in secretarial training, business-related subjects, and, more recently, computer programming. Above all, they spoke about the need for sponsorship of such training. In short, both basic skills training and skills upgrading required financial inputs that placed heavy burdens on already strained household resources.

Young boys and girls who "sit" at home did not face the same situations when they left school. Depending on their economic means, parents readily encouraged such young boys to continue schooling or supported their entry into training programs, trying to edge them closer to potentially better-paying or more secure formal-sector jobs. But whether young girls continued depended on a host of other factors: attitudes of parents, elder brothers, or uncles, and the needs of other children. Not all parents, especially fathers, were keen on daughters' working away from home or outside Mtendere. Older girls, according to another township study, "are considered both safe and more useful within households, where they can look after younger siblings and/or do the housework for a working mother, sister, or for that matter, their own family. At the same time, not being fully exposed to the harsh realities of the outside world . . . single girls gain more attraction as marriage partners for higher-income workers" (Hoppers 1985:195).

Generationally extended households encounter many tensions because of the different expectations that women and men, the young and the old, have about appropriate behavior. Crowded living conditions easily affront deeply held notions about propriety between the sexes and the generations, for example forcing a man to sleep in the same room as his wife and children and causing embarrassment about where to bathe and dress. And crowded living conditions prompted many young people to seek leisure and pleasure away from home, thus giving rise to parents' complaints over the difficulty of controlling them.

As if such domestic friction were not enough, many parents painfully realized that the young people who "sat" at home were much less likely than they themselves had been to become members of households in their own right and to own houses that might help establish their socioeconomic foothold in the city. If young men today are wage employed at all, they are unlikely to earn enough to establish and support households of their own. Their relatives may not have sufficient means to provide the amount of cash required for contracting a proper marriage, that is, to pay what the local court termed "dowry," namely the transfer of bridewealth that legitimates a marriage. In short, these young men are caught in a bind. So are young women. Because of the depressed economy and a gender ideology that encourages male initiative and female dependency, today's young women and their children may be less likely than their mothers to become part of conjugal units in their own right.

All the households in my sample that remained in Mtendere over the years contained young women who had children without being married. Such young women and the children remained members of their mother's household when their young fathers, unlike Katherine's husband, did not accept responsibility, refusing to pay "damages." Although pregnancies occur across all socioeconomic strata, their incidence among girls of poorer background is greater according to one observer, "because such girls often deliberately seek a boy-friend whose main function is to augment the poor provisions from home" (Hoppers 1985:194). As we saw in the discussion of the local court's renditions, both parties typically argued that they were "just playing." But pregnancy had serious consequences for girls, for it resulted in expulsion from school. The previous discussion also demonstrated that when such young women eloped and no "dowry" was transferred, they had no claims whatsoever to support from their partner. And so they began looking for another man from whom to get support. Such an outcome readily supported assumptions about young women's irresponsibility and sexual looseness.

Some of the young mothers I interviewed in Mtendere in 1989 who lived with their parents chose not to marry their children's young fathers, who had neither jobs nor resources. Instead they waited for "Mr. Right," who might "keep them nicely." Being kept nicely, we recall, meant receiving food, shelter, and clothing. Their wait might be long, for Zambian women, regardless of class and age, know not to expect much from men. Thus young women and young men are both in a bind, on account of their conflicting expectations about each other.

Young men doing radio repair

Young man doing piecework in garden on the outskirts of Mtendere

The tensions in the relations between the sexes and generations identified in 1950s urban scholarship are all too evident, if not more pronounced, in the reactions of young women and men (Epstein 1981; Hansen 1991; Powdermaker 1962). It is no wonder that some senior residents in Mtendere claim that young people are irresponsible. Young women in urban settings like Lusaka today enjoy considerably more freedom and mobility than their mothers did in their youth. Adolescents of both sexes meet away from home and in coeducational government schools; some went to national service camps together. They travel by public transportation across town and interact with persons from many different walks of life and backgrounds. It is in this light that one must view the concern of some mothers that their young daughters ought to undergo initiation. Troubled by their daughters' defiance of conventional norms, some senior women claim that young women readily become loose and sexually promiscuous because they have not been initiated and taught how to behave properly; thus they do not show respect for their seniors, do not work for the sake of their husbands, and do not know how to keep their husbands faithful by enhancing their own sexuality.[2]

Such mothers' wishes do not always come true. In 1988 Esther, whose coming-out ceremony I attended in 1984, "sat" at home, unmarried, with a two-year-old child and expecting another. She first became pregnant before finishing school, by a young man who reneged on his promise to marry her. The damages he was charged had not been paid entirely before Esther became pregnant again, this time by another man. He had agreed to marry her, and Esther was to join him after the birth of the baby. Like many other young women, Esther wanted to get married because of the respectability that marriage confers on childbearing and motherhood and because, like most young women, she hoped that a husband would support her and her children.

Most of the nine young women between the ages of fourteen and twenty-one with whom I had an informal group discussion in 1989 doubted the importance of initiation ceremonies, although only three of them had undergone one. "What is the use?" one of them argued "So many girls get damaged anyway." They all knew that men cannot always be relied upon. One young woman who was still attending school suggested that girls should "finish school first, take a course, work a bit, and then get married so as to be able to support themselves." Yet the rest argued that it is important first to marry—

"if you can get a husband"—after that came trade, and then perhaps a course. They all wanted real marriages—that is, with bridewealth—and not informal relationships, which may mean, as one of them said, "marriage for a day only," alluding to the insecurity of nonformalized marriages.

Adults who argued in favor of initiation were well aware that both women and men have sexual desires but that society blames women for provoking sexual promiscuity and, since the mid-1980s, for transmitting AIDS. Yet when mothers hold young women responsible for bringing such problems on themselves, they also express their own helplessness in the face of the social and economic forces that distract their attention from their responsibilities as mothers. Mothers who argue that initiation rites will turn young adult women into "good girls" hope that their daughters will marry properly and assume conventional roles as wives and mothers in the kind of cooperative conjugal relationships that their own need to assume larger burdens of income-generating responsibilities in many cases turned into an unattainable ideal. Almost inevitably, some mothers come to seem conservative, holding sex and motherhood as key to the construction of womanhood.

Perhaps because of disappointment on account of their own daughters' experiences of having children without being married, some Mtendere women were particularly keen to stage kitchen parties for daughters who reached the point of marriage without having had children. Except for the youngest, all of Agnes Siame's five daughters gave birth before marriage. And her son had to pay damages for making a schoolgirl pregnant. After some years of sexual bravado, he settled down with another woman, with whom he has had several children. Two of Agnes's daughters later married their children's fathers after the settlement of damages, and the oldest eventually married another man, whom she subsequently divorced; she has since lived for several years with another partner. They have all, at various times, descended on Agnes and Kapansa's home in Mtendere when they had problems on their own home fronts. In the late 1970s, the third-born child, a daughter, was made pregnant by a man more than fifteen years her senior when she was just fifteen years old and had not finished school. He paid damages and she went to live with him outside Lusaka. In 1984 I found her and her three children at her parents' home in Mtendere, where she had sought shelter because the hus-

band beat her too often. She did join him again, but subsequent years
saw her return to Mtendere several times for the same reason.

When in 1988 her youngest daughter was to marry a self-
employed man from another Lusaka township, Agnes organized a
kitchen party at a friend's home in the yards. This daughter had
dropped out of school and was always difficult for her mother to control, "moving about" with boys. Agnes was relieved to see her married and she told me proudly of the kitchen party, describing the foods
and drinks, the presents—"so many they only needed to buy cutlery," and the cost of the event, which her two oldest children (who
held white-collar jobs) had helped to pay. Yet her pride in being a
"good mother" was soon tinged with despair. The marriage did not
last long, and the young daughter took up with other men. This
mother's pride in her own accomplishments turned into lament on
account of the troubles her daughters' difficult lives caused her. "How
am I supposed to support all these children?" she asked, referring to
the frequent extension of the household. "What can I do?" she said.
"I have tried my best to educate my children. But the young ones
today have no respect for all the work you have done for them."

Disenchantment and Difference

My concern with the effects of Zambia's ongoing political and economic problems on township residents must not take precedence over
a consideration of the meanings of these processes to those who have
lived through them. Like many other settlements, Mtendere was a
special place to the senior generation who had participated in its establishment, yet at the same time it was enmeshed with the high-income
townships and the wider city in multiple networks of difference.
Residents of townships like Mtendere interact with fellow Zambians
of many different regional backgrounds from directors of firms to
managers of offices to mid- to upper-level employees in government
offices. Such Zambians make up the single largest segment of today's
employers of domestic servants, for whom a considerable number of
Mtendere men and a growing number of women are working, as they
also are working for a declining population of expatriates. Most township residents have at one time or another some contact with expatriates of many different nationalities, from Canada to Japan, who are
replacing the colonial white population of largely British and South

African background and who today staff the upper ranks in the offices of international development agencies and NGOs. And because of political and economic upheaval within the larger southern African region, refugees have come and gone. Mtendere hosted a noticeable population of Africans from Southern Rhodesia in the 1970s and South Africa during the 1970s and 1980s. While many of them have now returned to their countries of origin, Zaireans who are leaving their strife-ridden country have begun to take residence in townships like Mtendere. Although the scope of exposure is much wider in the capital, most rural areas except those that are very remote in terms of road access and transportation have for a long time experienced extensive exchanges of people, goods, and ideas (Colson and Scudder 1975:208).

Over the years, the developments in Zambia's political economy have made a township like Mtendere less and less able to contain within itself the peace that its name connotes. The senior generation's pride in living in the "nicest of Lusaka's compounds" is being undermined by contradictions in society at large. The township today is more occupationally diverse than it was when its earliest residents went to live there. In large part this can be attributed to the general housing shortage in Lusaka, which has prompted more white-collar workers like teachers, nurses, and bank clerks to seek accommodation in townships like Mtendere. The proportion of residents who now are tenants has increased in response to declining real income and rapid inflation of food and rental costs (Weinberger 1992:6).[3]

The overall insecurity of living fueled by these processes is manifesting itself in Mtendere, as it is in the rest of Lusaka, in the form of burglaries, theft, and even armed robberies.[4] Until recently, the township had no police, and some residents feared walking its unlit streets at night. Like their more privileged neighbors in the yards, Mtendere residents who can afford to build them now live behind perimeter walls, and everyone is concerned about the security of household objects in houses left unattended. Meanwhile, in nearby Kabulonga, the yard through which buses to Mtendere pass on their way to and from town, more women married to midlevel Zambian men have begun to conduct informal-sector work from home, for example as beauticians, hairdressers, fashion designers, or bakers (Hansen 1989a:226). In the mid-1980s, residents from both compounds and yards shopped in the same supermarkets and state shops in their search for the basic consumption goods that are used in most homes regardless of socioeconomic background, such as mealie meal, cooking oil, salt, sugar, soap, and detergent. In effect, socioeconomic differentiation within Mtendere is increasing at the same time as formerly distinct lifestyles between compounds and yards appear to be leveling out to some degree. Yet these processes are not affecting all residents in the same manner nor with the same consequences. In fact, the blurring of distinctions is most clearly evident in women's informal-sector activities and in the educational outlook for children.

Ideas of progress and of living better lives arise in interactions with persons from many different backgrounds, with whom Zambians have long been accustomed to living and mixing. Each generation has reached out differently, hemmed in by its own material and social circumstances and by the cultural politics of its time. The parents of today's young adults were keen to furnish their township homes and acquire smart clothing or at least "a Sunday best," to the extent to which men's wages and women's informal-sector earnings allowed them to pursue such ambitions.

Mtendere residents take enormous pride in household acquisitions, as I noticed in battles in the local court over objects like cupboards, beds, mattresses, bedsheets, and items of clothing. When after repeated trouble with her first husband Agnes Siame's oldest daughter moved into her parents' house in Mtendere in 1984, she brought along her furniture, television set, and pots and pans. Residents take much pride in and pay attention to the interiors of their dwellings, which are usually decorated, though not at the same expense. Mr. Lungu's living room displayed carved and painted curios, a framed award honoring his longtime service as an airport porter, and family photographs, including snapshots from his visit to London in 1985, compliments of the airline. Many homes had religious pictures on the walls. Although walls might never have been painted in some of the poorer homes, they almost all featured calendars, and many displayed cut-out photographs from magazines and decorations made out of recycled materials, for example metal wire, bottle caps, mealie meal sacks, and plastic shopping bags. Most living rooms that contained upholstered furniture, no matter the degree of wear, had antimacassars on couches and chairs and doilies and/or tablecloths on tables and cupboards. Many women do exquisite embroidery, and some made money from producing these pieces of handicrafts that create an identifiable style of township interior decoration.

Some households in Mtendere now have electricity, and television sets, together with the ubiquitous battery-operated radios, transmit information about events and ideas from the worlds beyond the capital and the nation into township living rooms. Although television sets are not widespread in Mtendere, they reach an audience much larger than a household's own members. Viewing practices are blurring long-held distinctions about gender, age, and space. What is more, electrical

Mrs. Lungu Jr. in the living room

lighting potentially changes the way and timing in which domestic space is used. And electric stoves and refrigerators might alter food preparation practices and eating habits. While these items were not widespread and had not been in use at the end of the 1980s for long enough for me to ascertain their effects, it was quite evident that such commodities are cultural objects that play important roles in the structuring and perhaps changing of women's and men's experiences of everyday life. To be sure, modern kitchen and household technology interacts with lifestyle ideas conveyed by television, magazines, books, and popular music to expand the horizon of today's young adults in places like Mtendere. Taken together, such objects and media are implicated in complex ways in constructing what it means to be a young Zambian in our late-twentieth-century world.

How do young residents of Mtendere perceive themselves in their encounters with so many others? How do they view living at the margins of a complex world that is interpenetrated by global commodity chains and rapid circulation of ideas? To be sure, the meanings that young people construct in their encounters with others and the

Mrs. Mumba doing wool embroidery of her own design on
mealie meal plastic sacking

world "outside" help to account for their lack of patience with their parents' pride in Mtendere as "the nicest of Lusaka's compounds." Young people know that there are alternatives to the world that they think their parents have taken for granted. They want in, they want access, and they reach out as best they can, given the material and social circumstances that circumscribe their lives and the gender conventions that are part of their socialization.

The meanings that young people in Mtendere construe about alternative lives arise in their encounters with difference at many overlapping levels of interaction: between parents and children, older and younger siblings, school dropouts and university graduates, residents of compounds and yards, villages and towns, nationals and expatriates, and local and "outside." But above all, gender is central to this entire series of distinctions, and it gives rise to marked differences in how late-twentieth-century life is experienced in a city like Lusaka. At issue are deep-seated normative cultural notions about women and men that keep engaging ideas from "outside" about freedom and access and in the process give them their Zambian gloss. Thoroughly Zambian manifestations of this uneasy dialogue, such as initiation rites and kitchen parties, as well as persistent troubles over premarital pregnancies and the difficulties of setting up independent households speak clearly about the accommodation, defiance, and despair that are among the compromises that as yet have prevented such gendered meanings from being pulled apart by their own contradictions. The result is a battle on the home front in which parents' despair on account of their misbehaving children is a dialogue about both custom and the economy.

Political Discord

Throughout the 1980s, the efforts of Mtendere residents at making a living and ensuring the future welfare of their children were thwarted in many ways. They were not alone in this experience; it was shared across rural and urban settings, reducing rural-urban income disparities and blurring previous life-style distinctions, while accentuating inequality in general. The economic crisis was the result not only of adverse world market trends that brought the country declining revenues from mineral exports but also of the politics of the government and its single party, UNIP.

cities and townships like Mtendere the ramifications of the gov-
‗‗‗lent's problems were experienced most directly in the accelera-
tion of consumer prices, especially of mealie meal, the urban staple
food. Subsidized meal prices became a contentious issue in the government's dealings with the IMF/World Bank, and between the government and the people, especially in towns where UNIP drew most of
its constituency. While Zambia's on-and-off-again relationship with
the IMF is a subject of inquiry in its own right, a few observations are
in order here (Bates and Collier 1993; Geisler and Hansen 1994).
Briefly, food riots prompted by the withdrawal of mealie meal subsidies took place on the copperbelt in December 1986. The subsidies
were reinstated but subsequently phased out in the late 1980s by
means of a coupon system intended to protect poor urban residents
against the introduction of economic prices for mealie meal. But on
June 25, 1990, riots over the high cost of living, especially food, began
in Lusaka and spread to the rest of the country.

Youth played a special role in the mealie meal riots that dramatized
the dilemma of their situation—the disjuncture between their need to
work and the availability of wage-labor jobs in an economy characterized by widespread formal unemployment and growing poverty.
Street vendors, mainly out-of-school youth, were the major force
behind the looting of state-owned stores in the copperbelt towns and
Lusaka. With tight household budgets and crowded housing, their
parents had difficulty "keeping" them, i.e., providing them with shelter, food, and clothing. But formal jobs were few and far between for
everyone, especially young school dropouts and school leavers with
secondary school certificates. Resorting to street selling as a way of
earning income, young vendors were subjected to government harassment. When they looted the state-owned stores, the street vendors
pointed at government as the source of their limited opportunities.

As these events demonstrate, the 1990 rioters were attacking the
government and the single-party system. In past years, Zambians had
been conditioned to attribute their problems to the former colonial
government, white South Africa and Rhodesia, and the world economy. Depending on the issue at hand, they also blamed "subversive"
foreigners, "Indian" businessmen, and women marketeers. But in
1990 they pointed to the political system as the source of their economic woes. They had been patient long enough and had grown
increasingly weary of the president's exhortations to continue tight-

ening their belts. In the graphic cynicism at which so many Zambians excel, they identified many of the problems. The international jet-setters spoke of "one Zambia, one airplane," referring to the few and irregular flights of the national carrier. Transportation became a major problem, especially between rural and urban areas. The deterioration of the national bus company had become so extensive in the late 1980s that IFA trucks, imported from East Germany, had become major passenger haulers. So many accidents occurred on these trucks that people in need of public transportation spoke of IFA as an "international funeral association." When, in one of the frequent police sweeps, marketeers were relocated from streets and public places to the bare ground outside of Lusaka's Soweto market in the late 1980s, they named the place Kambilombilo, drawing an obvious parallel to the resettlement center on the copperbelt where youth had been dumped without the provision of services. And they pinpointed widespread corruption in government when interpreting the acronym of BMW cars as "buy mandrax from Wina," a well-known politician, allegedly involved in drug smuggling between India and South Africa. Clearly, even cynicism was wearing thin. On the morning of June 3, 1990, a one-man coup was attempted, but it was curtailed within a few hours.

Mtendere township had originally been consolidated through planned, organized squatting by a group of UNIP people who in the late 1960s were able to benefit from tensions between ANC and UNIP in the years before the declaration of the one-party government at the end of 1972. Mtendere initially offered its UNIP-supporting settlers a space for peaceful party-line association while they went on arranging their urban livelihoods. But, as in many other urban and rural settings, over the years the postcolonial state and its local-level representation left a political void in Mtendere (Crehan and von Oppen 1988; Pottier 1988:96–110). The township party organization and its activities did not improve urban living arrangements. Overall, residents had to be cajoled into attending party functions. They were forced to pay party membership dues if they were to operate in township markets. And yet women's time was diverted from their trade when they had to line city streets and appear at the airport to greet visiting dignitaries.

The contradictions in the government's response were becoming all too evident in the face of growing economic pressures to make a

living. The government frequently scapegoated women street vendors who were selling daily provisions as the cause of Zambia's economic ills, and it identified secondhand clothing traders as a health
hazard in cholera cases. Traders interpreted such campaigns for what
they were, namely, efforts to distract their attention from the inade-
quacies of government-provided services. Yet how, residents asked,
could UNIP leaders talk about improving the welfare of "the common
man" and yet prevent women marketeers from earning a living?
There was growing resentment about the high-handed manner in
which the township's UNIP organization and its representatives had
behaved in the past, forcing people to attend public functions and clos-
ing the market for meetings.[5]

In response to public pressure, events in the wake of the 1990 coup
attempt led to a change in the constitution to allow other political parties to function. The old-guard UNIP supporters in Mtendere trod
carefully then, not pestering residents. Residents' appraisal of UNIP's
economic failures had clear political ramifications. The elections that
took place in October 1991 placed Mtendere in the hands of the win-
ning party, the Movement for Multi-Party Democracy (MMD) and
replaced the one-party regime with a multiparty government whose
MMD leadership is bent on replacing the country's centralized economy with a market-oriented one. Politics and economics interacted
closely in the move away from UNIP, as they continue to do in the residents' ongoing assessment of their new government. If the notion of
the market on which new government policies are being built favors
persons with capital and resources, the opportunity structure will
remain significantly biased against women. In this process, struggles
over access to housing and jobs by gender and generation will no
doubt remain contentious urban issues. As in the past, tensions over
these issues will likely make the home front an important site on
which women and men, the young and the old, continue to negotiate
their private troubles and public issues.

7 | The Makings of a Research Project

I like cities. Their diverse populations, institutions, and events encapsulate activities that spill into the wider society, bringing about active interchanges of people, things, and ideas. What attracted me to urban research was that such visual and spatial dynamics called into question the bounded notions of culture so characteristic of a previous era's anthropology. In fact, as an anthropology student in Denmark, I chose to study urban life in Africa in preference to village interaction after conducting undergraduate field research on social organization in rural southwestern Kenya in 1969. As an out-and-out urbanite, I realized from this brief rural research venture that the village did not engage me actively enough. This recognition drew my attention to the remarkable body of urban ethnography on late colonial Zambia, which considered the very flexibility and variability of urban social organization as a key to understanding the evolving nature of African urbanism.

Even though many consider Lusaka but a poor cousin compared to Harare in neighboring Zimbabwe or to Nairobi in Kenya, which is the tourist capital of Africa, Lusaka is one of my favorite cities. The downtown, where tall office buildings are replacing the remaining visible edifices from the colonial period, is but a small part of a built environment increasingly dominated by the rapid expansion of low-income settlements. Greenery and tropical flowers, perimeter walls and gates, dust, noise, crowds, and people on the move everywhere contribute to the excitement but also to the challenge of conducting

166

Chapter 7Chapter 7

urban research: how to account for local-level observations in a township like Mtendere when so many of its residents' activities spill out of the township and in turn are affected by that outside world. In this chapter I hope to share with my readers some of my enthusiasm about urban research. Specifically, I discuss how my comings and goings in Mtendere opened up Lusaka to me, creating an intellectual engagement in the flow of life. Alerting readers to what exists outside the immediate range of observations that have been highlighted so far, I turn now to the fieldwork context. And in the concluding chapter I bring some of my observations based on long-term field research to bear on widespread scholarly assumptions about Third World urbanization.

Few anthropologists begin their field research with the specific intention of conducting long-term work in the same setting, although many entertain wishes to return and in fact some do. Ten years lapsed between the beginning of my initial fieldwork and my return to Mtendere in 1981. During the intervening decade, I moved between continents and went back to school, and I was unsure about whether to locate my urban research interests in the metropolitan United States or to return to Zambia. My initial research in Lusaka, in 1971–1972, was concerned with the gender division in waged and nonwaged work, as well as within households in Mtendere. I did return, and over the years I extended my research interests in directions that I myself never anticipated when first carrying out field research in Mtendere.

As my work in the township developed, it directed my attention to important relationships that linked the township's low-income residents with people elsewhere, calling for the kind of multi-site research that for some years preoccupied me with investigations of the changing relationship between domestic servants and their employers and, more recently, inquiries into the local organization and consumption of secondhand clothing imported from the West (Hansen 1989a, 1994). These interests were not incidental to my work in Mtendere but caught my attention from the flow of everyday life as I returned to the township over the years. And I keep returning to the township, which continues to be the setting that significantly shapes my understanding of the concerns of low-income townspeople, that great majority of Zambia's urban population who are "the common man." As I see it, in fact, Mtendere is the very image of urban Zambia.

This chapter explains the methodological considerations that have been part of my work in Mtendere as it has developed over the years. They are very much a product of my growing understanding of local concerns, and they have evolved through an ongoing dialogue with members of my original household sample and other township residents whom I have come to know. In general, urban field research is an exciting challenge with regard to both methodology and logistics. And long-term urban field research adds particular twists to this challenge. Overall, the chapter has two main concerns. One has to do with the logistics of conducting urban research and the adjustments, both intentional and fortuitous, that took place as this study developed into a long-term project. The second is intersubjective and has to do with how the researcher and the people she studies respond to one another as they are caught up in time: structural, biographical, and situational. As such, the chapter telescopes several processes, some of which were distinct and others of which overlapped. In the final section, I address this issue by discussing some of the problems and potentials involved in doing long-term research in an urban setting like postcolonial Lusaka.

Households, Work, and the Economy

The subject of my initial field research in Lusaka, in 1971–1972, arose from unpublished observations made by some of the anthropologists associated with the Rhodes-Livingstone Institute during the late colonial period regarding the contributions of urban African women to household economies. While knowledge about women's important but unrecognized work was retained in the oral memory of institute staff and mentioned in passing in urban studies from the late colonial period, the nature of the economic roles of urban African women had not been examined in its own right (Epstein 1981:57–58, 309–12; Powdermaker 1962:181–89, 202–203).[1] I initiated my research in Mtendere township in order to illuminate the empirical scope and theoretical nature of such activities. Colleagues in Lusaka were instrumental in my selection of Mtendere township as the site of my research: it was a recent settlement and it was within fairly easy reach. They also helped me to identify contact persons in Mtendere.

After some exploratory visits to Mtendere, during which a long-term local woman resident agreed to work with me, we began the research with a household survey of economic activity in one of the township's four sections. Since neither plot maps nor aerial photographs of the township were available, we considered differentiation among house types to be fairly representative of the range of socioeconomic developments in the township. Identifying houses by plot numbers, we drew a sample based on house types: 33 percent of the sample of one hundred households lived in completed houses; 50 percent, in houses under construction; and the last 17 percent, on plots where little construction had taken place and residents lived in a single room or temporary shelter. This selection corresponded well with the actual distribution of houses in the township at the time, that is, some four years after it had first been established. The procedure we used is usually referred to as quota sampling (Moser and Kalton [1958] 1971:127–36). It differs from other random sampling methods in many ways but most fundamentally by the fact that, once the quotas are decided upon, the choice of actual sample units is left to the investigator.

In consultation with my assistant and colleagues, I developed a questionnaire, structured for the purpose of collecting basic demographic and socioeconomic information about the residents, such as household composition by sex, age, headship, marital status, ethnic background, education, religion, work history, and length of urban residence in Mtendere and elsewhere. Because I was still learning Nyanja, the lingua franca of Lusaka, my assistant played an important role in administering the questionnaire, as she spoke several local languages and also served as an interpreter when necessary. Aside from working with the questionnaire, we also engaged residents in more open-ended discussions. Our conversations followed a topical outline of questions, eliciting information about financial decision making and money arrangements, aspects of social interaction within the household and beyond it, such as associational and organizational activities in the neighborhood, the larger community, within the city, and in relationship to relatives in the countryside. We also talked about the residents' plans for the future. I used notebook and pen, rather than tape recorder, in gathering all data.

Most of the persons we spoke with, in this and subsequent research in Mtendere, were women. Women were more readily available, although if men were present, they usually listened and, occasionally, took the lead. When in later years I inquired in more detail into the township's formal history and political organization, I spoke mostly with men. This gender representation reflects that of Zambian society in general, where there are far fewer women than men in formal jobs across the economy, from political office to paid domestic service.

Throughout my research it has been a difficult task to obtain factual information about householders' economic resources and expenditures. I tried to get around this problem in various ways—for example by inviting select residents to list incomes and expenditures on a weekly basis—but without much success. One reason was probably that some residents were reluctant to divulge "things of the house," such as money matters; another may have been that few households actually shared a common purse. Some women said categorically that they had "no idea" of their husbands' or partners' incomes, others made guesses, and a few knew the exact amount to the point of showing me the pay slip. But for men as well as women who had nonwaged earnings, for instance, from informal-sector activity, all such estimates were difficult. Women explained the difficulty by speaking of money going "into the pot," that is, being spent immediately on satisfying daily food needs. This graphic explanation tells of the small earnings most women make from informal-sector activity, and it helps to explain why they rarely accumulate sufficient profit to expand their small-scale trade into business.

Although I found it difficult to collect detailed information about household resources and expenditures, I was able to learn enough about the money-allocation system between spouses to describe the household budgeting pattern current in the early 1970s: who was responsible for what kinds of purchases and what kind of allowance, if any, women received from men (Hansen 1975). Many women were explicit about one thing: the allowance men gave them was too small. Even if my overall characterization of household incomes and expenditures cannot be expressed in detailed terms, it describes the situation clearly: women had no customary claim on men's income; if they received an allowance, it might not cover daily household needs; and their own contributions to the household economy readily disappeared into the pot.

My observations from follow-up work during subsequent research phases showed the persistence of this pattern, yet with gender and generational relations increasingly strained because of Zambia's deteriorating economy. On my return in 1981, we identified ninety of the one hundred houses in which we had interviewed in 1971. The discrepancy is attributable partly to human error (mix-up or incorrect plot numbers) and partly to the regulation of the township according to a new layout established by the city council over the intervening years. In the houses that we identified by plot number and where we were able to make contact, we found forty-six of the same householders we had interviewed in 1971.[2] In the remaining houses, residents had changed. We interviewed in both sets of houses, adding new households to bring the sample up to one hundred, categorizing our groups as "original" ($N = 46$), "different" ($N = 35$) and "new" ($N = 19$). The presentation in this book draws primarily on the original sample, although I occasionally refer to the supporting samples when I wish to make particular points. Specifically, whenever I have referred to persons by name, I discuss members of the original sample.

Our subsequent follow-up studies have traced fluctuations in household size and composition, the different economic involvements of women and men, and the unfolding experiences of children into young adults who have fought an uphill battle over access to education, work, and marriage. These processes revolve critically around resources, in both a material and a social-organizational sense, and previous chapters demonstrate how I directed my concern toward understanding their negotiation.

During each phase of the research, my assistant and I undertook additional work. I have already mentioned how we conducted supporting household surveys in order to place my shrinking original sample in a broader context. We also pursued specific lines of inquiry into questions that arose as the research evolved over the years. For instance, because many more women were pursuing informal trade in 1981 than in 1971, we carried out a survey in the township's market with focus on the gender and age division of labor in market trades. In 1984, when conducting a survey about domestic service practices in some of Lusaka's high-income areas, I extended a brief survey into one of Mtendere's four sections in order to explore the extent and scope in a low-income area of paid domestic work as well as of poorly remunerated and unpaid work performed by young persons. I have hinted at the ambiguous nature of such practices in chapter 5.

My understanding of the household as a battlefront on which private troubles and public issues are negotiated in everyday life between women and men and across generations arose from informal discussions between friends in the township and from residents bringing personal problems to church friends or the party chairman. When such matters were not solved in informal familial forums or by township institutions, they were taken to the local court. Having witnessed much quarreling over such matters within the township over the years, I decided in 1988 to examine how the local court dealt with them. My assistant and I attended court proceedings at the nearby Chelston local court, to which Mtendere residents brought their troubles. I discussed the work of the court and its procedures with the presiding justice. In addition, I read transcriptions of court cases, taking notes on those involving Mtendere residents, particularly but not exclusively those concerning premarital pregnancy, divorce, and inheritance. A legal scholar might ask different questions of these documents and interpret them differently. Their relevance to this book was highlighted in chapter 5, in which I drew on my notes from the court as well as on my observations about gender relations within Mtendere to demonstrate the different construction of male and female in postcolonial Zambia.

How reliable are the observations collected by means of the procedures I have discussed above? Although they are not representative of all of low-income Lusaka, or urban Zambia in general, the range of activities and household social organizational practices I describe here is found throughout Lusaka's poor neighborhoods (e.g., Bardouille 1981; Jules-Rosette 1981; Munachonga 1988; Todd and Shaw 1980). I have extended my knowledge about Mtendere and its relationship within the city and to other low-income residential areas by interviewing officials, from the political setup in the township itself (including ward, branch, and other local functionaries of the party), various institutional contexts in Lusaka (for example, the district council, the national housing board, and the central statistical office), and nongovernmental organizations, such as religious and philanthropic groups involved with township work. The historical dimension of this book stems from my reading of archival sources from the colonial period and after independence, especially information concerning urban administration, housing, and work. While some of this research was conducted for a study concerned with domestic service, I have not ignored its relevance to the present project (Hansen 1989a).

Learning How: Logistics and Participation in Urban Life

Surveys, questionnaires, and open-ended interviews yield valuable information. The insights gained in these ways become more richly textured from participant observation. This time-honored anthropological approach to field research entails being present and getting involved in the flow of life. It adds flesh to the dry bones by illuminating questions—for example, about number of children, years of education, religious affiliation, and ethnic background. Participant observation reveals more about how lives actually are lived than do brief answers to pre-set questions. Through it, for instance, I have learned about the nature of parents' interaction with children, the significance of education to a person's job situation, membership of church and extra-church activity, and the relative insignificance of ethnicity in neighborhood and township interaction. I have learned most of what I know about interactional practices, and gender and generational relations from such participation as sitting inside or, more frequently, on the ground outside a resident's house talking with members and visitors about daily concerns, special projects, and plans; hanging out in the township's market; and walking its streets on our way to or from some activity.

Walking around in this manner, my assistant and I have looked in on and participated in many special events, among them celebrations on account of a newborn child, a young girl's initiation, and funerals. On many occasions, I enjoyed refreshments and meals in residents' homes. Through conversations prompted by such visits I have obtained detailed information concerning which commodities were scarce, what the current substitutes were, and how residents experienced their situation as consumers in relationship to the strained Zambian economy. One example of such insights describes the situation particularly clearly. One chilly July morning in 1981, a neighbor joined my assistant and me for tea at my assistant's house. We ate day-old bread, with which we were happy, for bread was a scarce item then, available mainly on the black market. And we had butter with the bread. This was a treat, for no one had tasted butter for a long time. My assistant's husband had brought the butter from his workplace. While we savored the butter, my friends joked that it definitely had come from Zimbabwe, for in Zambia everyone knows that "foreign is better." Their commentary was directed toward the shortcomings of the local manufacturing industry and the fact that Zambians since the colonial era have depended on imports for the satisfaction of many needs.

Participant observation is perhaps less straightforward in urban than in village research, where accommodations more readily get arranged in situ. I have never lived in Mtendere township itself in spite of several attempts to organize township accommodations. There are several reasons for this. The most immediate explanation is the concerns that my long-term assistant expressed for my well-being. The lack of water-borne sanitation and, until recently, electricity made her reluctant to house me. "You will get bored," she used to say, especially in the evenings when most Mtendere residents restrained their movements because of the insecurity in the township in general, where there were no telephones and no police. And nightlife was rowdy around the beer halls. "Why don't you stay with the Catholic fathers?" she said when we discussed this issue in 1981, referring to a Jesuit guest house she was familiar with because of her church connections. "They have got television and there are people there who know a lot about Zambia." The inquiries she made in the township on my behalf usually failed because of space constraints. Residents who owned houses already had many claims placed on their limited space from members of their own households, visitors, and actual and potential tenants. But above all they had a hard time figuring out why on earth I might prefer Mtendere over the low-density areas in which I usually stayed. Their apprehensions initially troubled me until I realized that they perceived my needs in terms of the material circumstances of a world into which only a few of them had been fully integrated. My participant observation in local activities did not change that perception. Our mutual constructions—theirs of me as another *mzungu* and mine of them as low-income township residents—in effect located us differently in the broader setting in which we all interacted.

Because I did not stay in the township, my field research in Lusaka has been of the commuting kind. Over the years, I have lived in several expatriate households, one of them Indian but most of them North American. All my hosts were academics who either taught at the University of Zambia or worked in some research capacity. Most of them lived around the university campus, some miles away from Mtendere as the crow flies. The actual road network is more complicated, especially since there was no public transportation between the township and the campus area.

I reached Mtendere in many different ways. During my first research phase, in 1971–1972, I commuted on a small Honda motorbike. In 1981, friends in Lusaka advised me to bring along a folding bicycle from the United States, for bicycles were extremely scarce in Zambia at that time. In 1984 and 1985, I frequently took the long route: going all the way into central Lusaka from the university on public transportation or by hitchhiking and then getting on the minibus destined for Mtendere at the main downtown market, then reversing the process on my return. I learned my way around Lusaka's main market, avoiding it when mounted police cleared illegal traders away, and at times waiting for transport during the late afternoon for what seemed liked an eternity. Sometimes I gave up and left, choosing to hitchhike in preference to waiting for hours at the market. But hitchhiking had its own uncertainties. The upkeep of the car fleet in Zambia leaves much to be desired, and the death rate from automobile accidents is among the highest in the world. By 1988 and 1989, the fleet of minibuses had deteriorated very badly, and the buses of the national bus company were few and far between. But the taxi business boomed as more taxi licenses were issued. During those two years, I commuted with relative ease by taxi, which brought me directly across from the university district to Mtendere in the morning but made for much waiting and searching for a taxi in the township on my return in the late afternoon.

Reaching Mtendere by these means, I have gained close-range insights into the importance of transport for residents of a large, physically spread-out city such as Lusaka. From conversations while traveling, I learned about people's reactions to current political and economic events. Regardless of whether I took a motorbike, bicycle, public transport, or taxi, I could not avoid noticing the panorama that was unfolding before my own eyes. What people carried to and from town on the bus, or as they walked alongside with their burdens, displayed the current availabilities, such as blankets or detergent. Three quarters of the passengers of a minibus would "drop" (the term used in Zambian English for getting off) at a supermarket on the periphery of Lusaka before reaching Mtendere because they saw shoppers carrying cans of cooking oil out of the store. I also saw the flip side of Zambia's erratic supply system, which revealed itself in the long lines of cus-

tomers who queued for hours in the hope of buying scarce but necessary commodities like sugar, salt, and soap. The pattern of movement
also reflected the cycling of purchasing power. Most wage workers are
paid at the end of the month, at which time buses were cramped and
even getting a taxi was difficult.

When, during the final phases of this research, I traveled by taxi, I
learned quite a bit about the possibility of a lucrative business, and its
not always legal links with suppliers of vehicles and spare parts. I also
learned about young men driving for long hours for a relative or
friend in the hope of getting into the taxi business or accumulating
start-up capital for some other venture. And I received many inquiries
about study possibilities in the United States and about what the
Danes were doing in Zambia. Managing traffic relationships requires
a range of skills that are crucial to accessibility in urban heterogeneous
settings (Hannerz 1980:104–5, 218–20). Such traffic skills in turn contribute to constructing culturally and class-specific notions of urban
space and opportunity. My own experiences convince me that Hannerz
is right when arguing that traffic poses important research questions
about the nature of urban relationships and interactions (1980:102). In
short, these different ways of getting to know Lusaka without a personal car taught me about the pleasures and frustrations that most
low-income residents encounter with regard to transportation.

Learning What: The Politics of Urban Research

I have stressed throughout this book that the struggle for resources
and access to means made Mtendere residents and their township part
of the overall sociopolitical urban setting rather than an enclave that
can be studied in its own right. When this struggle is projected onto
the structural level, it politicizes township life. An urban researcher
has to reckon with the state's attempt to control urban space and the
surveillance that it exacts through issuing research permits and questioning by persons in authority, including the party UNIP, its police,
and its vigilante groups. During the last half of the 1980s, UNIP institutionalized vigilante groups consisting of young men who were entitled to stop persons for questioning and to bring suspect individuals
to the attention of the police.

Research in any location, rural or urban, requires formal permissions and dealings with bureaucracies at many levels. In addition to

granting me a research permit through the immigration department and affiliation prior to my arrival, the Institute for African Studies at the University of Zambia (the successor to the Rhodes-Livingstone Institute) has provided me with letters of introduction to facilitate my entry into various places and institutions during all my studies in Lusaka. Seeking interviews with officials, I sometimes became mired in bureaucracy, yet at other times the process turned out to be smooth and easy. In that respect Zambia is no different from the United States, where the worst bureaucracy I ever encountered was the Immigration and Naturalization Service.

In my experience in Zambia, officials of the para-statal companies were the most difficult to gain access to, whereas officials of government institutions were much more readily available. My attempt to gain permission to work in Chelston local court in 1988 serves as an excellent example of this. Since telephones did not readily work, I approached the minister of justice without any prior appointment, carrying a letter of introduction and my calling card. After a few courtesies, he sent me straight on to an official at the high court, who immediately wrote a letter of permission. The official in charge of local courts willingly shared insights about court practices with me. He also sought to arrange for a court vehicle to take me directly to Chelston local court. That this did not materialize because the vehicles were either broken down or not available does not detract from the message of this incident: in general people are helpful.

The single most important aspect of field research regardless of location is to clear it properly with the authorities who are most immediately concerned with the locality under study. During each research period in Mtendere, I brought letters of introduction to the person who chaired the township UNIP branch, and my assistant and I called on persons at various levels of the local party hierarchy, including the market.

I may not have spent sufficient time on explaining my purpose in the township adequately each time, and in 1981 this became a problem. It was my first return after ten years' absence, during which time Zambia hosted freedom fighters from both Rhodesia and South Africa. Mtendere had several residents from both countries. Lusaka had experienced bombings instigated by the South African defense force. Suspicions readily arose as my assistant and I walked around in the township's unnamed streets, using plot numbers to identify the houses in which we had interviewed in 1971 and asking many questions about the whereabouts of former residents. Our visits to a local tavern caused gossip. In fact, we were stopped frequently and asked what we were doing.

One morning, some men from the special branch of the Zambia police force fetched us from the market right in the middle of an interview, took us to my assistant's house, and asked me to explain my activities. I showed whatever legitimation I carried and was driven back, bicycle and all, in a UNIP car to my residence in the university district so that I could produce my passport. I was told that the inquiry concerned my visa status, and the men left. At sunset, one of the men appeared at the gate, demanding to come inside. He requested my passport and credit cards, both of which I declined to deliver. He then demanded my notes and instructed me to appear in the special branch office at the Zambia police force headquarters at eight o'clock the next morning.

In the meantime, I had deposited one set of notes (I always made a carbon copy) together with my diary (which I always write in Danish) with trusted friends, whose advice I solicited. The next morning the research affiliation officer of the Institute for African Studies, also a good friend, and a colleague accompanied me to the appointment. The officer in charge asked why I was conducting research in a low-income township, why I had returned to the same place, specifically Mtendere, and why I studied poor women rather than women who had made it, and above all, why did I not study in a village as anthropologists used to do. It transpired that he had checked my notes carefully to see if my work focused on South Africans in particular. Zambia hosted the exiled South African National Congress. Was I an informer? Clearly, this was not the case.

With his apprehensions swept aside, the special branch officer and I had an interesting discussion about research priorities. His construction of Zambia as a developing country in which living and working opportunities were bound to change for the better made my research in a high-density urban area such as Mtendere and my attention to low-income women appear inappropriate. Such townships with their poverty and problems are places that the government does not like to be reminded about. As a striking commentary on the gulf between policy statements and actual livelihoods, this interchange has clarified my understanding of the uneasy relationship between the state and civil society in Zambia as well as of the ambiguous status that Western anthropologists hold in it.

My encounter with the special branch of the Zambian police force dramatizes that field research entails an exchange between the parties involved in which anthropologists and the people we study each construe the other but play very different roles in the process. This process of mutual interaction is perhaps more evident when researchers keep returning to the same locality and seek out residents whom they have come to know well from previous years. What becomes critical in such a research project is to a great extent the concerns that are crucial to local residents.

Because my ongoing study has come increasingly to grapple with residents' negotiations over material and social organizational resources, some processes slid from view, as they were not particularly pertinent to residents' attempts to secure their urban arrangements for living. These processes include phenomena that I certainly observed affecting some residents' lives at one time or another, such as healing practices and witchcraft accusations, which might have more salience for a researcher less bent than I on economic clarifications. They also include—and this I regret—a closer scrutiny of the increase in subletting, particularly questions about the livelihoods of tenants, to which I paid little attention because I was predominantly concerned with the households who remained in the township over the years.

My understanding of these processes is clearly biased in the direction of Mtendere residents by women's views, and I am pulled into the network from which they draw specific resources. Above all, I have come to understand the meaning and experience of township life to a woman from my long-term association with my assistant, who continuously has worked together with me, rather than for me. She provided my initial gender socialization into Lusaka and when relevant, she acted as my chaperone. As a well-respected long-term local resident, she facilitated my house visits and my access to township authorities. In this way, she was my most important local mentor. It is from her living room that I learned most of what I know about the texture of township life, of its joys, emotions, and trials, and of the challenges the material bases of this life pose to autonomous gender relations. Indeed, it is from within her household that I have come to understand how political one's personal life can be in Zambia.

History, Biography, and Situations

Long-term field research gives its investigator the opportunity to reconsider methodology in several ways.[3] The most obvious has to do with improving approaches in order to reckon with weaknesses or even mistakes in the research that was conducted previously. An example of this are the supporting samples I added to my research base while following up the experiences of the declining numbers of households in my original survey during subsequent years. Another way of improving one's approach to research consists of conducting new work, or exploring issues from different angles, perhaps as a result of concerns that arose after the departure from the research location.

Because my work in Lusaka has evolved over the years, it contains several such shifts—for instance, my survey in the market in 1981 and my growing interest in pursuing the question of how residents struggled over resources, which in 1988 took me to the local court. And in 1989 I singled out one particular group for special interviews about work and marriage: young adult daughters of the mothers I always had come back to. I also arranged some informal group discussions at which young Mtendere women educated me about their attitudes and actions in regard to men, money, and marriage. And although I much prefer to keep as low a profile as possible in relation to political officials, I interviewed several UNIP representatives in Mtendere in 1989, mainly to get their version of the history of the township, which I had pieced together more informally from residents during previous years.

The most challenging reconsideration that long-term research imposes on its practitioner is a product of the double encounter that fieldwork so obviously is about: the interaction between the people we study and the investigator herself. This interaction engages both parties with time in the three senses I distinguished at the outset of this book: historical, biographical, and situational. These different temporalities affect both the population under study and the researcher, and these processes intersect in complex ways. How much of what we study is a product of any single one of these processes and how much is attributable to their interaction? The remainder of my discussion explores this question with regard to the material presented in this book.

"How," asked Monica Wilson some twenty years ago, do we "combine a study of change through time, with emphasis on the flow of time, and the detailed analysis of relationships. . . . Static models are too far from reality to be useful, but how can we create a model that moves?" Her perceptive formulation, "zig-zag change," for movements that are not experienced as unidirectional but seem to reverse or even be suspended reckons with some of the difficulties that beset the study of time and people's experience of change (1976:399). So does Elizabeth Colson's discussion of the "reordering of experience" in the involvement with time on the part of both anthropologists and the people they study (1984). Still, the question of how to account for time and its experience remains an important issue in long-term studies, including my own. The "moving model" I have sought to apply in my own work views time and change in experiential and conceptual terms by integrating three different senses of time: historical, biographical, and situational.

My work has focused on several distinct but interconnected issues: gender relations and household dynamics, housing, and work. Through long-term research I have examined the nature of relationships between township and town and, to a much smaller degree, between city and countryside, and how these relationships have changed over time. I am particularly concerned with the direction such changes are taking and with what insights this may give us about the urbanization process and the kind of urbanism to which it is giving rise in Zambia.

The question concerning the direction of change is a tricky one, for it involves at least three different processes that I have discussed throughout this book: the effects that large-scale transformations of society are having on people's livelihoods; the way in which the stage in the household development cycle is affecting an individual's responses to changes in his or her circumstances; and the role that personal agency or even idiosyncrasy is having on a person's actions. These three processes intertwine in an individual's experience of his or her life, complicating analysis of the processes involved.

Adding up information collected through repeated follow-up inquiries about the unfolding experiences of members of my original household sample and in particular women, I suggested the use of a "work history" to examine the intersection of personal and household history with human agency (Hansen 1987). Such work histories tell us much about the direction of change in urban Zambia that synchronic research would hide from view. Through real life experiences these work histories inform us that the large-scale socioeconomic changes that stem from the deterioration of the country's economy have not bankrupted people's livelihoods. Instead, processes at the macro level have transformed local economic initiatives into an incessant chase after commodities, consumers, and credit.

When I left Mtendere in 1989, these processes had contributed to an increasing informalization of the overall economy, fueled by the recirculation of goods and commodities produced elsewhere rather than by local production. The gender division of labor in this economy placed men at its most lucrative positions, whereas women crowded its least profitable sectors, notably the resale of fruits, vegetables, and cooked foods. Proportionately more women past their childbearing years participated than did young women, thus gender and stage in the unfolding of the household development cycle do influence who works and where. And personal agency informed the drive to work, especially the ways in which women and men creatively, but differently, combined personal, social, and economic resources in their attempts to make a living.

Time will tell whether or not the much-hailed structural adjustment programs of the World Bank and the International Monetary Fund and the new multi-party government established in Zambia in 1991 will appreciably improve the livelihoods of low-income urban people in places like Mtendere. The ways in which historical and biographical time will intersect in their future reordering of experiences may perhaps produce a zigzag sense of change, if not new discontinuities or even breaks that will continue to challenge our scholarly search for models that move. To explore the direction such processes may take in the future, we must continue the kind of tracing that I have done over the last twenty years of urban residents' changing involvement with time, gender, and each other.

Conclusion:
A View from Lusaka

Through long-term research in a low-income township *Keeping House in Lusaka* has created its own story of people, their projects and plans, and their researcher. The observations I have made in this book about the unfolding of lives in Mtendere locate individual experiences of development over close to a twenty-year period in the mutual dynamics of Zambia's economic decline and cultural practices. Because some of these observations do not conform to widespread assumptions about the nature of Third World urbanization, housing, and the informal sector, they raise questions about the intellectual framing of such issues in the development literature. I use this conclusion to point to some of the insights that are to be drawn from this book and discuss their implications not only for how we understand the transformation of Third World cities like Lusaka but also for how we interpret their local cultural dynamics.

Housing

The social, political, and economic contexts for urban living in Zambia in the 1990s have changed considerably since the mid-1960s and early 1970s when urban planning solutions to the low-income housing question proposed owner-occupancy, often of the self-help kind. My work during twenty years in Mtendere demonstrates that rapid population growth combined with economic decline are turning home ownership into an exceedingly limited option for the next generation of urban residents. In fact, a growing proportion of Lusaka's low-income residents are finding shelter in rented rooms.

Past and present, housing was an important economic resource in the political and economic geography that shaped urbanism in Lusaka. Throughout Zambia's cities and towns, rental housing tied to jobs has always curtailed the development of owner occupancy except at the top and at the bottom of the opportunity structure. For the low-income population in a site-and-service settlement like Mtendere, a house of one's own not only embodied considerable investment by residents but also created socioeconomic space for people who were not part of the capital's shrinking formal wage-labor force. Indeed, such self-built housing had facilitated income-generating work from Lusaka's early colonial days, especially for women.

For the long-term residents whose lives I have followed over the years, owning a house in a low-income township such as Mtendere was an important asset, economically as well as socially. Once the township was legalized, a house of one's own offered security of tenure and provided the possibility for sublease, giving members of these households access to a larger number and more fluid sources of income, broader networks, and the ability to sustain reciprocity with members who came and went, whether they be young adult children, rural relatives, or both.

The relatively secure urban arrangements for living that long-term residents of Mtendere were able to establish for themselves are unlikely to be repeated by subsequent generations, including many of their own children, in Lusaka's faltering economy. Continued urban growth during the 1970s and 1980s combined with difficulties in both supplying and maintaining Lusaka's urban infrastructure. Barring overnight changes of the way in which the world does business with poor countries like Zambia, this process will no doubt continue in years to come when a slowdown in the overall rate of urbanization most likely will be outweighed by continued natural increase among the already resident urban population. These difficulties will become even more challenging for future urban generations as well as for newly arrived migrants from the rural areas. More of the capital's growing population will have to find housing on Lusaka's urban periphery, where there is little in the way of urban infrastructure and public services.

The major contributions to Lusaka's urban growth during the 1970s and 1980s came from increased squatting and the subdivision of plots and construction of rental rooms in low-income areas like Mtendere. It is likely that more and more of Lusaka's future urban residents will live in rented rooms and that the rate of commercialization of rentals that already is taking place now in site-and-service schemes and squatter settlements will increase dramatically in scope.

Prevailing housing policy has for a long time approached the low-income housing question with a number of problematic assumptions. They include the formulation of policy in terms of housing needs with reference to a quantifiable shortfall in low-income housing units. Such formulations are based on norms concerning household composition and occupancy status that tend to associate men with headship and view tenure as ownership. In short, the underlying vision views houses, even in low-income areas, as occupied by owners and headed by men who live with their wives and children.

A growing body of research from urban areas across the developing world has begun to qualify these assumptions (Edwards 1990; Gilbert 1993; Spiegel, Watson, and Wilkinson 1994; Varley 1995). Few low-income households conform to the ideal household envisioned in policy statements. As the households in Mtendere demonstrate, the housing needs of residents varied widely, depending on their family size, composition, stage in the household development cycle, and social and cultural practices that affected gender relations and authority. Specifically, the decline in formal employment combined with overall deterioration in Zambia's economy has put the second generation at more disadvantage than their parents and older siblings with regard to ownership of houses. Above all, because social and cultural practices in Zambia associate membership of houses with men, prevailing housing policy discriminates against women, ignoring their important role in the allocation of household resources. This role changes over the course of the household development cycle as wives and husbands become increasingly concerned with their own agendas. And household composition and size vary as members come and go, spouses split up or die, and some remarry. Last but not least, women are not always or only dependent members of male-headed households. As this book has demonstrated, the economic role of urban housing was particularly important to them.

Women and children relaxing. Different house types in the background.
House constructed of wood boards and metal sheets

Women and children relaxing. Different house types in the background.
Unfinished brick building constructed with rental of single rooms in view

These are important observations for urban planners to reckon with. Since the mid-1980s, Zambian government policy on housing has neglected the rental housing market in favor of owner-occupancy. Home ownership is typically associated with male headship of households and tends de facto to deny women access to houses in their own right. The renting out of rooms—in special settings like South Africa's migrant hostels and even bedholds (Ramphele 1993)—that is increasing in scope in many cities across Africa and the absentee landlordism and subletting that this book has shown in townships like Mtendere cast critical light on that assumption.

The time is long overdue for urban planners of low-income housing in rapidly growing cities like Lusaka to envision different scenarios than owner-occupied housing and to do so in terms that reckon with the gendered relationship to housing (Barnes 1990; Rakodi 1991). The low-income housing question in Africa's strained economies may well hinge on the rental housing market, which ought not to remain neglected at the policy level. Above all, rental housing might enable women to get housing in their own right, which would constitute an important step toward reducing the inequity of the present housing allocation system, most certainly in Zambia's urban settings.

The Informal Sector

Urban job prospects in Zambia in the 1990s have changed considerably since the mid-1960s and early 1970s when wage employment was the order of the day, at least for men, and policy questions concerning manpower development and technical skills took precedence over self-employment and small-scale trade. My long-term work in Mtendere demonstrates how married women extended their income-generating work from their own homes, yards, and streets into the township market and beyond. When I began my work in 1971, most husbands in these households were employed at the lower echelons of the wage economy. As the economy deteriorated, some husbands began to perform informal-sector work, sometimes as their sole occupation but more often as a sideline activity when the economic decline eroded the value of wages from formal jobs. Young adult children participated intermittently, turning the household into an arena from which different kinds of activities were staged, in very fluid arrangements as members came and went, occasionally cooperated, but usually pursued individual agendas.

The nature of such activities does not support rigid analytical distinctions between informal and formal sectors of the economy. Instead, such activities drew both their participants and their inputs from several sectors of the economy, rural as well as urban. And informal-sector participants depended for resource access on both household members and persons outside of households, which in turn involved them with institutions from across the urban economy.

Three observations of comparative significance for discussions of the informal sector's labor absorption potential arise from my long-term work in Mtendere. The first stems from the general nature of Lusaka's informal sector, in which trading activities far outnumber artisanry and small-scale production, particularly for women. The next two observations pertain specifically to the activity pattern of women's informal-sector work, which by and large is highly individual in its orientation and performed largely by women at an age when the needs arising from childbearing and childrearing assume less of their attention.

Taken together, these three observations clearly point to limitations in the expansion potential of Lusaka's informal sector. When allocating economic means and technical support, planners and development interventionists who believe the informal sector capable of absorbing ever larger numbers of the newly unemployed and fresh migrants from the countryside need to reckon with the limited diversification and constrained economic resources that this sector controls in Zambia. Above all, they need to appreciate how its resources are mobilized and by whom, when, and why. Long-term research illuminates the dynamics of these processes, which are too often masked in the rapid assessments conducted by development organizations.

Currently popular approaches, for example, regarding skills training for out-of-work female and male youth, predominantly in tailoring, carpentry, and tinsmithing in effect allocate skills to areas of petty production that already engage a large portion of the informal labor force. Development organizations bent on promoting micro-enterprises must do better than establish special skills-training projects that replicate these already limited solutions to youth unemployment. What is more, approaches that channel support to women's organizations are unlikely to reach their target—poor women—

because of the individual nature of so many women's informal-sector work. And approaches that target households headed by single women ignore the economic bind of many married women, namely their dependency on their husbands for resources. NGOs, for example, that typically seek out grass-roots organizations when entering the local scene with a view to enhancing opportunities for women, will find few such groupings here. They may instead create extra work for married women (Hansen 1982b).

The flaw of the last two approaches, at least with regard to Zambia, stems from ignoring cultural practices and expectations that define women's income-generating work as supplementation of household income rather than as autonomous economic activity. Long-term observations like mine reveal that adult women in a place like Mtendere know that they can neither rely on husbands' economic constancy nor keep the fruits of their household and income-generating work in cases of divorce and widowhood. So they take individual action and make their own arrangements, trusting neither men nor neighbors in cooperative activity.

Urban Bias

Zambia's rapid economic decline since the mid-1970s has affected urban and rural areas adversely, accentuating socioeconomic differentiation within society at large and reducing formerly more distinct disparities between the lives of the urban and the rural poor. Although the urbanization rate appears to have declined slightly during the last two decades, the country has seen extensive aggregate growth of the population living in cities in absolute terms (Wood 1986). Above all, the capital, Lusaka, has experienced continued population increase in the wake of the decline of economic activity in the mining towns in the copperbelt. Overall, Lusaka's expansion is a result of increase in the already resident urban population as well as of continued in-migration.

Why do so many Zambians choose town over country? They do so because of their perceptions of where they best can improve their circumstances. In spite of the country's declining economy over the last twenty years, many Zambians continue to consider cities to be the best places to find work, and Lusaka, the capital, more so than other towns. Urban women's and men's perceptions of what constitutes work, and their preferences for distinct types of work (for example,

Mtendere women's choice of small-scale trade over paid domestic service jobs), serve their needs and desires to improve their own and
their children's livelihood. Although such observations as these
reflect very local experiences, they cast important light on the changing nature of urban livelihoods.

The rapid growth of a city like Lusaka against the backdrop of
stagnating wage employment has been characterized as overurbanization by some (e.g., Gugler 1978). Overurbanization is not so much
a product of rapid urban growth as it is of misallocation of labor: too
many people eking out a living in jobs that contribute little to general welfare or national productivity, for example domestic servants
(Gugler 1988:78).

But what is productive labor? And which kinds of jobs contribute
to general social welfare? My long-term observations of how residents in one of Lusaka's many low-income settlements weathered
one of the fastest and most dramatic economic declines in postcolonial
Africa invite qualification of powerful assumptions behind the concept of overurbanization and a related notion, that of urban bias,
which I turn to below.

The notion of overurbanization discounts the significance of informal-sector work in general and women's nonpaid household work in
particular. Take the example of women's informal-sector work in
Mtendere, which very obviously contributed directly to household
welfare and indirectly to national productivity by enhancing the well-
being of both present and future workers. Although such work and
informal-sector activity in general is not accounted for in Zambia's
gross national product, today it puts far more people to work than
does the formal-wage sector.

The concept of overurbanization does not capture the dynamics of
ongoing socioeconomic transformations in a country like Zambia.
The social, economic, and political setting of urban Zambia and the
rural areas with which it is linked have changed in many ways since
the immediate post-independence years when large-scale economic
diversification through the construction of manufacturing plants
and factories employing wage labor were linked in a vision of economic growth. That vision never materialized, and today the informal sector, rather than wage labor, provides the most significant basis
for the making of a living for large segments of the population in
cities like Lusaka.

Overurbanization assumes that units of labor could be more productively applied elsewhere, particularly in agriculture (Flanagan 1993:113). This assumption is central to notions of urban bias that view cities as parasites on national resources and explain the urbanization process as taking place at the cost of rural development. In this view, the bias resulting from misallocation of resources to urban areas can be redressed only through an emphasis on rural development (Lipton 1977). Throughout the 1970s and 1980s the development policy followed in Zambia was informed by this strategy and set into motion by means of considerable loans, grants, and aid from international aid donors (Hansen and Ashbaugh 1991:215–22). Yet, over this same time, rural livelihoods declined rather than improved.

While much development intervention continues to be informed by notions of urban bias and of rural and urban areas representing distinct economic settings, recent scholarship has begun to demonstrate that such notions do not adequately characterize the complex socioeconomic relationships that are shaping rural and urban developments (Jamal and Weeks 1988). The notions of urban bias and a rural-urban gap are themselves biased by widely held views of what cities and rural areas ought to be like. The most deeply entrenched prejudice insists that *urban* means wage labor and *rural* implies subsistence cultivation. Confusing location with activity, such views ignore for the case of Zambia that the regional and broader international political economies from the colonial period onward have transformed both rural and urban livelihoods, setting into motion complex, historically changing, and regionally diverse interchanges between them. What is more, such views ignore the long-term effects of national policy on resource allocation and the fact that Zambia does not have a labor-intensive agricultural sector that will readily absorb an ex-urban labor force at a subsistence level.

Such anti-urban views are based on the assumption that rural areas can easily absorb a superfluous urban workforce. But in the rural Zambian case, there are few labor-intensive agricultural settings to perform that function. Access to rural land depends on claims that are socially and culturally constructed and have to be maintained during the absence of migrants. Rights to land have to be established, which is to say that urban residents bent on rural retirement spend considerable time and effort either on maintaining claims or establishing them in preparation for their moves from the city (Ashbaugh

1996). Finally, these moves are not always made with a view to engaging in agricultural toil; sometimes people plan to undertake small-scale entrepreneurship in a service-related activity or trade. In effect, not all rural dwellers are subsistence cultivators; some make a living from government work (for example, as teachers, nurses, or extension workers), from the informal sector, or from wage labor for farmers engaged in cash cropping (rather than subsistence cultivation) or on commercial farms, which in several of Zambia's provinces have placed land beyond the access of local and prospective cultivators. Rural and urban areas have been interdependent for a long time in Zambia; development orthodoxy concerning rural subsistence cultivation has a hard time grappling with that fact.

A View from Lusaka

While the colonial past certainly is relevant for purposes of understanding the forces that shaped contemporary cities in Zambia, the future of a city like Lusaka is best assessed not along the lines of a colonial urban tradition but along those of a postcolonial Zambian one. The population growth of Zambia's major towns and cities after independence has been so rapid that the country's urbanization rate today is about the highest in sub-Saharan Africa, and Lusaka is one of the fastest-growing cities in the world. This casting of Zambia's urban demographic map is still unfolding and unlikely to be stopped by administrative intervention.

This growth has occurred against the backdrop of a marked decline in employment opportunities in industry and manufacturing as well as in agricultural production. At the same time, the government, its party, and its para-statal agencies assumed greater importance in various institutional contexts affecting the lives of its citizens. But the government of the Second Republic also left many voids. While resources in Zambia became more scarce than ever, they also became increasingly maldistributed.

The postcolonial pattern of urban growth and the nature of urbanism that resulted from these processes display an urban fabric that has its roots in the past but is qualitatively different. Today, squatter settlements and lack of wage employment are no longer explained away as undesirable but are acknowledged as alternative ways of making out in the city. Whether such settlements will be considered as the norm—that is, as typical urban living arrangements rather than as alternatives—will depend on the ability of the government of the Third Republic to tackle the structural forces that continue to reproduce unequal access to housing and to work. Meanwhile, low-income residents throughout Zambia's towns continue much in the manner of Mtendere's residents, making their own arrangements as best they can both for housing and work.

While Lusaka may represent an exaggerated case of these processes and the experiences of long-term Mtendere residents may appear special because of home ownership, the development of urbanism as a Zambian way of life in Lusaka offers unique insights into processes that are unfolding elsewhere on the continent. Questions concerning urban housing and work are of top priority—for example, in the new South Africa. A new urban agenda is being established, and this book's observations about the social and political importance of place attachment in the struggle over urban housing and work by gender and generation will no doubt provide insight into this agenda.

At the same time as it addresses broader themes about low-income housing, the informal sector, and gender questions that arise from ongoing Third World urbanization elsewhere, *Keeping House in Lusaka* concerns very recognizable Zambian experiences. Involving dynamic interactions between urban institutions such as housing and work, individual experiences by women and men of distinct generations, and a shared history of postcolonial economic decline, the story of Mtendere is deeply lodged in its specific regional, historical, and cultural context.

The questions this book raises about Zambian experiences concern the store of knowledge, the political attitudes, and the gender beliefs that Mtendere residents draw upon as members of Zambian society. Their humor-laced cynicism about politics and class, the *apamwamba* and the yards, draws upon their experiences as urban residents during the long, lean years of the Second Republic. The cultural form of some of their experiences points to the dilemma of the present: the experience of inequity that results from being citizens of a poor country that remains dependent on the West in many ways.

In their efforts directed toward keeping house in Lusaka during the declining economic years of the Second Republic, most long-term Mtendere residents showed considerable resourcefulness. Their experiences during those years were the complex outcomes of sometimes overlapping but certainly interwoven situational, biographical, and structural processes. The interaction of these three senses of time is demonstrated most dramatically through their conjuncture in diverging gender and generational experiences.

Rather than displaying ties that bind, members of these households more often demonstrated lines that divided. Such divisions contributed to the anguished conflicts between parents and grown or half-grown children, as well as to tensions in conjugal relationships. Disappointed over their children's lack of opportunities, some parents revealed their own vulnerability. Thus when a daughter became pregnant, her dilemma brought out conservative reactions in many parents, mothers in particular. The cultural overtones of these reactions speak directly and with an immediacy both about contradictions in the gender domain on the home front and in society at large and about difficult economic times.

Urban initiation rites and kitchen parties highlight some of the contradictory experiences of peripheral living, in short, of the uneasy Zambian encounter with modernity. While taking fairly similar cultural form in their focus on advising women about their proper role, reinvented initiation rites and "new" traditions such as kitchen parties have different reference points, one to the past and the other to the unfolding present. That is to say, urban initiation rites celebrate conservative notions of women's proper roles, recalling a societal order and structure that has long been gone. Kitchen parties, for their part, innovate on the cultural theme of body politics, displaying a competitive performance plot into which flow objects of modernity: cutlery, tableware, and electric pots. Pointing in two different directions, the significance of such re-created rituals revolves around women, highlighting both the centrality and tensions around gender and the generational relations on the home front and in society at large. Such experiences are among those that this book has argued contribute to making urbanism in Lusaka recognizably Zambian.

Notes

Introduction

1. Cha-cha-cha was a popular dance in Zambia in the 1960s. After the failure of nonviolent actions to achieve independence, the name *cha cha cha* was given to a secret plan made by the United National Independence Party (UNIP), one of the two African political parties, for a popular revolt against colonial rule.
2. For different analytical formulations of temporalities, see Guyer (1988) and Heald (1991) in studies of the effects of socioeconomic change in rural Cameroon and Kenya.
3. Harvey (1973) and Castells (1977) are among the chief theoreticians to examine the political dimensions of urban space in the Western capitalist world, particularly the role of the state in the production of urban space, serving the interests of capital accumulation. Conventional anthropology has tended to view spatial patterns as reflective of the sociocultural order. This static view is being challenged in recent work, including urban research, which views space as socially constituted and seeks to understand the meaning of urban spaces through the knowledge of the people who live in them. For discussion, see Lawrence and Low (1990) and Rotenberg and McDonogh (1993).
4. On Zambia's changing political economy, see Bates and Collier (1993), Gertzel et al. (1984), Woldring (1984), Wood (1990), and Young and Loxley (1990).

1. Colonial Lusaka

1. These, and all other names used throughout this book except in chapter 5, are fictional. Most of them are common regional names, and some of them appear in my previous publications.

2. Some of the major works on the copperbelt include Berger (1974), Burawoy (1972), Harries-Jones (1975), Higginson (1989), Parpart (1983), and Perrings (1979).

3. Conceptualizations of colonial cities also include works outside Africa. See King (1989).

4. The mining companies had invited United Missions in the Copperbelt to operate health services and welfare work in the compounds, but they took over these functions in the early 1950s.

5. Useful overviews are available in Hannerz (1980), van Donge (1985), and Werbner (1984).

6. For some of these discussions, see Argyle (1991), Magubane (1969, 1971), and Matongo (1992).

7. Lusaka did not become a municipality until 1927. I use the term *municipality* throughout this chapter in preference to the less straightforward term *local authority township*.

8. The censuses of 1911, 1921, 1931, 1946, 1951, and 1956 concern the European, Asian, and "colored" communities. They make only limited reference to Africans and then mainly to African men in wage employment (Bettison 1959:8–9).

9. According to the Employment of Natives Ordinance of 1929, children under fourteen years of age could be employed only if the secretary for native affairs issued a license. This ordinance was revised in 1933 in accordance with International Labour Organisation conventions.

10. For a study of gender, housing, and prostitution in colonial Nairobi, see White (1990).

11. Bettison used a poverty datum line (PDL) concept to assess the adequacy of African wages against their cost of living in his 1957 Lusaka survey. Excluding rent (assuming it to be paid by employers), he found that only 15 percent of households with children were above the PDL (1959:98).

12. A total of 80.5 percent of the market women interviewed by Nyirenda were married. The proportion of female single heads of households in Lusaka at that time was 13.1 percent (1957:42).

13. For example, Cliffe (1979), Mitchell (1959), Moore and Vaughan (1994), Richards (1940), van Velsen (1960), and Watson (1958).

2. A House of One's Own

1. Southern Rhodesia became known as Rhodesia in 1965 when the white minority government unilaterally declared itself independent of Great Britain.

2. Lusaka's city council was replaced by a district council as a consequence of the Local Administration Act of 1980. For an overview of urban local administration in Zambia, see Rakodi (1988b), who highlights the lacking administrative capacities in the local government apparatus and the

incompetence of the urban local government in Lusaka in particular. I use the term *city council* when discussing developments prior to 1980 and the term *district council* for the subsequent period.

3. According to Wood (1986:169), the Asian population comprised 5.2 percent of Lusaka's non-Zambian-born population in 1969. It is unclear whether this figure includes the long-resident local Asian population or refers only to international migrants from Asia.

4. See note 11 in chapter 1.

5. Discussions include Hoek-Smit (1982), Jules-Rosette (1981:173–99), Pasteur (1979), Rakodi (1988a), and Schlyter (1991a). The Lusaka Housing Project Unit replaced the Squatter Control Unit, working with the council in implementing the squatter upgrading project. The project involved considerable community participation. The Housing Project Unit produced a series of valuable working papers, detailing various aspects of the upgrading process.

6. In addition to references cited in the bibliography, my discussion of Mtendere's early development draws on my notes from unpublished city council reports, held in the Special Collection of the University Library, the University of Zambia. Besides discussing the township's early developments with Mtendere residents and representatives of the township's UNIP organization, I also interviewed the chief squatter controller and city council staff.

3. URBAN ARRANGEMENTS FOR LIVING

1. I have taken the general meaning of the expression *urban arrangements for living* from Leeds (1974:75). Unlike him, I do not imply that households form cooperating units.

2. See chapter 7 for a detailed discussion of the methodological aspects of my research as well as its development during follow-up studies.

3. It is very possible that some of the ten house plots that I was unable to identify in 1981 might have been eliminated by commercial and service development in the township during the intervening decade.

4. Because people do not readily admit it, the incidence of polygyny may be higher than what I was told. It is difficult to assess the extent of polygyny, since co-wives do not always live together in the city. Some men have second wives in the countryside, and some co-wives resided in other townships in Lusaka.

5. Siyolwe (1994) offers interesting insights into the recent involvement of middle-class Lusaka women in this trade.

6. There is growing attention to these economic activities also in the West. See, for example, Portes, Castells, and Benton (1989), Redclift and Mingione (1985), and Sassen (1991).

7. The International Labour Organisation conducted studies of the informal sector in several African countries during the 1970s, including

Kenya (ILO 1972) and Zambia (ILO 1977). Hugh Macmillan reminded me of Richard Jolly (1993:709).

8. The United States Agency for International Development is conducting a worldwide project, Growth and Equity through Microenterprise Investments and Institutions (GEMINI) that focuses on the promotion of microenterprises in developing countries. For a discussion of the general ideas that guide this project, see Liedholm and Mead (1987). To my knowledge, the project has not yet covered Zambia. For findings from Zimbabwe, see McPherson (1991).

4. On the Home Front

1. For a discussion of this shift, see Moore (1988:1–11).

2. A protracted discussion from 1976 onward, involving a government-established legal commission, acrimonious debates in parliament, and news media features, preceded the passing of this law. For background, see Coldham (1983) and Longwe (1990). For an assessment of the new law and problems in its implementation, see Mindolo Ecumenical Foundation (1991) and Mwanza (1990).

3. Munachonga's observations (1988) on gender and household budgeting 1982–1983 parallel my own.

4. Zambian writer Norah Mumba used her own experiences as a widow who was a victim of property grabbing in her novel (1992).

5. See Jules-Rosette (1980) for a women's purity rite performed by the Vapostori, an indigenous African church in Marrapodi/Mandevu township in Lusaka. She also makes cursory observations about girls' initiation rites among non–church members. In the late 1980s, Jan Simonsen observed girls' initiation ceremonies among Mambwe migrants in Lusaka's John Howard township (1993:53–58).

6. Elizabeth Colson reminded me of this.

7. This sentence paraphrases arguments from newspapers: Letters to the Editor, "Adolescents Should Not Attend Kitchen Parties," *Zambia Daily Mail*, November 27, 1984, and M. Mapulanga, "Kitchen Parties Turned into Beer Dens," *Times of Zambia*, December 5, 1985.

8. The title of the first edition of Brelsford's book was *The Tribes of Northern Rhodesia* (1956). The idea of seventy-three tribes dates from a memorandum by J. Moffat Thomson (1934), which accompanied a tribal map drawn by the director of surveys, W. C. Fairweather.

9. A possible exception was reported to me by Anneke Touwen, who in the late 1980s conducted research in Lamba villages off the copperbelt where "Senegalese" men have married local women. The issue at stake was the participation of Lamba women in an ongoing debate about Zambia's gender-biased naturalization laws (personal communication, January 30, 1992). The children of a foreign wife married to a Zambian husband

become Zambian citizens, whereas the children of a Zambian woman married to a foreign husband do not. Ultimately, this issue has less to do with ethnicity than with civil rights and economic access.

5. Private Troubles and Public Issues

1. Damages are fines paid for impregnating a young woman.
2. According to information provided by Elizabeth Colson.
3. This practice appears to differ from that observed by Elizabeth Colson in the Tonga-speaking local courts in the Southern Province in the early 1970s. She reports that justices interrupted litigants, telling them "to stick to facts, not to digress, and that only the issues cited in the summons might be raised" (1976:26–27).
4. In 1988, I sat in on court proceedings and studied an entire year's court records (April 1987–May 1988), making a list of all cases brought in by Mtendere residents and taking notes on particular disputes. The court records for this period contained approximately six hundred cases, among which I took notes concerning one hundred that involved Mtendere residents. The court records do not indicate ethnicity but list place of birth, such as Lusaka or the village, and chief's area, in which the parties were born. The majority of names that appear in the cases in this chapter are common in the Eastern Province among such groups as Nsenga, Chewa, Tumbuka, and Ngoni. Among the names appearing in this chapter that are used in other regions are Mutale and Mwila (Bemba), Poloti (Lamba or Kaonde), Sitali (Lozi), Sinyinda (Tonga or Lozi); I am uncertain about the derivation of Nfonse.
5. Parpart notes a very similar situation in her study of Epstein's court records from the copperbelt 1950–1955 (Parpart 1988:127).
6. In 1987, one U.S. dollar was worth around eight Kwacha (K).
7. Epstein suggests that *ihuli* (plur. *amahuli*) on the copperbelt in the 1950s might derive from the Afrikaans word *hoer* ("whore") (1981:311).
8. Personal communication, letter of November 25, 1985.
9. One recent case that attracted dramatic attention involved widows of the Zambia National Football Team, who perished in an air disaster in Gabon in 1993. In a march to State House, widows complained of greedy relatives seizing their belongings. This practice, they argued, was "a sordid reminder that the nation is still bogged down in a primitive culture which condones harassment of widows and children" (*Times of Zambia*, July 31, 1993). For discussion, see Nkwilimba and Clarke (1994).
10. Information campaigns and lobbying activity in both rural areas and towns were carried out by women's groups before the new act was passed, especially by the Zambia Association for Research and Development (ZARD). See, for example, Longwe and Clarke (1990). The Intestate Succession Act of 1989 gives the surviving children the highest priority

among the beneficiaries. They are entitled to 50 percent of the estate. The
surviving spouse and parents have the next highest priority. They are
entitled to equal shares.

6. City Limits?

1. Forced repatriation to the countryside ceased to be an issue of public discussion in December 1990 when former president Kaunda amended the
constitution to allow other parties to function and elections were scheduled.

2. Women's use of "love medicine" in order to enhance their sexual attrac-
tiveness to men has been discussed by Keller (1978) and Jules-Rosette
(1981:129–63). As a result of the growing incidence of AIDS in Zambia,
men's preference for "dry sex" is drawing some attention. Women facilitate "dry sex" by ingesting herbs that dry out the vagina. For a discussion of problems entailed in this practice, see Nyirenda (1992).

3. Almost half of Weinberger's sample of ninety-three households in
Mtendere in 1990 were tenants. Her sample was categorized by women's
trading activity and composed of around 40 percent women who traded
in the market, 40 percent in the streets, and 20 percent from homes and
yards (1991:2–3 and table 1; 1992:6).

4. Crime statistics are far too unreliable to demonstrate the pervasive sense
of insecurity in urban Zambia. For want of a better indication I quote an
excerpt from the U.S. State Department Travel Advisory: "Crime is high
and travelers should take basic precautions. Travel at night should be
avoided even on major city streets and main highways. Except for airlines
public transport is unreliable and unsafe" (United States Department of
State 1988).

5. I was not in Zambia during that period. This paragraph paraphrases observations by Elisabeth Weinberger (personal communication, July 3, 1991).

7. The Makings of a Research Project

1. I am grateful to the late Jaap van Velsen for encouraging me to pursue
this line of research.

2. Ann Schlyter, who began studying thirty-six houses in George township in Lusaka in 1969, found the original builders still living in nine of
these houses when she returned in 1985—that is, twenty-five years
after her initial observations (Schlyter 1986:4).

3. Long-term field research has given rise to a special body of literature,
especially on changing rural livelihoods, among which some of the most
well-known works are Colson (1971), Colson and Scudder (1975, 1988),
Foster et al. (1978), Scudder (1983), and Scudder and Colson (1978). For
long-term urban research especially concerned with questions of housing, see Schlyter (1991b).

Bibliography

Ambler, Charles. 1990. "Alcohol, Racial Segregation, and Popular Politics in Northern Rhodesia." *Journal of African History* 31:295–313.

Amis, Philip. 1984. "Squatters or Tenants: The Commercialisation of Unauthorised Housing in Nairobi." *World Development* 12, no. 1: 87–96.

———. 1990. "Key Themes in Contemporary African Urbanisation." In P. Amis and P. Lloyd, eds., *Housing Africa's Urban Poor*, pp. 1–31. Manchester: Manchester University Press.

Amis, Philip, and Peter Lloyd, eds. 1990. *Housing Africa's Urban Poor*. Manchester: Manchester University Press.

Appadurai, Arjun. 1990. "Disjuncture and Difference in the Global Cultural Economy." *Public Culture* 2, no. 2: 1–24.

Argyle, John. 1991. "*Kalela, Beni, Asafo, Ingoma,* and the Rural-Urban Dichotomy." In A. D. Spiegel and P. A. McAllister, eds., *Tradition and Transition in Southern Africa: Festschrift for Philip and Iona Mayer*, pp. 65–86. Johannesburg: Witwatersrand University Press.

Armor, M. 1958. *Unauthorised Locations in Lusaka Urban District.* Lusaka: Boma.

Armstrong, William, and Terence G. McGee. 1985. *Theatres of Accumulation: Studies in Asian and Latin American Urbanization.* London: Methuen.

Ashbaugh, Leslie. 1996. "The Great East Road: Gender, Generation, and Urban-to-Rural Migration in the Eastern Province of Zambia." Ph.D. diss., Northwestern University.

Bamberger, Michael, Biswapriya Sanyal, and Nelson Valverde. 1982. *Evaluation of Site and Services Projects: The Experience from Lusaka, Zambia.* World Bank Staff Working Paper no. 548. Washington, D.C.

Banda, Gabriel. 1990. *Adjusting to Adjustment in Zambia: Women's and Young People's Responses to a Changing Economy.* Oxfam Research Paper no. 4. Oxfam UK and Ireland.

Bardouille, Raj. 1981. "The Sexual Division of Labour in the Urban Informal Sector: Case Studies of Some Townships in Lusaka." *African Social Research* 32:29–54.

Barnes, Sandra T. 1990. "Women, Property, and Power." In P. R. Sanday and R. G. Goodenough, eds. *Beyond the Second Sex: New Directions in the Anthropology of Gender*, pp. 255–80. Philadelphia: University of Pennsylvania Press.

Barth, Fredrik. 1967. "On the Study of Social Change." *American Anthropologist* 69, no. 6: 661–69.

Bates, Robert. 1976. *Rural Responses to Industrialization: A Case Study of Village Zambia*. New Haven: Yale University Press.

Bates, Robert H., and Paul Collier. 1993. "The Politics and Economics of Policy Reform in Zambia." In R. H. Bates and A. O. Krueger, eds., *Political and Economic Interactions in Economic Policy Reform: Evidence from Eight Countries*, pp. 387–443. London: Blackwell.

Bates, Robert H., and Anne O. Krueger, eds. 1993. *Political and Economic Interactions in Economic Policy Reform: Evidence from Eight Countries*. London: Blackwell.

Becker, Charles M., Andrew M. Hamer, and Andrew R. Morrison. 1994. *Beyond Urban Bias in Africa: Urbanization in an Era of Structural Adjustment*. Portsmouth, N.H.: Heinemann.

Berger, Elena L. 1974. *Labour, Race, and Colonial Rule: The Copperbelt from 1924 to Independence*. Oxford: Clarendon Press.

Berry, Sara. 1985. *Fathers Work for Their Sons: Accumulation, Mobility, and Class Formation in an Extended Yoruba Community*. Berkeley: University of California Press.

——. 1989. "Social Institutions and Access to Resources." *Africa* 19, no. 1: 41–55.

Bettison, David. 1959. *Numerical Data on Urban Dwellers in Lusaka, Northern Rhodesia*. Rhodes-Livingstone Communications no. 16.

Boswell, David M. 1969. "Personal Crises and the Mobilization of the Social Network." In J. C. Mitchell, ed., *Social Networks in Urban Situations*, pp. 245–96. Manchester: Manchester University Press.

Bradley, Kenneth. [1935] 1981. "Lusaka, the New Capital of Northern Rhodesia." *IN SITU: Journal of the Zambia Institute of Architects* 36:3–24.

Brelsford, Vernon. 1956. *The Tribes of Northern Rhodesia*. Lusaka: Government Printer.

——. 1965. *The Tribes of Zambia*, 2nd ed. Lusaka: Government Printer.

Bromley, Ray, and Chris Gerry, eds. 1979. *Casual Work and Poverty in Third World Cities*. New York: John Wiley.

Browne, G. St. Orde. 1933. *The African Labourer*. London: Oxford University Press.

Burawoy, Michael. 1972. *The Colour of Class on the Copper Mines: From African Advancement to Zambianization*. Zambian Papers no. 7. Institute for African Studies, University of Zambia.

Butler, L. G. 1958. "A Lusaka African Community: Chilenje." Parts 1 and 2. *Northern Rhodesia Journal* 3, no. 5: 442–48 and no. 6: 534–40.

Castells, Manuel. 1977. *The Urban Question: A Marxist Approach.* Cambridge: MIT Press.

Chanock, Martin. 1985. *Law, Custom, and Social Order: The Colonial Experience in Malawi and Zambia.* Cambridge: Cambridge University Press.

———. 1991. "A Peculiar Sharpness: An Essay on Property in the History of Customary Law in Colonial Africa." *Journal of African History* 32:65–88.

Clark, Gracia, ed. 1988. *Traders Versus the State: Anthropological Approaches to Unofficial Economies.* Boulder: Westview Press.

Cliffe, Lionel. 1979. "Labour Migration and Peasant Differentiation: Zambian Experiences." In B. Turok, ed., *Development in Zambia*, pp. 149–69. London: ZED Press.

Coldham, Simon. 1983. "The Law of Succession in Zambia: Recent Proposals for Reform." *Journal of African Law* 27, no. 2: 162–68.

———. 1989. "The Wills and Administration of Estates Act 1989 and the Intestate Succession Act 1989 of Zambia." *Journal of African Law* 33, no. 1: 128–32.

Collins, John. 1986. "Lusaka: The Historical Development of a Planned Capital, 1931–1970." In G. J. Williams, ed., *Lusaka and Its Environs: A Geographical Study of a Planned Capital City in Tropical Africa*, pp. 95–137. Handbook Series no. 9. Lusaka: Zambia Geographical Association.

Colson, Elizabeth. 1971. *The Social Consequences of Resettlement.* Manchester: Manchester University Press.

———. 1976. "From Chief's Court to Local Court." In M. J. Aronoff, ed., *Freedom and Constraint: A Memorial Tribute to Max Gluckman*, pp. 15–29. Assen: Van Gorcum.

———. 1980. "The Resilience of Matriliny: Gwembe and Plateau Tonga Adaptations." In L. S. Cordell and S. J. Beckerman, eds., *The Versatility of Kinship*, pp. 359–74. New York: Academic Press.

———. 1984. "The Reordering of Experience: Anthropological Involvement with Time." *Journal of Anthropological Research* 40, no. 1: 1–13.

Colson, Elizabeth, and Thayer Scudder. 1975. "New Economic Relationships Between the Gwembe Valley and the Line of Rail." In D. Parkin, ed., *Town and Country in Central and Eastern Africa*, pp. 190–210. London: Oxford University Press.

———. 1988. *For Prayer and Profit: The Ritual, Economic, and Social Importance of Beer in Gwembe District, Zambia, 1950–1982.* Stanford: Stanford University Press.

Comaroff, John L. 1980. "Bridewealth and the Control of Ambiguity in a Tswana Chiefdom." In J. Comaroff, ed., *The Meaning of Marriage Payments*, pp. 161–96. New York: Academic Press.

———. 1987. "Sui Genderis: Feminism, Kinship Theory, and Structural 'Domains.' " In J. Collier and S. Yanagisako, eds., *Gender and Kinship:*

Essays Toward a Unified Analysis, pp. 53–85. Stanford: Stanford University Press.

Comaroff, John L., and Simon Roberts. 1977. "Marital and Extra-Marital Sexuality: The Dialectics of Legal Change among the Kgatla." *Journal of African Law* 21:97–123.

Commins, Stephen, Michael Lofchie, and Rhys Payne, eds. 1986. *Africa's Agrarian Crisis*. Boulder: Lynne Rienner Publishers.

Cooper, Frederick, ed. 1983. "Urban Space, Industrial Time and Wage Labor in Africa." In F. Cooper, ed., *Struggle for the City: Migrant Labor, Capital and the State in Africa*, pp. 7–50. Beverly Hills: Sage Publications.

Copeman, E. A. 1956. "Memoirs of Abandoned Bomas." *Northern Rhodesia Journal* 3, no. 2: 139–41.

Crehan, Kate, and Achim von Oppen. 1988. "Understandings of Development: An Arena of Struggle." *Sociologica Ruralis* 28, no. 2/3: 113–45.

Dahl, Gudrun, and Anders Hjort. 1984. "Development as Message and Meaning." *Ethnos* 29, no. 3/4: 165–84.

Davison, Jean, ed. 1988. *Agriculture, Women, and Land: The African Experience*. Boulder: Westview Press.

Doxiades Associates. 1969. *A Special Program of Action for Resettlement of Squatters. I. Lusaka*. Lusaka: Ministry of Local Government and Housing.

Drakakis-Smith, David, ed. 1990. *Economic Growth and Urbanization in Developing Areas*. London: Routledge.

Drourega, S. J. 1927. "Initiation of a Girl in the Acenga Tribe Katondwe Mission, Luengwa District, Northern Rhodesia." *Anthropos* 22:620–21.

Dumont, Jean-Paul. 1992. *Visayan Vignettes: Ethnographic Traces of a Philippine Island*. Chicago: University of Chicago Press.

Economist Intelligence Unit (EIU). 1992. *Zambia: Country Profile 1992–1993*. London: Business International Limited.

Edwards, M. 1990. "Rental Housing and the Urban Poor: Africa and Latin America Compared." In P. Amis and P. Lloyd, eds., *Housing Africa's Urban Poor*, pp. 253–79. Manchester: Manchester University Press.

Elson, Diane, ed. 1991. *Male Bias in the Development Process*. Manchester: Manchester University Press.

Epstein, Arnold L. 1953. "The Role of African Courts in Urban Communities of the Northern Rhodesia Copperbelt." *Rhodes-Livingstone Journal* 13:1–17.

——. 1958. *Politics in an Urban African Community*. Manchester: Manchester University Press.

——. 1981. *Urbanization and Kinship: The Domestic Domain on the Copperbelt of Zambia, 1950–1956*. New York: Academic Press.

Fabian, Johannes. 1983. *Time and the Other: How Anthropology Makes Its Object*. New York: Columbia University Press.

Ferguson, James. 1985. "The Bovine Mystique: Power, Property, and Livestock in Rural Lesotho." *Man*, n.s. 20: 647–74.

———. 1990a. *The Anti-Politics Machine: "Development," Depoliticization, and Bureaucratic Power in Lesotho*. Cambridge: Cambridge University Press.

———. 1990b. "Mobile Workers, Modernist Narratives: A Critique of the Historiography of Transition on the Zambian Copperbelt." Parts 1 and 2. *Journal of Southern African Studies* 16, no. 3: 385–412 and no. 4: 603–21.

Fetter, Bruce. 1984. "The Missing Migrants: African Seeds in the Demographer's Field." *History in Africa* 11:99–111.

Flanagan, William G. 1993. *Contemporary Urban Sociology*. Cambridge: Cambridge University Press.

Folbre, Nancy. 1986. "Hearts and Spades: Paradigms of Household Economics." *World Development* 14, no. 2: 245–55.

Fortes, Meyer. 1949. "Time and Social Structure: An Ashanti Case Study." In M. Fortes, *Social Structure*. Reprinted in M. Fortes. 1970. *Time and Social Structure and Other Essays*. London: Atlone Press.

———. 1958. "Introduction." In J. Goody, ed., *The Developmental Cycle in Domestic Groups*, pp. 1–14. Cambridge: Cambridge University Press.

Foster, George, Thayer Scudder, Elizabeth Colson, and Robert Van Kemper, eds. 1978. *Long-Term Field Research in Social Anthroplogy*. New York: Academic Press.

Freund, Paul J. 1986. "Health Care in a Declining Economy." *Social Science and Medicine* 23, no. 9: 875–88.

Fry, James. 1979. *Employment and Income Distribution in the African Economy*. London: Croom Helm.

Geisler, Gisela. 1992. "Who Is Losing Out? Structural Adjustment, Gender, and the Agricultural Sector in Zambia." *Journal of Modern African Studies* 30, no. 1: 113–39.

Geisler, Gisela, and Karen Tranberg Hansen. 1994. "Structural Adjustment, the Rural-Urban Interface, and Gender Relations in Zambia." In S. Pressman, N. Aslanbeigui, and G. Sommerfield, eds., *Women in the Age of Economic Transformation: Gender Impacts of Reform in Post-Socialist and Developing Countries*, pp. 95–112. London: Routledge.

Gertzel, Cherry (with Carolyn Baylies and Morris Szeftel). 1984. *The Dynamics of the One-Party State in Zambia*. Manchester: Manchester University Press.

Geschiere, Peter. 1992. "Kinship, Witchcraft, and 'the Market': Hybrid Patterns in Cameroonian Societies." In R. Dilley, ed., *Contesting Markets: Analyses of Ideology, Discourse, and Practice*, pp. 159–79. Edinburgh: Edinburgh University Press.

Gibbon, Peter, Kjell J. Havnevik, and Kenneth Hermele. 1993. *A Blighted Harvest: The World Bank and African Agriculture in the 1980s*. Trenton: Africa World Press.

Giddens, Anthony. [1979] 1983. *Central Problems in Social Theory: Action, Structure, and Contradiction in Social Analysis*. Reprint, Berkeley: University of California Press.

Gilbert, Alan. 1993. *In Search of a Home: Rental and Shared Housing in Latin America*. Tucson: University of Arizona Press.

Gilbert, Alan, and Josef Gugler, eds. 1992. *Cities, Poverty, and Development: Urbanization in the Third World*. Oxford: Oxford University Press.

Gladwin, Christina, ed. 1991. *Structural Adjustment and African Women Farmers*. Gainesville: University of Florida Press.

Gluckman, Max. 1945. "The Seven Year Research Plan of the Rhodes-Livingstone Institute." *Rhodes-Livingstone Journal* 4:1–32.

——. 1961. "Anthropological Problems Arising from the African Industrial Revolution." In A. Southall, ed., *Social Change in Modern Africa*, pp. 67–82. Oxford: Oxford University Press.

Goody, Jack, ed. 1958. *The Developmental Cycle in Domestic Groups*. Cambridge: Cambridge University Press.

Gugler, Josef. 1988. "Overurbanization Reconsidered." In J. Gugler, ed., *The Urbanization of the Third World*, pp. 74–92. Oxford: Oxford University Press.

Gugler, Josef, and William G. Flanagan. 1978. *Urbanization and Social Change in West Africa*. Cambridge: Cambridge University Press.

Guyer, Jane I. 1981. "Household and Community in African Studies." *African Studies Review* 24, no. 2/3: 87–137.

——. 1988. "The Multiplication of Labor: Historical Methods in the Study of Gender and Agricultural Change in Modern Africa." *Current Anthropology* 29:247–72.

——, ed. 1987. *Feeding African Cities*. Manchester: Manchester University Press.

Guyer, Jane I., and Pauline Peters. 1987. Introduction to J. Guyer and P. Peters, eds., *Conceptualizing the Household: Issues of Theory and Policy in Africa*, pp. 197–214. Special issue of *Development and Change* 18, no. 2.

Hannerz, Ulf. 1980. *Exploring the City: Inquiries Toward an Urban Anthropology*. New York: Columbia University Press.

Hansen, Karen Tranberg. 1975. "Married Women and Work: Explorations from an Urban Case Study." *African Social Research* 20:777–99.

——. 1980. "The Urban Informal Sector as a Development Issue: Poor Women and Work in Lusaka, Zambia." *Urban Anthropology* 9:199–225.

——. 1982a. "Lusaka's Squatters: Past and Present." *African Studies Review* 25, no. 2/3: 117–36.

——. 1982b. "Planning Productive Work for Married Women in a Low-Income Settlement in Lusaka: The Case for a Small-Scale Handicrafts Industry." *African Social Research* 33:211–23.

——. 1984. "Negotiating Sex and Gender in Urban Zambia." *Journal of Southern African Studies* 10, no. 2: 219–38.

——. 1985. "Budgeting Against Uncertainty: Cross-Class and Trans-Ethnic Redistribution Mechanisms in Urban Zambia." *African Urban Studies* 21:65–74.

——. 1987. *"The Work History": Disaggregating the Changing Terms of Poor Women's Entry into Lusaka's Labor Force*. Working Papers on Women in International Development no. 134. East Lansing: Michigan State University.

——. 1989a. *Distant Companions: Servants and Employers in Zambia, 1900–1985*. Ithaca: Cornell University Press.

——. 1989b. "The Black Market and Women Traders in Lusaka, Zambia." In J. L. Parpart and K. Staudt, eds., *Women and the State in Africa*, pp. 143–59. Boulder: Lynne Rienner Publishers.

——. 1990. "Labor Migration and Urban Child Labor During the Colonial Period in Zambia." In B. Fetter, ed., *Demography from Scanty Evidence: Central Africa in the Colonial Era*, pp. 219–34. Boulder: Lynne Rienner Publishers.

——. 1991. "After Copper Town: The Past in the Present in Urban Zambia." *Journal of Anthropological Research* 47, no. 4: 441–56.

——. 1992. "Gender and Housing: The Case of Domestic Service in Lusaka, Zambia." *Africa* 62, no. 2: 248–65.

——. 1994. "Dealing with Used Clothing: *Salaula* and the Construction of Identity in Zambia's Third Republic." *Public Culture* 6, no. 3: 503–23.

——. Forthcoming. "Washing Dirty Laundry in Public: Local Court, Custom, and Gender Relations in Post-Colonial Zambia." In Kathleen Sheldon, ed., *Courtyards, Markets, and City Streets: Urban Women in Africa*. Boulder: Westview Press.

Hansen, Karen Tranberg, and Leslie Ashbaugh. 1991. "Women on the Front Line: Development Issues in Southern Africa." *Women and International Development Journal* 2:205–40.

Haraven, Tamara K. 1982. *Family Time and Industrial Time*. Cambridge: Cambridge University Press.

Harries-Jones, Peter. 1975. *Freedom and Labour: Mobilization and Political Control on the Zambian Copperbelt*. Oxford: Blackwell.

——. 1977. " 'A House Should Have a Ceiling': Unintended Consequences of Development Planning in Zambia." In S. Wallman, ed., *Perceptions of Development*, pp. 138–53. Cambridge: Cambridge University Press.

Hart, Keith. 1973. "Informal Income Opportunities and Urban Employment in Ghana." *Journal of Modern African Studies* 11:61–89.

Harvey, David. 1973. *Social Justice and the City*. Baltimore: Johns Hopkins University Press.

Heald, Suzette. 1991. "Tobacco, Time, and the Household Economy in Two Kenyan Societies: The Teso and the Kuria." *Comparative Studies in Society and History* 33, no. 1: 130–57.

Heisler, Helmuth. 1974. *Urbanisation and the Government of Migration*. London: C. Hurst.

Higginson, John. 1989. *A Working Class in the Making: Belgian Colonial Labor Policy, Private Enterprise, and the African Mineworker, 1907–1951*. Madison: University of Wisconsin Press.

Himonga, Chuma N. 1985. "Family Property Disputes: The Predicament of Women and Children in a Zambian Urban Community." Ph.D. diss., London School of Economics and Political Science.

———. 1987. "Property Disputes in Law and Practice: Dissolution of Marriage in Zambia." In A. Armstrong, ed., *Women and Law in Southern Africa*, pp. 56–84. Harare: Zimbabwe Publishing House.

Hobson, Dick. 1979. *Showtime: A History of the Agricultural and Commercial Society of Zambia*. Lusaka: Agricultural and Commercial Society of Zambia.

———. 1985. "Autobiographical Notes by Vernon Brelsford, Edited and Introduced by Dick Hobson." Unpublished manuscript.

Hoek-Smit, Marja. 1982. *Community Participation in Squatter Upgrading in Zambia: The Role of the American Friends Service Committee in the Lusaka Housing Project*. Philadelphia: American Friends Service Committee.

Hoppers, Wim. 1985. *From School to Work: Youth, Non-Formal Training and Employment in Lusaka*. The Hague: Centre for the Study of Education in Developing Countries.

International Labour Organisation. 1972. *Employment, Incomes and Equality: A Strategy for Increasing Productive Employment in Kenya*. Geneva: ILO.

———. 1977. *Narrowing the Gaps: Planning for Basic Needs and Productive Employment in Zambia*. Addis Ababa: ILO/JASPA (Jobs and Skills Programme for Africa).

———. 1986. *Youth Employment and Youth Employment Programmes in Africa. A Comparative Sub-Regional Study: The Case of Zambia*. Addis Ababa: ILO/JASPA.

Jackman, M. E. 1973. *Recent Population Movements in Zambia. Some Aspects of the 1969 Census*. Zambian Papers no. 8. Institute for African Studies, University of Zambia.

Jamal, Vali, and John Weeks. 1988. "The Vanishing Rural-Urban Gap in Sub-Saharan Africa." *International Labour Review* 127, no. 3: 271–92.

Jules-Rosette, Bennetta. 1975. "Marrapodi: An Independent Religious Community in Transition." *African Studies Review* 18:1–16.

———. 1979. "Alternative Urban Adaptations: Zambian Cottage Industries as Sources of Social and Economic Innovation." *Human Organization* 38, no. 3: 225–38.

———. 1980. "Changing Aspects of Women's Initiation in Southern Africa: An Exploratory Study." *Canadian Journal of African Studies* 13, no. 3: 389–405.

———. 1981. *Symbols of Change: Urban Transition in a Zambian Community*. Norwood, N.J.: Ablex Publishing Corporation.

Kasongo, Anthony B., and A. Graham Tipple. 1990. "An Analysis of Policy Towards Squatters in Kitwe, Zambia." *Third World Planning Review* 12, no. 2: 147–65.

Kay, George. 1967. *A Social Geography of Zambia*. London: University of London Press.

Keller, Bonnie B. 1978. "Marriage and Medicine: Women's Search for Love and Luck." *African Social Research* 26:489–505.

———. 1979. "Marriage by Elopement." *African Social Research* 27:565–85.

King, Anthony D. 1976. *Colonial Urban Development: Culture, Social Power, and Environment*. London: Routledge.

———. 1989. "Colonialism, Urbanism, and the Capitalist World Economy." *International Journal of Urban and Regional Research* 13, no. 1: 1–18.

———. 1990. *Urbanism, Colonialism, and the World Economy: Cultural and Spatial Foundations of the World System*. London: Routledge.

King, Kenneth J. 1977. *The African Artisan: Education and the Informal Sector in Kenya*. London: Heinemann.

Larsson, Anita, and Ann Schlyter. 1993. *Gender Contracts and Housing Conflicts in Southern Africa*. National Swedish Institute for Building Research, Research Report SB:66.

Lawrence, Denise L., and Setha M. Low. 1990. "The Built Environment and Spatial Form." *Annual Review of Anthropology* 19:453–505.

Leeds, Anthony. 1974. "Housing-Settlement Types, Arrangements for Living, Proletarianization, and the Social Structure of the City." In W. A. Cornelius and F. M. Trueblood, eds., *Latin American Urban Research*, 4:67–100. Beverly Hills: Sage Publications.

Lemarchand, Rene. 1988. "The State, the Parallel Economy, and the Changing Structure of Patronage Systems." In D. Rothchild and N. Chazan, eds., *The Precarious Balance: State and Society in Africa*, pp. 149–70. Boulder: Westview Press.

Liedholm, Carl, and Donald Mead. 1987. *Small-Scale Industries in Developing Countries: Empirical Evidence and Policy Implications*. Michigan State University Development Paper no. 8. East Lansing: Michigan State University.

Lipton, Michael. 1977. *Why Poor People Stay Poor: Urban Bias in World Development*. Cambridge: Harvard University Press.

Longwe, Sara H. 1990. "Lessons from the Struggle to Give Women Equality Under the Law: Reforming the Law on Inheritance in Zambia." Paper presented at Women, Law and Development Conference on Networking for Empowerment in Africa, Harare, Zimbabwe.

Longwe, Sara H., and R. Clarke. 1990. "Research Strategies for Promoting Law Reform: Lessons from Changing the Law on Inheritance in Zambia." Paper presented at seminar on research methodology, organized by the Women and Law in Southern Africa Research Project, Harare, Zimbabwe.

MacGaffey, Janet. 1983. "How to Survive and Become Rich Amidst Devastation: The Second Economy in Zaire." *African Affairs* 82, no. 328: 351–66.

———. 1991. *The Real Economy of Zaire*. Philadelphia: University of Philadelphia Press.

Macmillan, Hugh. 1993. "The Historiography of Transition on the Zambian Copperbelt—Another View." *Journal of Southern African Studies* 19, no. 4: 681–712.

Maembe, Edward, and Jim Tomecko. 1987. *Economic Promotion in an Integrated Upgrading Project: The Case of Kalingalinga Township, Lusaka*. IAS Commissioned Studies Reports no. 1, Institute for African Studies, University of Zambia.

Magubane, Bernhard. 1969. "Pluralism and Conflict Situations in Africa: A New Look." *African Social Research* 7:529–54.

——. 1971. "A Critical Look at the Indices Used in the Study of Social Change in Colonial Africa." *Current Anthropology* 12:419–31, 439–45.

Mair, Lucy. 1951. "A Yao Girl's Initiation." *Man* 51:60–63.

Martin, Antony. 1972. *Minding Their Own Business: Zambia's Struggle Against Western Control*. London: Hutchinson.

Martin, Richard J. 1974. "Housing in Lusaka." In N. R. Hawkesworth, ed., *Local Government in Zambia*, pp. 53–94. Lusaka: City Council.

Matejko, Alexander. 1976. "Blacks and Whites in Zambia." *Ethnicity* 3, no. 4: 317–37.

Matongo, Albert B. K. 1992. "Popular Culture in a Colonial Society: Another Look at Beni and Kalela Dances on the Copperbelt, 1930–64." In S. N. Chipungu, ed., *Guardians in Their Time: Experience of Zambians Under Colonial Rule, 1890–1964*, pp. 180–217. London: Macmillan.

McPherson, Michael A. 1991. "Micro and Small-Scale Enterprises in Zimbabwe. Results of a Country-Wide Survey." GEMINI Technical Report no. 25.

Mindolo Ecumenical Foundation. 1991. *A Seminar on Widowhood, Law of Succession, and the Church in Zambia*. Kitwe: Mindolo Ecumenical Foundation.

Mills, C. Wright. [1959] 1970. *The Sociological Imagination*. Reprint, Harmondsworth, UK: Penguin Books.

Mingione, Enzo. 1991. *Fragmented Societies: A Sociology of Economic Life Beyond the Market Paradigm*. London: Blackwell.

Miracle, Marvin. 1962. "Apparent Changes in the Structure of African Commerce, Lusaka 1954–1959." *Northern Rhodesia Journal* 5, no. 2: 170–75.

Mitchell, J. Clyde. 1956. *The Kalela Dance*. Rhodes-Livingstone Papers no. 27.

——. 1959. "Labour Migration in Africa South of the Sahara: The Causes of Labour Migration." *Bulletin of the Inter-African Labour Institute* 6, no. 1: 12–47.

——. 1987. *Cities, Society, and Social Perception: A Central African Perspective*. Oxford: Clarendon Press.

Moore, Henrietta L. 1988. *Feminism and Anthropology*. Minneapolis: University of Minnesota Press.

Moore, Henrietta L., and Megan Vaughan. 1987. "Cutting Down Trees: Women, Nutrition, and Agricultural Change in the Northern Province of Zambia, 1920–1986." *African Affairs* 86:523–41.

——. 1994. *Cutting Down Trees: Gender, Nutrition, and Agricultural Change in the Northern Province of Zambia, 1890–1990.* Portsmouth, N.H.: Heinemann.

Moser, C. A., and G. Kalton. [1958] 1971. *Survey Methods in Social Investigation*, 2nd ed. London: Heinemann Educational.

Moser, Caroline O. N. 1978. "Informal Sector or Petty Commodity Production: Dualism or Dependence in Urban Development?" *World Development* 6, no. 9/10: 1041–65.

––, ed. 1987. *Women, Human Settlements, and Housing.* London: Tavistock.

Mulwanda, Mpanjilwa, and Emmanuel Mutale. 1994. "Never Mind the People, the Shanties Must Go: The Politics of Urban Land in Zambia." *Cities* 11, no. 5: 303–11.

Mumba, Norah M. 1992. *A Song in the Night: A Personal Account of Widowhood in Zambia.* Lusaka: Multimedia Publications.

Munachonga, Monica. 1988. "Income Allocation and Marriage Options in Urban Zambia." In D. Dwyer and J. Bruce, eds., *A Home Divided: Women and Income in the Third World*, pp. 173–94. Stanford: Stanford University Press.

Muntemba, Maud. 1977. "Thwarted Development: A Case Study of Economic Change in Kabwe Rural District of Zambia, 1902–70." In R. Palmer and N. Parsons., eds., *The Roots of Rural Poverty in Central and Southern Africa*, pp. 345–64. Berkeley: University of California Press.

Murray, Colin. 1981. *Families Divided: The Impact of Migrant Labour in Lesotho.* Cambridge: Cambridge University Press.

——. 1987. "Class, Gender, and the Household: The Development Cycle in Southern Africa." *Development and Change* 18:235–49.

Mwanza, Iris. 1990. " 'Give Me a Little Peace of Mind.' The Law of Succession and the Intestate Succession Act, 1989." Unpublished obligatory essay submitted in partial fulfillment of the LL.B. degree to the School of Law, University of Zambia.

Ncube, Welshman. 1987. "Underprivilege and Inequality: The Matrimonial Property Rights of Women in Zimbabwe." In A. Armstrong, ed., *Women and Law in Southern Africa*, pp. 3–34. Harare: Zimbabwe Publishing House.

Nelson, Nicki. 1978/79. "Female-Centered Families: Changing Patterns of Marriage and Family Among Buzaa Brewers of Mathare Valley." *African Urban Studies* 3:85–103.

Netting, Robert McC., Richard Wilk, and Eric J. Arnould, eds. 1984. *Households: Comparative and Historical Studies of the Domestic Group.* Berkeley: University of California Press.

Nkwilimba, Mapanza, and Roy Clarke, eds. 1994. *Gabon Aftermath: The Mistreatment of the Football Widows.* Lusaka: ZARD.

Norwood, H. C. 1975. "Informal Industry in Developing Countries." *Town Planning Review* 46:83–94.

Nyirenda, A. A. 1957. "African Market Vendors in Lusaka, with a Note on the Recent Boycott." *Rhodes-Livingstone Journal* 22:31–63.

Nyirenda, Meya J. 1992. *An Investigation of the Behavioral Aspects of the "Dry Sex" Practice in Lusaka Urban.* Edited by Ilse Mwanza and Nkandu Leo. Lusaka: Society of Women and AIDS in Zambia.

O'Connor, Anthony. 1983. *The African City.* London: Hutchinson.

Onimode, Bade, ed. 1989. *The IMF, the World Bank, and the African Debt.* London: ZED Press.

Palmer, Ingrid. 1991. *Gender and Population in the Adjustment of African Economies: Planning for Change.* Geneva: International Labour Office.

Parpart, Jane L. 1983. *Labor and Capital on the African Copperbelt.* Philadelphia: Temple University Press.

——. 1988. "Sexuality and Power on the Zambian Copperbelt: 1926–1964." In S. B. Stichter and J. L. Parpart, eds., *Patriarchy and Class: African Women in the Home and the Workforce,* pp. 115–38. Boulder: Westview Press.

Parpart, Jane L., and Kathleen Staudt, eds. 1989. *Women and the State in Africa.* Boulder: Westview Press.

Pasteur, David. 1979. *The Management of Squatter Upgrading.* Farnborough: Saxon House.

Peattie, Lisa R. 1987. "An Idea in Good Currency and How It Grew: The Informal Sector." *World Development* 15, no. 7: 851–60.

Perrings, Charles. 1979. *Black Mineworkers in Central Africa: Industrial Strategies and the Evolution of an African Proletariat in the Copperbelt, 1911–41.* New York: Africana.

Peters, Pauline. 1983. "Gender, Development Cycles, and Historical Process: A Critique of Recent Research on Women in Botswana." *Journal of Southern African Studies* 10, no. 1: 100–122.

Phiri, Elizabeth C. 1993. *Violence Against Women in Zambia.* Lusaka: YWCA Council of Zambia.

Portes, Alejandro, Manuel Castells, and Lauren A. Benton, eds. 1989. *The Informal Economy: Studies in Advanced and Less Developed Countries.* Baltimore: Johns Hopkins University Press.

Pottier, Johan. 1988. *Migrants No More: Settlement and Survival in Mambwe Villages, Zambia.* Bloomington: Indiana University Press.

Potts, Deborah, with C. C. Mutambirwa. 1991. "High-Density Housing in Harare: Commodification and Overcrowding." *Third World Planning Review* 13, no. 1: 1–25.

Powdermaker, Hortense. 1962. *Coppertown: Changing Africa. The Human Situation on the Rhodesian Copperbelt.* New York: Harper and Row.

Rakodi, Carole. 1988a. "Upgrading in Chawama, Lusaka: Displacement or Differentiation?" *Urban Studies* 25:297–318.

———. 1988b. "The Local State and Urban Local Government in Zambia." *Public Administration and Development* 8:27–46.

———. 1990. "After the Project Has Ended: The Role of a Non-Governmental Organization in Improving the Conditions of the Urban Poor in Lusaka." *Community Development Journal* 25, no. 1: 9–20.

———. 1991. "Cities and People: Towards a Gender-Aware Urban Planning Process?" *Public Administration and Development* 11:541–59.

Ramphele, Mamphela. 1993. *A Bed Called Home: Life in the Migrant Labour Hostels of Cape Town*. Cape Town: David Philip.

Redclift, Nanneke, and Enzo Mingione, eds. 1985. *Beyond Employment: Household, Gender, and Subsistence*. London: Basil Blackwell.

Republic of Zambia. 1965. Circular 17/65. Ministry of Local Government and Housing.

———. 1966. Aided Self-Help Housing on Site and Service Schemes. Circular 59/66. Ministry of Local Government and Housing.

———. 1967a. Report of the City Engineer to the Housing Committee. May. City of Lusaka.

———. 1967b. Report of the City Engineer to Estates Committee. July. City of Lusaka.

———. 1967c. A Socio-Economic Survey of Kalingalinga. Department of Community Development, Ministry of Co-Operation, Youth and Social Development.

———. 1968. Report of Acting Town Clerk to Site and Service Resettlement Committee. January. City Council.

———. 1969. Urban Budget Survey, Lusaka, Zambia. Lusaka: Central Statistical Office.

———. 1971. *Second National Development Plan, January 1972–December 1976*. Lusaka: Government Printer.

———. 1975. *Self-Help in Action: A Study of Site-and-Service Schemes in Zambia*. Research Study no. 2. Lusaka: National Housing Authority.

———. 1981a. Provision of Community Facilities in the Upgraded and Site-and-Service Areas Under the Lusaka Housing Project Unit. April 14. Council Report by Director of Housing and Social Services to the Social Services Committee.

———. 1981b. *1980 Census of Population and Housing. Preliminary Report*. Lusaka: Central Statistical Office.

———. 1985. *1980 Population and Housing Census of Zambia*. Analytical Report, vol. 3, *Major Findings and Conclusions*. Lusaka: Central Statistical Office.

———. 1990. *1990 Census of Population, Housing and Agriculture*. Preliminary Report. Lusaka: Central Statistical Office.

———. 1991. *Women and Men in Zambia: Facts and Figures*. Lusaka: Central Statistical Office.

Rex, John. 1974. "The Compound, the Reserve, and the Urban Location: The Essential Institutions of Southern African Labour Exploitation." *Southern African Labour Bulletin* 1:4–17.

Richards, Audrey I. 1940. *Bemba Marriage and Present Economic Conditions*. Rhodes-Livingstone Papers no. 4.

——. 1982. *Chisungu: A Girl's Initiation Ceremony among the Bemba of Zambia*, 2nd ed. London: Tavistock.

Roberts, Andrew. 1976. *A History of Zambia*. London: Heinemann.

Roberts, Richard, and Kristin Mann. 1991. "Law in Colonial Africa." In K. Mann and R. Roberts, eds., *Law in Colonial Africa*, pp. 3–58. Portsmouth, N.H.: Heinemann.

Roeber, Carter A. 1995. "Shylocks and Mabisinesi: Trust, Informal Credit, and Commercial Culture in Kabwe, Zambia." Ph.D. diss., Northwestern University.

Rogers, Barbara. 1980. *The Domestication of Women: Discrimination in Developing Countries*. New York: St. Martin's Press.

Roitman, Janet L. 1990. "The Politics of Informal Markets in Sub-Saharan Africa." *Journal of Modern African Studies* 28, no. 4: 671–96.

Rotenberg, Robert, and Gary McDonogh. eds. 1993. *The Cultural Meaning of Urban Space*. Westport, Conn.: Bergin and Garvey.

Rothchild, David, and Naomi Chazan, eds. 1988. *The Precarious Balance: State and Society in Africa*. Boulder: Westview Press.

Rothman, Norman C. 1972. "African Urban Development in the Colonial Period: A Study of Lusaka, 1905–1964." Ph.D. diss., Northwestern University.

Sampson, Richard. [1960] 1982. *So This Was Lusaakas: The Story of the Capital of Zambia to 1964*. Reprint, Lusaka: Multimedia Publications.

Sandbrook, Richard. 1982. *The Politics of Basic Needs: Urban Aspects of Assaulting Poverty in Africa*. Toronto: University of Toronto Press.

——. 1993. *The Politics of Africa's Economic Recovery*. Cambridge: Cambridge University Press.

Sanjek, Roger. 1982. "The Organization of Households in Adabraka: Toward a Wider Comparative Perspective." *Comparative Studies in Society and History* 24, no. 1: 57–103.

Sano, Hans-Otto. 1990. *Big State, Small Farmers: The Search for an Agricultural Strategy for Crisis-Ridden Zambia*. Copenhagen: Centre for Development Research.

Sanyal, Biswapriya. 1981. "Who Gets What, Where, Why, and How: A Critical Look at the Housing Subsidies in Zambia." *Development and Change* 12:409–40.

——. 1991. "Organizing the Self-Employed: The Politics of the Urban Informal Sector." *International Labour Review* 130, no. 1: 39–56.

Sassen, Saskia. 1991. *The Global City*. Princeton: Princeton University Press.

Schlyter, Ann. 1986. "Commercialization of Housing in Upgraded Squatter Areas. A Preliminary Presentation of the Case of George, Lusaka, Zambia." Paper presented at International Research Conference on Housing Policy, the National Swedish Institute for Building Research, Gavle, Sweden, June 10–13, 1986.

———. 1991a. *Twenty Years of Development in George, Zambia*. Stockholm: Swedish Council for Building Research.

———. 1991b. "Time Series Analysis: A Longitudinal Study of Housing Quality in Lusaka." In A. G. Tipple and K. G. Willis, eds., *Housing the Poor in the Developing World: Methods of Analysis, Case Studies, and Policy*, pp. 62–80. London: Routledge.

Schoffeleers, J. M., and I. Linden. 1972. "The Resistance of the Nyau Societies to the Roman Catholic Missions in Colonial Malawi." In T. O. Ranger and I. N. Kimambo, eds., *The Historical Study of African Religion*, pp. 252–73. Berkeley: University of California Press.

Schuster, Ilsa M. Glazer. 1979. *New Women of Lusaka*. Palo Alto: Mayfield Publishing.

———. 1982. "Marginal Lives: Conflict and Contradiction in the Position of Female Traders in Lusaka, Zambia." In E. G. Bay, ed., *Women and Work in Africa*, pp. 105–26. Boulder: Westview Press.

Scudder, Thayer. 1983. "Economic Downturn and Community Unravelling." *Culture and Agriculture* 18:16–19.

Scudder, Thayer, and Elizabeth Colson. 1978. "Long-Term Field Research in Gwembe Valley, Zambia." In George Foster, Thayer Scudder, Elizabeth Colson, and Robert Van Kemper, eds., *Long-Term Field Research in Social Anthropology*, pp. 227–54. New York: Academic Press.

Seidman, Ann. 1974. "The Distorted Growth of Import-Substitution Industry: The Zambian Case." *Journal of Modern African Studies* 12:601–31.

Serpell, Robert. 1993. *The Significance of Schooling: Life-Journeys in an African Society*. Cambridge: Cambridge University Press.

Sethuraman, S. V. 1981. *The Urban Informal Sector in Developing Countries*. Geneva: International Labour Organisation.

Seymour, Anthony. 1976. "Squatters, Migrants, and the Urban Poor: A Study of Attitudes Towards Inequality with Special Reference to Squatter Settlements in Lusaka, Zambia." Ph.D. diss., University of Sussex.

Simmance, Alan F. J. 1974. "Urbanization in Zambia." *Journal of Administration Overseas* 13:498–509.

Simons, Jack H. 1979. "Zambia's Urban Situation." In B. Turok, ed., *Development in Zambia*, pp. 1–25. London: ZED Press.

Simonsen, Jan K. 1993. "Uwinga: An Exploratory Study of Mambwe Marriage Rituals." Cand. polit. thesis, University of Oslo.

Siyolwe, Yolisha W. 1994. "Makwebo Women: A Study of the Socio-Economic Activities of a Select Group of Women Traders in Lusaka, Zambia, 1980–1990." Master of Letters thesis, University of Oxford.

Skinner, Reinhard J., and Michael J. Rodell, eds. 1983. *People, Poverty and Shelter: Problems of Self-Help Housing in the Third World.* London: Methuen.

Smith, Joan, Immanuel Wallerstein, and Hans Dieter Evers, eds. 1984. *Households and the World Economy.* Beverly Hills: Sage Publications.

Smith, Joan, and Immanuel Wallerstein, eds. 1992. *Creating and Transforming Households.* Cambridge: Cambridge University Press.

Southall, Aidan. 1961. "Introductory Summary." In A. Southall, ed., *Social Change in Modern Africa*, pp. 1–46. London: Oxford University Press.

Spiegel, Andrew, Vanessa Watson, and Peter Wilkinson. 1994. "Domestic Fluidity and Movement Patterns Among Cape Town's African Population: Some Implications for Housing Policy." Paper presented at the Centre for African Studies, University of Cape Town.

Stadler, A. W. 1979. "Birds in the Cornfield: Squatter Movements in Johannesburg, 1944–1947." *Journal of Southern African Studies* 6, no. 1: 93–123.

Starr, June, and Jane F. Collier. 1989. "Introduction: Dialogues in Legal Anthropology." In J. Starr and J. F. Collier, eds., *History and Power in the Study of Law: New Directions in the Study of Law*, pp. 1–28. Ithaca: Cornell University Press.

Stoller, Paul. 1994. "Ethnographies as Texts/Ethnographers as Griots." *American Ethnologist* 21, no. 2: 353–65.

Stren, Richard, with Vikram Bhatt, Larry Bourne, Jorge E. Hardoy, Patricia McCarney, Roger Riendeau, Luc-Normand Tellier, Rodney White, and Joseph Whitney, eds. 1992. *An Urban Problematique: The Challenge of Urbanization for Development Assistance.* Toronto: Centre for Urban and Community Studies, University of Toronto.

Stromgaard, Peter. 1985. "A Subsistence Economy Under Pressure: The Bemba of Northern Zambia." *Africa* 55, no. 1: 39–58.

Thøgersen, Karsten, and Jørgen E. Andersen. 1983. *Urban Planning in Zambia: The Case of Lusaka.* Copenhagen: Royal Danish Academy of Fine Arts, School of Architecture.

Thomson, Betty Preston. 1954. *Two Studies in African Nutrition.* Rhodes-Livingstone Papers no. 24.

Thomson, J. Moffat. 1934. *Memorandum on the Native Tribes and Tribal Areas of Northern Rhodesia.* Lusaka: Government Printer.

Timberlake, Michael, ed. 1985. *Urbanization in the World Economy.* Orlando: Academic Press.

Times of Zambia. 1981. Feature about demonstration by miners' wives in Chililabombwe. July 10, p. 1.

——. 1985. "Kitchen Parties Turned into Beer Dens." December 5.

——. 1987. "Poor in Homes Predicament." December 7, p. 2.

——. 1992a. "Leave Lobola Alone." June 19, p. 3.

——. 1992b. "Excessive Lobola Puts off Marriages." July 1, p. 6.

———. 1993. Feature article about the plight of the widows of the national football team. July 31, p.1.

Tipple, A. Graham, and Kenneth G. Willis, eds. 1991. *Housing the Poor in the Developing World: Methods of Analysis, Case Studies and Policy.* London: Routledge.

Todd, Dave, Alfred Mulenga, and Chris Mupimpila. 1979. *Businesses in Lusaka's Markets and Recommendations for Their Assistance.* Lusaka Housing Project Evaluation Team and Urban Community Research Unit, Working Paper no. 37. Institute for African Studies, University of Zambia.

Todd, Dave, and Anthony Mulimbwa. 1980. *An Evaluation of the Legal Framework of Public Participation in the Management of Human Settlements in Zambia.* Lusaka: Urban Community Research Unit, Institute for African Studies, University of Zambia.

Todd, Dave, and Christopher Shaw. 1980. "The Informal Sector and Zambia's Employment Crisis." *Journal of Modern African Studies* 18, no. 3: 411–25.

Tumbo-Masabo, Zubeida, and Rita Liljeström, eds. 1994. *Chelewa, Chelewa: The Dilemma of Teenage Girls.* Uppsala: Scandinavian Institute of African Studies.

Turner, John F. C. 1965. "Lima's Barriadas and Corralones: Suburbs Versus Slums." *Ekistics* 19:152–55.

———. 1972. "Housing as a Verb." In J. F. C. Turner and R. Fichter, eds., *Freedom to Build,* pp. 148–75. New York: Macmillan.

Turrel, Robert. 1984. "Kimberley's Model Compounds." *Journal of African History* 25:59–75.

UNDP (United Nations Development Programme). 1993. *Human Development Report 1993.* New York: Oxford University Press.

United States Department of State. 1988. State Department Travel Advisory: Zambia. July 14 update. Unpublished computer printout.

Vail, Leroy, and Landeg White. 1991. "The Possession of the Dispossessed: Songs and History among Tumbuka Women." In L. Vail and L. White, *Power and the Praise Poem,* pp. 231–77. London: James Currey.

van Binsbergen, Wim M. J. 1981. "Cults of Affliction in Town and the Articulation of Modes of Production." In W. van Binsbergen, *Religious Change in Zambia,* pp. 236–65. London: Kegan Paul International.

van Donge, Jan Kees. 1985. "Understanding Rural Zambia Today: The Relevance of the Rhodes-Livingstone Institute." *Africa* 55, no. 1: 60–76.

van Velsen, Jaap. 1960. "Labour Migration as a Positive Factor in the Continuity of Tonga Tribal Society." *Economic Development and Cultural Change* 8:265–78.

———. 1964. *The Politics of Kinship: A Study in Social Manipulation Among the Lakeside Tonga of Nyasaland.* Manchester: Manchester University Press.

——. 1975. "Urban Squatters: Problem or Solution." In D. Parkin, ed., *Town and Country in Central and Eastern Africa*, pp. 294–307. London: Oxford University Press.

Varley, Ann. 1995. "Neither Victims nor Heroines: Women, Land, and Housing in Mexican Cities." *Third World Planning Review* 17, no. 2: 169–82.

Watson, William. 1958. *Tribal Cohesion in a Money Economy*. Manchester: Manchester University Press.

Weekly Post. 1992. "Squatters Get Council Ultimatum." August 14–20, p. 2.

Weinberger, Elisabeth. 1991. Frauen als Kleinstunternehmer in Lusaka, Zambia. Unpublished work report. September.

——. 1992. Frauen als Kleinstunternehmer in Lusaka, Zambia. Unpublished work report. February.

Welsh, David. 1971. "The Growth of Towns." In M. Wilson and L. Thompson, eds., *The Oxford History of South Africa*, Vol. 2, *South Africa 1870–1966*, pp. 172–243. Oxford: Clarendon Press.

Werbner, Richard P. 1984. "The Manchester School in South-Central Africa." *Annual Review of Anthropology* 13:157–85.

Western, John. 1985. "Undoing the Colonial City?" *Geographical Review* 3:335–57.

White, C. M. N. 1953. "Conservatism and Modern Adaptation in Luvale Female Puberty Ritual." *Africa* 23, no. 1: 15–25.

White, Luise. 1990. *The Comforts of Home: Prostitution in Colonial Nairobi*. Chicago: University of Chicago Press.

Wilk, Richard, ed. 1989. *The Household Economy: Reconsidering the Domestic Mode of Production*. Boulder: Westview Press.

Wilkinson, Peter. 1983. "Providing 'Adequate Shelter': The South African State and the 'Resolution' of the African Urban Housing Crisis, 1948–1954." In D. C. Hindson, ed., *Working Papers in Southern African Studies*, vol. 3. Johannesburg: Ravan Press.

Wilson, Elizabeth. 1963. "Lusaka: A City of Tropical Africa." *Geography* 48:411–14.

——. 1992. *The Sphinx in the City: Urban Life, the Control of Disorder, and Women*. Berkeley: University of California Press.

Wilson, Godfrey. 1941 and 1942. *An Analysis of the Economics of Detribalization in Northern Rhodesia*. Rhodes-Livingstone Papers nos. 5 and 6.

Wilson, Monica. 1976 "Zig-Zag Change." *Africa* 46, no. 4: 399–409.

Wirth, Lewis. 1938. "Urbanism as a Way of Life." *American Journal of Sociology* 4:2–24.

Woldring, Klaas, ed. 1984. *Beyond Political Independence: Zambia's Development Predicament in the 1980s*. The Hague: Mouton.

Wood, Adrian P. (with G. P. Banda and D. C. Mundende). 1986. "The Population of Lusaka." In G. J. Williams, ed., *Lusaka and Its Environs: A*

Geographical Study of a Planned Capital City in Tropical Africa, pp. 164–88. Handbook Series no. 9. Lusaka: Zambia Geographical Association.

Wood, Adrian P., ed. 1990. *Dynamics of Agricultural Policy and Reform in Zambia*. Ames: Iowa State University Press.

World Bank. 1992. *World Tables*. Baltimore: Johns Hopkins University Press.

Young, Roger, and John Loxley. 1990. *Zambia: An Assessment of Zambia's Structural Adjustment Experience*. Ottawa: North-South Institute.

Zambia Daily Mail. 1984. "Adolescents Should Not Attend Kitchen Parties." Letter to the editor, November 27.

———. 1992. "Free Houses Coming—Sata." July 24, p. 1.

Index

Acquired Immune Deficiency Syndrome (AIDS), 133, 142, 146, 155
African metropolis, 1, 3, 13
African National Congress (ANC), 43, 64; and mass mobilization, 53
African suburbs, 28, 31, 37; Matero, 28; New Chilenje, 28, 36, 38. *See also* Residential areas, Lusaka
African Urban Housing Ordinance, 28, 39
Agricultural resettlement, 143; Kambilombilo, 143, 163
Agriculture, commercial: cash cropping, 144; colonial, 5, 44; peasant cultivation, 44; postcolonial, 5, 144; women's role, 44
AIDS. *See* Acquired Immune Deficiency Syndrome
Alcohol distilling: *kachasu*, 79, 80, 85, 109, 145. *See also* Beer brewing; Beerhalls
ANC. *See* African National Congress
Apamwamba, 68, 116, 193. *See also* *Mayadi* (yards)
Apartheid: development, 28
Appadurai, Arjun, 8

"Back-to-the-land." *See* Agricultural resettlement.
Bardouille, Raj, 91, 101, 171
Beer brewing: *chibuku*, 109, 110; women in Mtendere, 79, 80, 85
Beerhalls, 42, 110; gender, 40; Mtendere, 109; oldest, 36, 40; politics, 43; profits, 28
Berry, Sara, 8, 96
Bettison, David, 22, 23, 37, 38, 39, 40, 41, 51
Bridal showers. *See* kitchen parties
Bridewealth, 137, 138, 139, 152; "dowry," 124, 126, 127, 128, 129, 136; *lobola*, 124; and "proper marriage," 128, 136, 137, 138, 139. *See also* Divorce; Marriage
Broken Hill (now Kabwe), 22, 29, 38

Case studies: Banda, Mrs., 104; Esther's coming-of-age and pregnancies, 111–12, 120–21, 154; Lungu household, 146–47, 150, 158–59; Mbebe household, 72–73; Mubanga, Mrs., 21, 36–38, 41, 42, 47, 72; Nyirenda, Salome, 101–102; Njovu, Anna, 122; Phiri

household, 145; Sakala household, 146; Siame household, 71,
93, 116, 121, 136, 138, 155–56,
158; Simpemba household,
99–100, 102, 105–106, 152; Zulu,
Mr., 21, 35–36, 37, 38, 41, 72
Census of African population, 23,
32–33, 49–50, 196n8
Chanock, Martin, 118, 119
Children: education, 38, 148, 150;
food riots, 162; migration to town,
44, 45; unpaid household work,
76–101; with parents, 38. See also
intergenerational relations
Churches, 16, 36; charismatic, 42; in
dispute mediation, 120, 121, 126;
in Mtendere, 65, 67, 107–109;
supporting destitutes, 122;
Watchtower movement, 43
Colonial city, 1; administrative headquarters, 1; colonial company
towns, 29; criticism of concept, 13,
21–22; definition, 23–24, 196n3
Colson, Elizabeth, 7, 10, 138, 144,
180, 198n6, 199n2
Comaroff, John, 95, 138
Commercialization of housing. See
Rental housing
"Common man," 9, 47, 116, 164,
166
Compound: meaning today, 68; messengers', 35, 37; Mtendere the
"nicest," 61, 68–69, 157, 161; origin, 24–25, 27; place attachment,
73. See also Residential areas
Conjugal relations: court cases, 119,
121, 122, 123, 124–31; status of
union, 124, 127; tensions, 98, 101,
103, 106, 135. See also Domestic
domain; Gender relations;
Marriage; Sexuality
Consumption: food, 6, 44, 77, 83, 93,
98, 106, 110, 144; clothing, 35,
122, 124, 158; household com-

modities, 158, 160, 194; secondhand clothes, 166
Copperbelt towns, 13, 28, 29, 48,
117; declining employment, 114,
189; education, 38; growth, 29;
housing, 51; migration from, 6,
50, 114; research, 22. See also
Mining industry
Courts: African urban (colonial),
30; case method, 119; conjugal
cases, 123–31, 135; Chelston local
court, 65, 118, 121; fines ("damages"), 120, 121, 123, 152; gender
distinctions in cases, 118, 124;
informal (family forums),
120–21; insult/defamation cases,
119, 123, 131–33; mavuto
("trouble"), 120, 133–36, 137;
procedures, 122–23, 139
Custom: court, 130, 138–39; language, 17, 118–19; reconstituted
notions, 138. See also "Tradition"
Customary law, 118–19, 123; divorce,
136, 137, 140; marriage, 137

Debt, foreign: 12, 57, 191
Dependents. See Live-in relatives
Development: agricultural, 12, 20;
community development, 109;
informal sector, 86–87, 92,
188–89; priorities, 190–91;
research, 7, 20; support of squatter
upgrading, 57–58. See also IMF;
NGOs; Urban bias; World Bank
Dispute mediation. See Courts
Divorce: 17, 76, 85, 97, 102, 127. See
also Marriage
Domestic domain: domestic science,
38, 42; tensions, 30. See also
Conjugal relations; Marriage
Domestic service, 31, 38; ballroom
dancing, 36, 42, 43; Mtendere
men, 77; research, 166, 170, 171;
wages, 51; women's attitude, 79,

83, 85, 99, 190; Zambian employers, 156

Economic decline: 5–9, 12, 81–82, 87,
89, 93, 94; lack of recovery,
141–42, 148, 181; rural effects, 6,
7; UNIP, 161; urban effects, 6, 114.
See also Postcolonial economy
Education: colonial towns, 38;
decline, 18; gender, 76, 148,
151; Mtendere, 78; school
leavers/drop-outs, 150–51, 162;
skills training, 188; postcolonial
expansion, 17, 48, 148
Electricity: Mtendere, 65, 71,
159–60
Employment of Natives Ordinance,
196n9
Environment, built: architecture, 7,
165; colonial, 13, 23–24, 31, 36,
51; space, 7, 8, 60
Epstein, A. L., 22, 29, 30, 40, 98, 119,
136, 167
Ethnic groups, 73, 75; Bemba, 36,
37; Chewa, 37, 112, 116; Chokwe,
112; Kunda, 112; Lozi, 115;
Luvale, 112; Mambwe, 105;
Mwenye (Indians), 116; Ngoni,
35, 37, 122; Nsenga, 37, 105, 112;
stereotypes, 115–16; Tonga, 137;
Wazungu (Europeans), 116, 173;
Yao,112. *See also* Languages,
Zambian; Urban ethnicity

Ferguson, James, 7, 30, 45
Flanagan, William, 7, 8, 191
Food riots, 162
Freedom fighters, 176, 177. *See also*
Political destabilization, regional

Gender: colonial construction, 42;
ethnicity, 116–17; housing, 39–42,
45, 69, 102–106, 185; migration,
45–46; politics, 139–40; squatting,

39. *See also* Informal sector, Wage
labor; Women
Gender relations, 14, 15; authoritar-
ian structure, 16–17, 98–103,
113; cultural norms, 17, 46; privi-
leging men, 92, 102, 134–35;
return migration, 145–47. *See
also* Conjugal relations;
Domestic domain; Households;
Marriage; Sexuality
Geschiere, Peter, 8
Giddens, Anthony, 10, 11
Gluckman, Max, 22, 114
Gugler, Josef, 8, 10, 60, 190
Guyer, Jane, 6, 95, 96, 102, 195n2

Hannerz, Ulf, 29, 175
Hart, Keith, 86
Home front, 94, 117, 161, 170. *See
also* Conjugal relations; Domestic
domain; Gender relations;
Households
Household budget survey. *See*
Research methodology
Household samples. *See* Research
methodology
Households, 4, 9, 11, 151; allowance,
79, 97–98, 198n3; definition,
95–96; development cycle, 10, 11,
18, 92, 97–102, 142, 146, 152,
181; female headed, 76, 84, 145;
gender relations, 94–106; non-
bounded, 16, 70. *See also* Conjugal relations; Domestic domain;
Gender relations; Home front
Housing: access, 10, 59, 60, 193;
allowance (subsidy), 51, 59;
biographies, 71–76; construction,
68, 72–73, 193; economic asset, 4,
92, 94, 103; employer-provided, 4,
14, 24, 39, 51, 184; gender, 4,
39–42, 45, 69, 103–106, 186;
Lusaka *vs.* copperbelt, 28, 31;
place attachment, 73; private

ownership, 14–15, 28–29, 47, 51;
rental, 105, 157, 178, 184, 185,
187; sale, 4, 105; security of
tenure, 104; self-help, 47, 51, 184;
servants' quarters, 25, 31, 35, 37,
67; shortage, 51, 53, 60, 105, 184;
social asset, 4, 94. *See also* Site-
and-service schemes; Squatting;
Urban planning
Housing (Statutory and Improvement Areas) Act of 1974, 57

Identity, 119; gender 120, 131,
134–36; personal, 135
ILO. *See* International Labour
Organisation
IMF. *See* International Monetary
Fund
Informal sector: definition, 87, 188;
development, 13, 34; differences,
31, 87–88; gender, 15, 46, 71, 83,
91–93, 100, 101, 184, 187–89;
limited specialization, 87–93,
187–89, 190; middle-class
involvement, 157; postcolonial
growth, 51, 150; scholarship,
85–87, 197n7; state, 15, 92. *See
also* Self-employment; Small-
scale trade; "Suitcase" trade
Initiation rites: modern urban, 16,
18, 111–12, 154–55, 161, 172,
194, 198n5; Njau dance, 112
Intergenerational relations: parental
problems, 69, 161; tensions, 16,
17–18, 142, 147–56, 194; sexuality, 152, 154. *See also* Children
International Labour Organisation
(ILO), 86, 143, 197n7. *See also*
Informal sector
International Monetary Fund
(IMF): Zambia, 162; structural
adjustment programs (SAP), 86,
92, 181. *See also* World Bank
Intersubjectivity, 10, 19, 167

Intestate Succession Act of 1989, 97,
103, 140, 198n2, 199n10

Jules-Rosette, Benetta, 43, 73, 91,
101, 114, 171, 198n5

King, Anthony, 8, 24, 196n3
Kitchen parties, 16, 18, 112–14, 155,
156, 161, 194, 198n7

Land (Conversion of Titles) Act of
1975, 57–58
Land tenure: change of law, 57–58;
informal use, 64–65; occupancy
title, 70. *See also* Agriculture,
commercial; Land Act
Languages, Zambian: Bemba, 37,
114; Nyanja, 64, 123, 168; Tonga,
123. *See also* Ethnic groups;
Urban ethnicity
Leeds, Anthony, 70, 197n1
Legal ordinances, colonial: employment, 33, 44; housing, 33, 40;
migration, 33, 34; trade, 40. *See
also* African Urban Housing
Ordinance; Employment of
Natives Ordinance
Leisure activities, 29, 35–36, 42; gendered nature, 42; subscription parties, 43, 114. *See also* Social interaction; Voluntary associations
Live-in relatives, 38, 71, 76, 81, 100,
142, 150
Livingstone: former capital, 13;
schools, 38
Local court, Chelston. *See* Courts
Local/global interaction, 8, 18; cultural complexity, 8; dilemma of,
193–94; global influences, 17,
159–61; hybridization, 8;
inequity, 141; tensions of, 142,
156–61
Long-term field research. *See*
Research methodology

Lusaka: distinctions from copperbelt, 13, 14, 22, 23, 51; history,
  13, 22–29; limited colonial
  research, 22; planning as capital,
  1, 13, 24
Lusaka City/District Council:
  Mtendere township, 61, 65;
  squatter upgrading, 57, 60; urban
  administration, 196n2. See also
  Urban planning

Macmillan, Hugh, 30, 45
Marriage, 16, 17, 37, 40, 76, 100;
  "proper," 128–29, 135,
  137–39, 152. See also Bride-
  wealth; Conjugal relations;
  Domestic domain; Divorce;
  Gender relations; Polygyny;
  Widowhood
Matrilineality, 72, 73, 97; inheri-
  tance, 103. See also Intestate
  Succession Act
Mayadi, 69, 80, 116. See also
  Residential areas; Yards
Micro-enterprises. See Informal
  sector
Migration: colonial history, 5; inter-
  national, 50; interurban, 73–76;
  migrant labor, male, 24, 33; postcolonial, 50; regional (southern
  African), 71–72, 73, 115, 157;
  remittances, 44; return (urban to
  rural), 6, 143–47; rural-urban, 5,
  34, 37; women migrants, 38, 44,
  45–46. See also Legal ordinances;
  Rural-urban interaction
Mills, C. Wright, 9
Mining industry: companies, 13,
  48; employment decline, 6, 114;
  export, 5, 12; nationalization, 12,
  48; research on, 22. See also
  Copperbelt towns
Mitchell, J. Clyde, 22, 29, 116, 144,
  196n13

MMD. See Movement for Multi-
  Party Democracy
Moore, Henrietta, 98, 117, 144,
  196n13, 198n1
Movement for Multi-Party
  Democracy (MMD), 164. See also
  Party politics; Third Republic
Mtendere township: churches,
  65, 67, 107–109; clinic, 61, 63,
  65, 80; electricity, 65, 71,
  159–60; history of 60–69;
  "nicest" compound, 61, 68–69,
  157, 161; role of UNIP, 64–67,
  81, 99, 109, 122, 142, 163–64;
  site-and-service scheme, 47–69,
  184; schools, 61, 63, 65, 78, 80;
  self-employment, 77–82; wage
  labor, 77–78, 79, 83, 143. See
  also Compound; Residential
  areas, Lusaka
Mwenye (Indians), 116. See also
  Ethnic groups

NGOs. See Nongovernmental
  Organizations
Nongovernmental Organizations
  (NGOs): development priorities,
  7; Mtendere, 109, 151; skills-
  training, 151, 188–89; squatter
  upgrading, 58; women, 188–89.
  See also Development

One-party state, 9; attitude to
  researchers, 175–78; "back-to-
  the-land," 143–44; dismantling,
  11–12, 18, 65, 142; economic crisis, 161–63; formation, 11, 55;
  political dissent, 162–64; role in
  townships, 65–67; special branch
  of police, 177–78. See also Party
  politics; UNIP
Overurbanization, 60, 190–91

Parpart, Jane, 92, 199n5

Party politics: colonial, 29; mass mobilization in townships, 53; political culture, 115; political discord, 162–64. *See also* ANC; MMD; UNIP

Patrilineality, 97, 105

Political destabilization, regional, 12, 48, 157, 176–77

Polygyny, 76, 81, 84, 98–99, 100, 135. *See also* Marriage

Population growth, 5, 34, 50; Lusaka, 48, 184, 189, 190; post-colonial, 55; sex ratio, 50

Postcolonial economy, 2, 4, 5–6, 8, 12, 18, 48, 55; lack of recovery, 141–42. *See also* Economic decline

Powdermaker, Hortense, 30, 98, 144, 167

Premarital pregnancy, 18, 110, 142, 152, 154–55, 194; "damages" (fines), 120–21, 123, 152

Prostitution, 199n7; Belgian Congo, 116; girlfriends, 137; unmarried women, 134. *See also* Sexuality

Rakodi, Carole, 58, 60, 187

Rental housing, 60, 65; elsewhere in Africa, 60, 187; Mtendere, 157, 185, 187.

Research methodology: case method, 119, 171; household budget study, 97–98, 169; house-hold samples, 73, 80–81, 84–85, 100, 110, 142, 144–45, 168–71; long-term field research, 18–19, 166–81; multi-site research, 166, 170; participant observation, 172–75; permissions, 175–78

Residential areas, Lusaka, 27, 28; Bauleni, 58; Chaisa/Chipata, 57; Chawama, 57; Chibolya, 28; George, 57; Helen Kaunda, 65; John Laing, 60; Kabulonga, 157;

Kabwata, 24, 27, 31, 36, 40, 60; Kalikiliki, 65; Kalingalinga, 58, 61, 64, 69, 77; Kaunda Square, 55; Libala, 36, 37; Maploto, 28; Marrapodi/Mandevu, 43, 55, 114; Matero, 60; Misisi, 60; New Kanyama, 28; Old Chilenje, 28, 36, 60; *See also* Compound; *Mayadi* (yards); Mtendere

Residential segregation: colonial, 27, 35, 37; postcolonial, 51, 65

Rhodes-Livingstone Institute: cop-perbelt research, 29–31; criticism, 30, 196n6; on gender, 30, 45–46, 167; methodology, 30; scholarship 13–14, 22, 176, 196n5

Richards, Audrey, 111, 136, 196n13

Ritual practice: cleansing of wid-ows, 104; healing, 43, 178; pos-session, 43

Rural-urban interaction, 6, 44, 191, 192; circulation of children, 110; economic exchange, 83, 110–11; effects of migration, 44–45; income disparities, 6, 144, 189; scholarship, 45. *See also* Migration.

Sanjek, Roger, 4

SAP. *See* Structural adjustment program

Schlyter, Ann, 4, 60

Schuster, Ilsa. 76, 91, 148

Second Republic, 65, 69, 192, 193; disenchantment, 69, 163. *See also* UNIP

Secondhand clothing: commercial import, 36; consumption, 166; rural trade, 83; sourcing, 36, 80; sales, 36, 79

Self-employment, 86–87; Mtendere, 77–79, 85; shift from wage labor, 81–82. *See also* Informal sector; Small-scale trade; "Suitcase" trade

Self-help housing. *See* Site-and-service schemes; Squatting
Sexuality, 17, 117, 135; adultery, 124, 128, 134; "bitching," 132–33, 134–35, 136; extramarital relations, 98; initiation rituals, 111; kitchen parties, 113; sexual behavior, 98, 154; women's vulnerability, 102, 152. *See also* Conjugal relations; Gender relations; Identity; Prostitution
Shebeens. See Beerhalls
Site-and-service schemes: introduction, 47, 53, 55, 57; growth, 59; Mtendere, 47–69, 184. *See also* Housing; Urban planning
Small-scale trading, 11, 15, 79, 83, 87, 99, 101, 103. *See also* Informal sector; Self-employment; "Suitcase" trade
Social interaction: gender segregated, 16, 106, 111–114; hospitality, 110; neighborhood, 107. *See also* Leisure; Voluntary associations
Socioeconomic differentiation, 6, 116, 158, 161, 189, 192; housing access, 59–60; among low-income residents, 6, 7
Southall, Aidan, 23
Squatting: copperbelt, 31, 46; definition, 27–28; demolition, 59–60; development, 13, 14, 27, 34; different types, 27, 31, 37; growth in Lusaka, 53, 56, 59; housing advocates, 57; lack of tenure, 53, 60; single heads of households, 46, 58; South Africa, 28. *See also* Housing; Urban planning
Street names, Lusaka: Cairo Road, 2, 13, 23, 35; Chachacha Road, 1; Freedom Way, 1; Great East Road, 27, 37, 64; Haile Selassie Avenue, 2; Los Angeles Boulevard, 2; Saddam Hussain Boulevard, 2

Structural adjustment program (SAP), 86, 181. *See also* IMF; World Bank
"Suitcase" trade, 83–84, 85, 88, 116. *See also* Informal sector; Self-employment; Small-scale trade

Third Republic, 193. *See also* MMD
Third World urbanization, 2, 4, 7, 20; homogenization, 8; scholarship, 8, 12, 166, 183; Third World city, 8, 21, 183. *See also* Urbanization
Time: analytical construct, 9, 10; experiential category, 9–10, 19; modalities, 9–11, 18–19, 167, 179–81, 194; spatial metaphors, 10–11
"Tradition," 16, 18, 124, 139, 194. *See also* Custom

UNIP. *See* United National Independence Party
United National Independence Party (UNIP), 55; and ANC, 43, 53, 65; decline, 161–63; Mtendere, 64–67, 81, 99, 109, 120, 122, 142, 163–64. *See also* One-party state; Party politics; Second Republic
Urban administration. *See* Lusaka City/District Council; Urban planning
Urban areas. *See* Compound; Copperbelt towns; Housing; Residential areas, Lusaka; Residential segregation; Urban planning; Yards
Urban arrangements for living, 87, 94, 118; definition, 70, 197n1
Urban bias, 20, 189–92
Urban ethnicity, 29, 73, 75, 113, 114–17; ethnic stereotypes, 115–16; southern African backgrounds, 114. *See also* Ethnic groups

Urban living conditions, surveys:
Bettison report (Lusaka) 1957,
37, 39, 41, 51; budget survey
1969, 77; colonial government
report 1944, 33–34; Kalingalinga
study (1967), 61; labor market
survey 1986, 93, 142
Urban planning, 13, 60; assumptions behind, 185–87; colonial
period, 24–29; low-income
housing, 14–15, 47, 51–69; new
agenda, 193; South African contrasts, 13, 25, 28, 29; squatter
upgrading, 53, 57–60. See also
Housing; Site-and-service
schemes; Squatting
Urbanism: as a way of life, 3, 7, 8,
9, 20, 21, 165, 180, 193, 194;
Lusaka, 13, 30–43; mining towns,
13; the West, 7. See also African
metropolis
Urbanization: colonial growth, 34,
44–46; history, in the West, 7;
postcolonial rates, 4–9, 48, 144,
192; Zambian historiography, 45.
See also Third World urbanization; Urban planning

Voluntary associations, 16, 42–44;
funeral associations, 42–43;
"homeboy" groups, 42, 115;
Kalela, 29, 43. See also Leisure;
Social interaction

Wage labor: Lusaka, 31, 38;
Mtendere 77–78, 79, 83, 143. See
also Domestic service; Gender
Wages: all-inclusive, 51; cash and
rations, 51, 196n11; decline, 142;
housing subsidy, 59
Wazungu (sing., mzungu)
(Europeans), 116, 173. See also
Ethnic groups
Widowhood, 76, 84, 103–104, 145.
See also Marriage
Wilson, Godfrey, 22, 29, 144
Wilson, Monica, 9, 179–80
Wirth, Louis, 7
Witchcraft accusations, 104, 123,
133, 178
Women: education, 38, 76, 79;
migration, 33, 38, 44–45; small-
scale trade, 41, 46, 77; wage labor,
41, 50, 79, 83. See also Conjugal
relations; Gender; Gender rela-
tions; Informal sector; Marriage;
Sexuality
World Bank, 5; market economies,
86; structural adjustment pro-
grams, 181; squatter upgrading,
57–58; Zambia, 162. See also IMF

Yards, 69, 112, 116, 156, 157, 158,
161, 193. See also Mayadi;
Residential areas, Lusaka